CENTRAL ROUTE TO THE PACIFIC.

CENTRAL ROUTE TO THE PACIFIC.

Pl. 1.

U of M

G. H. Heap del.

P. S. Duval & Co. lith. Phil^a

RAFTING ACROSS GRAND RIVER.

CENTRAL ROUTE

TO THE

PACIFIC,

FROM THE

VALLEY OF THE MISSISSIPPI TO CALIFORNIA:

JOURNAL OF THE EXPEDITION

OF

E. F. BEALE, SUPERINTENDENT OF INDIAN AFFAIRS IN CALIFORNIA, AND GWINN HARRIS HEAP,

FROM

MISSOURI TO CALIFORNIA, IN 1853.

BY

GWINN HARRIS HEAP.

PHILADELPHIA:
LIPPINCOTT, GRAMBO, AND CO.
1854.

Entered according to the Act of Congress, in the year 1853, by
LIPPINCOTT, GRAMBO, AND CO.,
in the Office of the Clerk of the District Court of the United States in and for the Eastern District of Pennsylvania.

PHILADELPHIA:
T. K. AND P. G. COLLINS, PRINTERS.

CONTENTS.

239817

LIST OF PLATES.

CENTRAL ROUTE TO THE PACIFIC.

INTRODUCTORY.

On the third day of March, 1853, Congress passed a law appropriating $250,000 for the purpose of carrying into effect a plan which E. F. Beale, Superintendent of Indian Affairs for the State of California, had proposed for the better protection, subsistence, and colonization of the Indian tribes within his superintendency.

The President having given his approval to this plan, Mr. Beale was instructed to proceed forthwith, by the shortest route, to his superintendency, and to select lands most suitable for Indian reservations. He was also directed, in connection with this plan, to examine the Territories of New Mexico and Utah, where their frontiers and those of California lie contiguous, and to ascertain whether lands existed there to which the California Indians might, with advantage, be removed.

Mr. Beale having, in a few days, collected a small party, and my duties calling me at this time to California, I gladly availed myself of his invitation to join the expedition, which promised to be replete with interest, not only because he proposed traversing a large tract of unexplored country, but also from its being one of the routes in contemplation for a railway from the Valley of the Mississippi to our Pacific possessions.

In the journal now offered to the public, I have endeavored to give a correct representation of the country which we traversed; and, although I do not pretend to do justice to the subject, I trust that these notes will not be altogether without value, particularly at a time when the public mind is engrossed with a

2

subject of such stupendous magnitude as the establishment of a trans-continental railway. It was a source of frequent regret to us, that circumstances which it is not necessary to explain here, had put it out of our power to provide instruments for a more scientific survey of this route; and I have, therefore, avoided to state anything, even in the form of a surmise, the correctness of which could only be ascertained by instrumental survey. It is often difficult to determine heights and grades with perfect accuracy, even with the assistance of instruments; random assertions, made upon mere supposition, would, therefore, be entirely without value. The information I claim to give is such only as I believe will be found reliable and useful, particularly to emigrants; to them, any new light thrown upon the geography of the interior of our continent, cannot fail to be interesting, and they will find this journal a faithful delineation of the country through which our route led us.

In regard to the map accompanying this book, I wish to state that the portion which differs from any hitherto published, is the section embraced between the mouth of Huerfano River, in west long. 103° 20′, and Little Salt Lake, in west long. 113°. No survey has been published of this region, and all information regarding it has heretofore been derived exclusively from the reports of trappers and Indian traders. Without claiming for it any extraordinary degree of accuracy, it will be found, I hope, much more correct and reliable than any map hitherto published. Almost hourly notes, with the constant use of the compass, and a correct estimate of distances, were, in the absence of instruments, my means of delineating the topography of the country which we traversed. The other portions of the map are copied from the best and latest surveys.

The route selected by Mr. Beale was, in conformity with his instructions, the shortest and most direct to California; and it also enabled him to examine, with the least delay, the localities to which it was believed that the Indians of California might be removed with advantage to themselves, should suitable lands for the purpose be found.

The following is a synopsis of the route he designed taking:

The starting-point was Westport, in Missouri; from thence, leaving the River Kanzas on our right, we were to proceed to Fort Atkinson on the Arkansas, crossing the head-waters of the Osage and Neosho. From Fort Atkinson, our course was up the left bank of the Arkansas, as far as the River Huerfano, which joins the Arkansas about forty-five miles above Bent's Fort; thence up the Huerfano to the Sangre de Cristo Mountains, and through them to Fort Massachusetts on Utah Creek, in the north of New Mexico. After leaving Fort Massachusetts, we were to proceed up the valley of San Luis, lying between the Sangre de Cristo Mountains and the Sierra Mojada on the east, the Sierras Blanca and Sahwatch on the north, and the Sierra de San Juan on the west. Up this valley to the Sahwatch Valley, through the Coochatope Pass in the Sahwatch Mountains, and down the River Uncompagre to the Grand River Fork of the Great Colorado, in Utah Territory. Thence across the River Avonkaria and the Green River Fork of the Colorado, through the Wahsatch Mountains to the Mormon settlements near Little Salt Lake and the Vegas de Santa Clara. From this point we would travel on the old Spanish trail leading from Abiquiú, across the desert, to the River Mohaveh, where we intended to leave it, and enter into the Tulare Valley in California, through Walker's Pass, in the Sierra Nevada.

We left Washington on the 20th of April, and arrived at St. Louis the 2d, Kanzas the 5th, and Westport the 6th of May.

Westport is a thriving place, situated four miles from Kanzas; and emigrants from Missouri to California and Oregon make either this place or Independence their starting-point. At both towns all necessary supplies can be obtained at reasonable rates, and their merchants and mechanics being constantly required to supply the wants of travellers on the plains, keep on hand such articles as are best adapted for an overland journey. Kanzas, a newer place, is also thriving, and a fine river-landing. At Westport, I had the pleasure of meeting with a very courteous gentleman, Count Cypriani, ex-governor of Leghorn. He was preparing for an expedition to California, *via* Fort Laramie, the South Pass, Great Salt Lake, and Carson's Valley. His party consisted of eleven persons of education and science, and an escort of mountain men; and his outfit was in every respect well appointed and complete. If the observations of this accomplished gentleman should be given to the public, they will be a valuable addition to the scanty knowledge we possess of the interior of our country. He has had much experience as a traveller, having already visited the greater portion of both the continents of the western hemisphere, as well as those of Europe, Asia, and Africa.

CHAPTER I.

JOURNEY FROM WESTPORT TO THE RIVER HUERFANO.

Our party was composed of twelve persons, viz:—

E. F. Beale, Superintendent of Indian Affairs in California.
G. Harris Heap.
Elisha Riggs, of Washington.
William Riggs, "
William Rogers, "
Henry Young.
J. Wagner.
J. Cosgrove.
Richard Brown (a Delaware Indian).
Gregorio Madrid (a Mexican).
Jesus Garcia, "
George Simms (colored man).

May 10, 1853. The train started from Westport in the afternoon, with directions to proceed to Council Grove, and await our arrival there. Mr. Beale accompanied it a few miles into the prairie, and returned after dark.

With a view to making a rapid trip, we had dispensed with everything that was not absolutely necessary for our wants; and our outfit, therefore, was of the simplest description.

May 15. All our arrangements being completed, we started from Westport at 3 P.M. A party of ladies and gentlemen accompanied us a few miles into the prairie, and drank a "stirrup cup" of champagne to the success of our journey. The weather was bright and clear, and, after a pleasant ride of twelve miles over prairies enamelled with flowers, we encamped at thirty minutes after six P. M. on Indian Creek, a tributary of the Kanzas, fringed with a thick growth of cottonwoods and willows. Day's march, 12 miles.

May 16. Moved camp at 5 A. M. The morning was cloudy. George Simms, who superintended the culinary department, procured milk from a neighboring Caw Indian's hut, which, with dried buffalo tongue, enabled us to make a hearty breakfast. An excellent and well-beaten road, as broad and smooth as a turnpike, led us through a green rolling prairie. Although we saw many prairie hens and plovers, we were too impatient to overtake our train to waste time in shooting them. Arrived at 9 hours 30 min. A. M. at Bull Creek, twenty-three miles, where we found two log-huts, good water and grass, and some cottonwood and willow trees.

After a short rest, we continued on to Garfish Camp, twenty-two miles, over a rolling prairie, covered with rich herbage—but noticed little timber. Passed many water-holes. The weather was cool, with a pleasant southerly wind. Around our encampment the grass was knee-high, but no wood was found nearer than half a mile; a few dry bushes, eked out with "buffalo chips," sufficed to prepare our supper. The Santa Fé mail stage was stopping here when we arrived, and proceeded on its way to Independence shortly after. Day's march, 45 miles; total distance from Westport, 57 miles.

May 17. The morning was ushered in with the wind from the southward, ladened with heavy clouds, and accompanied by occasional showers of rain. Mr. Beale went in search of a mule, which had drawn her picket-pins in the night, and taken the "back track" towards Westport; but, after a ride of seven miles he was compelled to relinquish the pursuit. Numerous prairie wolves surrounded the camp all night. Arrived at "One Hundred and Ten" at 45 minutes after 10 A. M. The wind veered to southeast, still accompanied by rain, and the weather was cold and unpleasant. "One Hundred and Ten" is so named from its being at that distance from Fort Leavenworth. This hamlet is composed of a few log-houses situated in a hollow, near a small stream shaded by cottonwoods. The inhabitants are Shawnees, but at this time nearly all the men were absent; the women appeared neat and respectable. Prairie hens and plovers were numerous; but we were still too near the settlements for nobler game. Continued our route at 1 P. M.; the road still led over a beautiful rolling country, the grass good, and occasional pools of water. At 4 P. M. encamped at Dragoon Creek, after a ride of twelve miles. It is a small brook, well shaded by cottonwoods and oaks, and grass grows luxuriantly on its banks. A few Caw Indians at this place came into our camp hoping to exchange horses with us, and were quite disappointed at our refusal to trade. They were fine-looking men, well proportioned, and athletic. The chief, whose portrait I offered to sketch, seemed delighted with the idea, and hastened to his camp for his rifle, which he was more anxious to have correctly represented than himself. He presented us a paper with a very complacent air, evidently thinking that it contained strong recommendations of his tribe, and himself in particular. It was written by some mischievous emigrant, who advised all travellers to beware of this great chief, who was none other than a great rascal, and great beggar. We did not undeceive him as to its contents, and he left us, seeming perfectly satisfied with the impression he had created. Day's travel, 35 miles; distance from Westport, 92 miles.

May 18. We had a severe thunder and rain storm, which lasted all night; the wind blew strong from the southward, and the lightning was incessant and vivid. One of those balls of fire which sometimes descend to the earth during violent thunderstorms, fell and exploded in our midst. The mules, already terrified by the constant peals of thunder, became frantic with fear; and when this vivid light was seen, accompanied with a report like the crack of a rifle, neither picket-pins nor hobbles could hold them; they rushed through the camp overturning everything in their course—their ropes and halters lashing right and left, and increasing their panic. They were stopped by an elbow of the creek, where they were found a few minutes after, huddled together, and quivering with fear. It was fortunate for us that they did not take to the open prairie, as we would have had much difficulty in recovering them. This was our first experience in a *stampede*, and to prevent a recurrence of such accidents we after this placed the animals in the centre, and, dividing our party into twos and threes, slept in a circle around them. By using such precautions we were never subjected to this annoyance again, except once, after entering the country of the Utahs. At dawn, the wind veered to the westward, and blew very cold. Before sunrise, we resumed our journey, and in twelve miles crossed a fine clear stream, and in fourteen miles reached another. A ride of twenty-five miles brought us to a hollow, where, finding good water, we encamped. Resting but a short time we continued our journey, and in ten miles, over a rich rolling country, arrived at Council Grove, where our train was waiting for us.

Council Grove is situated in a rich grassy bottom, well watered, and heavily timbered. It is a settlement of about twenty frame and log houses, and scattered up and down the stream are several Indian villages. At a short distance from the road is a large and substantially built Methodist mission-house, constructed of limestone, which is found here in inexhaustible quantities. This stone is excellent as a building material, and lies in strata of from six inches to three feet in thickness: lintels and arches are made of it as it is extracted from the quarries, which extend for fifteen miles up the stream. Day's march, 32 miles; total distance, 122 miles.

May 19. We now considered ourselves fairly embarked on our journey, for until leaving Council Grove we felt as if we were still within the boundaries of civilization. Even the huts which we passed occasionally on the road, though inhabited only by Indians, removed that sense of utter loneliness which impresses the traveller upon the boundless prairie. Mr. Beale had selected only such men as were inured by long habit to the privations and hardships which we expected to encounter. One, the Delaware, was an experienced hunter, and to his unerring rifle we owed, during the journey, many abundant repasts, when otherwise we would have been upon short allowance.

While at Council Grove, we had some mules shod, and the provisions that had been consumed on the journey from Westport, were replaced. The animals having been well packed, and our arms and ammunition inspected, we bid adieu to Council Grove in the morning, and after a pleasant ride of seventeen miles encamped near water in a hollow on the roadside. The weather was fine, a cool breeze refreshing the air. Some prairie hens, ducks, and plovers were shot. In the afternoon, after travelling fifteen miles, we encamped near the "Lost Spring." The grass along the road was good, and we passed several pools which probably dry up in midsummer.

Since our departure from Westport we had seen many graves on each side of the road, and some of the camping-places had the appearance of village graveyards. The cholera raged on the plains a few years ago, occasioning a fearful mortality, and these mounds remain to attest its ravages. Through carelessness or haste, they were often too shallow to protect their contents from the wolves, and it frequently happened that he who in the morning was hastening forward in health and spirits towards the golden bourn, was ere night a mangled corpse, his bones scattered, by the savage hunger of the wolf, over the plain.

It was now deemed prudent to keep guard, as we were approaching Indian hunting-grounds, and were liable at any moment to meet a predatory band. Eight of the party kept watch, each man being relieved every hour. Day's march, 32 miles; distance from Westport, 154 miles.

May 20. The night was cold and frosty. Started soon after sunrise, and, after travelling sixteen miles, encamped on Cottonwood Creek; a pretty brook, lined with cottonwood and oak trees, and alive with small fish, some of which were caught with a hook and line.

Resumed our march at noon, and travelled over a flat uninteresting country with little water. This day saw antelope for the first time. Met Major Rucker, and Lieutenants Heath and Robinson on their way from New Mexico to Fort Leavenworth. They informed us that at a short distance in advance of us were large bands of buffalo. Encamped, as the sun was setting, on a brook called Turkey Creek, where we found an abundant supply of water, but no wood. We here overtook Mr. Antoine Leroux, on his way to Taos, and considered ourselves fortunate in securing the services of so experienced a guide. He did not join us at once, as he was desirous of seeing his train safely over one or two bad places in advance of us, but promised to overtake us in a day or two. Day's march, 35 miles; distance from Westport, 189 miles.

May 21. Raised camp at sunrise, and after a ride of thirty miles stopped to noon on the Little Arkansas. This stream is difficult to cross during a continuance of heavy rains, but has little water in it at this season. Passed good water and grass in twelve miles from last camp.

We were all on the lookout for buffaloes. It was five days since we had left Westport, and as yet our eyes had not been gladdened by the sight of even one. Hoping to fall in with them more readily by diverging from the beaten track, I left the party soon after sunrise, and turning to the left, went a few miles in the direction of the Arkansas. After a ride of two hours, I observed afar off many dark objects which resembled trees skirting the horizon, but, after a closer scrutiny, their change of position convinced me that they were buffaloes. I slowly approached them, and, in order to obtain a nearer view without giving them the alarm, dismounted, and, urging my horse forwards, concealed myself behind him. I thus got within a hundred yards of the herd. Bands of antelope and prairie wolves were intermingled with the buffaloes, who had come down to a rivulet to drink. Of the latter some were fighting, others wallowing, drinking, or browsing. I was just congratulating myself upon my *ruse* in getting so near to them, this being my first sight of these noble animals, when my horse, suddenly raising his head, uttered such a sonorous neigh as put the whole troop to flight. Away they galloped, one band after another taking the alarm, until the whole herd, numbering several thousand, was in motion, and finally disappeared in clouds of dust. Despairing of getting such another opportunity for a shot, I reluctantly turned my horse's head in the direction where I supposed the rest of the party to be. A few hours' ride brought me back to them. They too had fallen in with buffaloes, and, in their eagerness to secure the first prize, each man had taken two or three shots at a straggling old bull, an exile from the herd; he fell, pierced with twenty-three balls. He was, however, too old and tough to be eaten, and was left for his friends the cayotes.

Buffaloes now became such an ordinary occurrence that the novelty soon wore off, and we had more humps, tongues, and marrow-bones than the greatest gourmand could have desired.

In the afternoon travelled ten miles to Owl Creek, one of the head-waters of the Neosho, where we found good grass and timber, but no water. Passed many pools, much muddied by buffaloes. Mr. Leroux joined us here, but remained behind again to see his train across this creek.

Early in the evening, another rain and thunderstorm broke over us, and lasted all night; the grass, and everything metallic, threw off sparks of electricity; the rain descended in torrents, and it was with difficulty that a fire could be kindled. A more unpromising prospect could scarcely be imagined. Some endeavored to secure the packs and provisions, whilst others, stoically resigning themselves to their fate, wrapped their dripping blankets around them, and slept in spite of the storm. Day's march, 40 miles; distance from Westport, 229 miles.

May 22. Moved camp without breakfast, for, notwithstanding the rain, no water for making coffee had been caught. The day broke clear and bright, and large bands of buffaloes being in our vicinity, Mr. Beale and myself went out for a hunt. On ascending the ridge which inclosed the bottom in which we were encamped, long lines of these animals could be seen quite near, walking with solemn tread, and occasionally stopping to browse or to roll; but, as we approached them to windward, they soon took the alarm, and, wheeling round, galloped off to rejoin the scattered herds in the plain. We rode some distance down the deep bed of Owl Creek, and having got to leeward of a large herd, endeavored to approach them in the Indian manner, by creeping on our hands and knees. By approaching them to leeward, and remaining perfectly motionless whenever they raise their heads to sniff the air, or evince any alarm, hunters have succeeded in getting sufficiently near to strike them with their ramrods. We, however, could only get within rifle-shot, and Mr. Beale wounding one, though not mortally, he made his escape with the rest of the band. Indians, in chasing the buffalo, use only the most practised horses; guiding them with their knees, their long lances ready for use, they rush at full speed in the midst of a herd, and piercing the animal under the shoulder, so as to penetrate the heart, they leave him to fall, and continue the chase, often killing ten or twelve in the course of a single run.

We had already overtaken and passed several large wagon and cattle trains from Texas and Arkansas, mostly bound to California. With them were many women and children; and it was pleasant to stroll into their camps in the evening and witness the perfect air of comfort and being-at-home that they presented. Their wagons drawn up in a circle, gave them at least an appearance of security; and within the inclosure the men either reclined around the camp-fires, or were busy in repairing their harness or cleaning their arms. The females milked the cows and prepared the supper; and we often enjoyed the hot cakes and fresh milk which they invited us to partake of. Tender infants in their cradles were seen under the shelter of the wagons, thus early inured to hard travel. Carpets and rocking-chairs were drawn out, and, what would perhaps shock some of our fine ladies, fresh-looking girls, whose rosy lips were certainly never intended to be defiled by the vile weed, sat around the fire, smoking the old-fashioned corn-cob pipe.

Although Mr. Beale and myself overtook camp at a late hour, we travelled a few miles farther, and encamped for the night on Walnut Creek, an insignificant brook at this season, but which is difficult to cross after rains. This is the point at which emigrants to Oregon and California, from Texas and Arkansas, generally strike this road. They prefer the route which leads them through the South Pass—to the one on the Gila, or Cooke's route, where little or no timber or water are found for long distances. Mr. Leroux again rejoined us here with the intention of remaining with us. In the evening, the Delaware brought in the humps, tongues, and marrow-bones of two fat buffalo cows. Day's march, 42 miles; distance from Westport, 271 miles.

May 23. We were again on the road at sunrise, and travelled thirty-one miles to the Pawnee Fork of the Arkansas. The sun was excessively hot, but towards noon its heat was tempered by a pleasant breeze from the northwest; crossed many gullies, which carry water only after heavy rains. We passed, on the right of the road, a remarkable *butte*, or spur of the hills, projecting into the plain, and presenting a broad surface of smooth rock, thickly inscribed with names. This landmark is known as "The Pawnee Rock."

In twenty miles from last camp, we came to a well-wooded ravine, after which the country became more undulating. Pawnee Fork was swollen and turbid from the late rains, but we got good water from a spring near the camp. The Delaware brought in a fine antelope and a hare, and during our noon camp shot an old buffalo cow, much bitten by wolves.

Encamped in the evening near a pond on the roadside, where we found good pasturage, but no wood; *bois de vache* served us for fuel. Just before dark an enormous wolf boldly trotted into camp, but a ball from the Delaware's rifle sent him scouring over the plains, minus a leg. Several bands surrounded camp all night, keeping up a dismal howling. Day's march, 40 miles; distance from Westport, 311 miles.

May 24. Travelled steadily from $5\frac{1}{2}$ A. M. until noon, when we encamped near a water-hole on the roadside. The country was flat and uninteresting. Passed through many prairie-dog villages, whose active little inhabitants sat in their holes, with only their heads appearing above the surface, barking at us with the appearance of great wrath at our intrusion. Saw several bands of antelopes and wolves; but all the buffaloes had disappeared. Resumed our journey at 5 P. M., and traversed level plains, devoid of interest, until 9 P. M., when we reached the Arkansas. It was quite dark when we encamped, and we spread our blankets without supper. The rain commenced falling at midnight, and continued until morning, accompanied by a high wind. We were, of course, far from comfortable, having no shelter whatever from the storm; but to Mr. Leroux, who was taken suddenly ill, this inclement weather was particularly distressing. He was attacked with pleurisy, and his sufferings were so great that he felt convinced that this place would be his grave. Day's march, 45 miles; total distance from Westport, 356 miles.

May 25. We were glad to saddle up at sunrise, and in five miles reached Fort Atkinson, where Major Johnson, the officer in command, gave us a cordial reception. Several large bands of Indians, of the Cheyenne and Arapahoe tribes were congregated around the fort, awaiting the arrival of Major Fitzpatrick, Indian Agent, whom they daily expected. As it continued to rain without intermission all day, we concluded to pass the night in the fort, where Major Johnson had provided comfortable accommodations for us. Orders had just been received to remove this post to Pawnee Fork of the Arkansas, one hundred miles nearer the settlements. It will there be of very little service, for it is already too near to the frontiers. The timber at Pawnee Fork being mostly cottonwoods, it is not suitable for building purposes; though at Fort Atkinson there is none whatever nearer than fifteen miles; and it was with some difficulty that we obtained a few small logs for our men, who were encamped at a short distance, under tents, borrowed from the fort. All the houses are in a dilapidated condition; a few are built of adobes (sun-dried bricks), but the greater part are constructed of sods. Emigrants frequently stop here to settle their difficulties with Indians, and with each other, Major Johnson administering justice in a prompt and impartial manner. A few days before our arrival, a quarrel having occurred between a party of emigrants and some Cheyenne Indians, which ended in blows, Major Johnson, upon investigation, finding that an American was the aggressor, immediately ordered him back to the States. Mr. Leroux being still too ill to continue the journey, remained here under the care of the surgeon of the post; and Mr. W. Riggs, desiring to return to the States, took leave of us at this point. Day's travel, 5 miles; whole distance, 361 miles.

May 26. Although it still continued to rain, we left Fort Atkinson at noon, and travelled up the left bank of the Arkansas. The trail from Independence to Santa Fé crosses the Arkansas ten miles above Fort Atkinson; and there is another crossing five miles higher up. The rain continued without intermission, and at 7 P. M. we encamped, after a rapid ride of thirty-five miles. Found but little wood, which was difficult to kindle, and made a wretched supper. The rain poured on us all night without cessation, completely saturating our blankets. The Arkansas was rising fast. Day's march, 35 miles; making 396 from Westport.

May 27.—Heavy rain all night; raised camp at 6.30 A. M., and until nine o'clock our route was up the left bank of the Arkansas. The country offered no variety. The river bottom in which we travelled was very sloppy from the late rains; coarse grass we found in abundance. It is not as nourishing as the drier grass of the prairie, which the mules are more partial to. We passed during the morning several large parties of emigrants for California with cattle. Their stock was in good condition, and travelled steadily at the rate of fifteen miles a day. Encamped near an emigrant train at noon to dry our packs and clean our arms. We had killed some ducks, which, with milk and butter from the emigrants, enabled us to make an excellent dinner. Day's march, 20 miles; total distance, 416 miles.

May 28.—It rained lightly all night. Started at 6 A. M., and travelled up the left bank of the Arkansas nineteen miles over a rolling country. The constant emigration on this route has destroyed nearly all the timber on the left bank of the Arkansas. The emigrants burn more wood than they need, and frequently by their carelessness destroy much valuable timber, as well as set fire to the prairies. There are many cottonwood trees on the islands of the Arkansas, and on its right bank. Encamped on an island formed by the rise of the river. The Delaware killed a fine antelope and some ducks. Went twelve miles farther in the afternoon, and encamped on an island (Chouteau's Island). The river was everywhere fordable. On the left shore, opposite to us, was a large emigrant train, whose cattle were in splendid condition; they supplied us abundantly with milk. The country over which we travelled this day was broken, with low hills and dry ravines running towards the river. They had some cottonwood trees in them, also large quantities of drift-wood, showing that they discharge much water during rains, and come from a comparatively wooded country. Day's travel, 31 miles; 447 from Westport.

May 29.—At sunrise, recrossed the river to its left bank; grass still coarse and rank. The water of the Arkansas is very similar in color and taste to that of the Missouri. As we coasted up the left bank the grass became coarser and scantier. Passed a singular slaty mound on the right of the road, resembling a pyramid in ruins. Encamped at noon near a slough of the river. There was no wood near enough for use; but the general resource in such cases on the plains was scattered in abundance around us. The sun was very hot, but at times tempered by a light breeze from the northwestward. A wagon and cattle train of emigrants encamped near us. In the afternoon, we ascended the river eight miles, and encamped near the stream in coarse, wiry grass, as in fact it has been for several days past. The country a few miles from the river has scanty grass and dry arid soil. In the evening, we had a large company of emigrants on each side of us. Day's travel, 36 miles; whole distance, 483 miles.

May 30.—Raised camp soon after sunrise, and after travelling twenty miles, encamped in the "Big Timbers" on the Arkansas. The grass on the plains was coarse, and not very abundant on the river. This place is a favorite resort of the Indians in winter. They here find a good shelter from the bitterly cold winds which then sweep over these plains, and their horses can always pick up a living along the river. This grove of cottonwoods extends for several miles. They are large and grow close together. The weather was cloudy in the morning, but clear at noon; wind southwest. We passed this morning two wagon and cattle trains for California *via* Great Salt Lake. Washington Trainor, of California, with a large number of cattle, and about fifty fine horses and mules, camped near us. We travelled twelve miles in the afternoon, and encamped at 7 P.M. The country had become more interesting and rolling, and we had occasionally beautiful views of the Arkansas. The grass improved as we ascended the river, and we had now an abundance of timber, particularly where we encamped for the night. We passed in the afternoon the old trading-post established by Hatcher for the convenience of trading in winter with the Indians at the "Big Timbers." This place was abandoned when Bent's Fort was given up, and is now in ruins. Saw many deer, but killed only a few ducks. Day's travel, 32 miles; total distance, 515 miles.

May 31. Swarms of mosquitoes prevented much sleep. Thunder and lightning north and south of us all night. Started at sunrise; the sky was clear and weather cool, with a bracing wind from the northwest; in a few hours it veered to the southwest. At ten o'clock, we had our first view of the Spanish Peaks, distant about seventy miles. Travelled up the left bank of the Arkansas, and obtained at times several picturesque views of the river, which is occasionally hemmed in by rocky cliffs. The country was more rolling, stony, and dry than on the preceding day. Saw many deer and antelopes. At ten o'clock, we passed the mouth of Purgatoire River, flowing into the Arkansas from the southwestward. Beds of excellent coal have been discovered on this stream, which will be of inestimable value hereafter. At twelve, encamped on "Lower Dry Creek," where we found scanty dry grass and water in pools. The Delaware brought in two fine antelopes. Travelled ten miles in the afternoon, and encamped three miles above Bent's Fort. We rode all through the ruins, which present a strange appearance in these solitudes. A few years ago this post was frequented by numerous trappers and Indians, and at times exhibited a scene of wild confusion. It is now roofless;

for when the United States refused to purchase it, the proprietors set it on fire to prevent its becoming a harbor for Indians. The adobe walls are still standing, and are in many places of great thickness. They were covered with written messages from parties who had already passed here to their friends in the rear; they all stated that their herds were in good condition, and progressing finely. Day's march, 35 miles; distance from Westport, 550 miles.

June 1. The weather in the morning was pleasant, and the wind from the northwest cooled by passing over the snow-clad peaks of the Rocky Mountains. According to our maps, we were now within an easy day's travel of the mouth of the Huerfano (Orphan's River), and were impatient to reach that point, as we there intended to diverge from the beaten track, and, leaving the Arkansas behind us, traverse the plains lying between that river and the base of the Spanish Peaks, Sangre de Cristo Mountains, and the Sierra Mojada.

Started before sunrise; the road leading occasionally on the Arkansas bottom, but more frequently over the upper plain. The bottom was covered with an abundance of coarse grass, whereas, on the plain, it was scanty, and in bunches. Proceeding four miles we crossed Upper Dry Creek, which is seven miles from Bent's Fort; and, in twelve more, passed a large pond. Many large bands of antelope and deer bounded away on either side as we advanced. At half-past twelve we ascended a remarkable spur, which projects into the river-bottom, and can be seen for fifteen miles below; it bears northeast from the Spanish Peaks. From this point we could mark the course of Timpas Creek from the mountains to its junction with the Arkansas. On the right bank of the Timpas, near its mouth, are several singular buttes, two of which are conical, and the remainder flat-topped. Our noon camp was two miles below the Timpas, and about twenty-eight above Bent's Fort. As this was the distance from Bent's Fort at which the mouth of the Huerfano was placed on our maps, we expected to reach it before dark; but found that we would have to travel sixteen or seventeen miles farther up the Arkansas. In fact, from this point until we reached the Mormon settlement on Little Salt Lake, we could place no reliance on the maps. Crossed the Arkansas one mile above the mouth of the Timpas, and had no difficulty in fording it, though, without due caution, animals are liable to get entangled in quicksands. The grass on the plains west of the Arkansas was more abundant and of a better quality than that on the side we had just left; there was also much grama grass and cactus. The water of the Timpas, which was found in holes only, was cool, but slightly brackish. The night was bright and starry, and illuminated during part of the evening by a beautiful aurora borealis. Day's travel, 30 miles; distance from Westport, 580 miles.

June 2. Left the Timpas at early dawn, and discerned at a distance of fifteen miles several high buttes, bearing due west, in a line with the southern end of the Sierra Mojada; towards these we now directed our course. The country was gradually rolling towards the buttes, and covered with abundant bunch grass; the prickly pear, or cactus, which grows in clusters close to the ground, was at times very distressing to our mules; their constant efforts to avoid treading on this annoying plant gave them an uneasy, jerking gait, very harassing to their riders during a long day's march. Upon reaching the summit of the buttes, a magnificent and extensive panorama was opened to our view. The horizon was bounded on the north by Pike's Peak, northwest and west by the Sierra Mojada, Sangre de Cristo Mountains, and Spanish Peaks; to the south and east extended the prairie, lost in the hazy distance. On the gently undulating plains, reaching to the foot of the mountains, could be traced the courses of the Arkansas and Sage Creek by their lines of timber. The Apispah, an affluent of the Arkansas, issuing from the Sierra Mojada, was concealed from sight by a range of intervening buttes, while the object of our search, the Huerfano, flowed at our feet, distant about three miles, its course easy to be distinguished from the point where it issued from the mountains to its junction with the Arkansas, except at short intervals, where it passed through cañons in the plain. Pike's Peak, whose head was capped with eternal snows, was a prominent object in the landscape, soaring high above all neighboring summits.

Descending the buttes to the Huerfano, we encamped on it about five miles above its mouth. A bold and rapid stream, its waters were turbid, but sweet and cool; the river-bottom was broad, and thickly wooded with willows and cottonwoods,

M 10 U

Pl. II. P. 27.

G. H. Heap del. Lith. of P.S. Duval & Co. Phil.

SPANISH PEAKS.

Huerfano Butte.

U of M

interlaced with the wild rose and grape-vine, and carpeted with soft grass—a sylvan paradise. This stream was about twenty-five yards in breadth, and five feet deep close to the bank. Bands of antelope and deer dotted the plain, one of which served us for supper, brought down by the unerring rifle of Dick, the Delaware.

This camp was to us a scene of real enjoyment; a long and tedious march, over plains of unvarying sameness, was over, and we were now on the eve of entering upon a new and unexplored country, which promised to the admirers of nature a rich and ever-varying treat. The hunters of the party also looked forward with impatience to reaching the mountains, where game of every description was said to abound, and where it would not be necessary to exercise the great patience and perseverance, without which it is difficult to approach deer and antelope on the plains; the Delaware possessed both these requisites in perfection, and gave us daily proofs of his skill. We noticed, whilst travelling along the same route with emigrants, that although game was at times comparatively scarce near the road, it was not owing to the number they destroyed, but rather to the constant *fusillade* which they kept up on everything living, from a buffalo to a goffer, and from a grouse to a blackbird.

In the afternoon, we continued up the Huerfano about a mile, and crossed over to the left bank; the ford was good and but three feet deep. Fine grama grass grew on the upper plain on each side of the river, and an abundance of rich grass on the bottom land. A large growth of cottonwoods line the banks of this stream for twelve miles above its mouth, though higher up it is not so heavily timbered. It is hemmed in at intervals by picturesque bluffs of sandstone.

The following are the bearings of the mouth of the Huerfano; Pike's Peak, northwest; northern Spanish Peak, south-southwest; southern Spanish Peak, south by west. General course of the river, from southwest to northeast. Day's journey, 28 miles; total, 608 miles.

CHAPTER II.

ROUTE FROM HUERFANO RIVER TO COOCHATOPE PASS.

June 3. Our camp the preceding night was a mile below the lower end of the cañon through which the Huerfano forces a passage; this chasm is about ten miles in length, and the ground on each side is much cut up by deep and rocky ravines running into it. I rode up to its entrance to sketch; the scenery was wild and beautiful; wild turkeys flew away at my approach, and the startled deer rose from their beds in the grass at the bottom of the cañon, making their escape up a ravine to the plain. A line of bluffs runs parallel to the Huerfano on the west from two to five miles distant, and wagons should travel at their base to avoid the broken ground nearer the stream; a thick growth of dwarf pines and cedars covers their summits. The wagon trail from the Greenhorn and Hardscrabble settlements on the upper Arkansas approaches the Huerfano below this cañon, leaves it there, and returns to it above.

After a ride of twenty-four miles up the left bank we encamped to noon on a gully where we found water in rocky hollows; the pasturage was excellent, as in fact it had been since reaching the Huerfano, for we had not seen better since leaving Council Grove. The scenery, as we approached the country between the Spanish Peaks and the Sierra Mojada, was picturesque and beautiful; mountains towered high above us, the summits of some covered with snow, while the dense forests of dark pines which clothed their sides, contrasted well with the light green of the meadows near their base. All day, heavy clouds had been gathering on the mountain-tops, portending a storm; at noon it broke, covering them with snow, and soon after swept over the plains. Here it rained in torrents, accompanied by a westerly wind, which blew with such fury as to

Pl. III.

P. 28.

G.H.Heap del.

P.S.Duval & Co. Lith. Philª

LOWER MOUTH OF HUERFANO CAÑON.

U of M

G.H. Heap del.

P.S. Duval & Co. lith. Phil[a]

HUERFANO BUTTE.

U.of M.

render it impossible for man or beast to face it; at the crossing of Apache Creek, a small affluent of the Huerfano, we were compelled to turn our backs to the gale and wait patiently for its subsidence. Long before the rain had ceased on the plains, the mountain tops were again glittering in the setting sun, the newly fallen snow sparkling in his beams, tinged with a rosy hue. Soon after dark we encamped on the Huerfano, in the midst of luxuriant grass. Our packs and bedding had got wet, the ground was spongy and boggy, and, although the rain had ceased, a heavy dew fell during the night, which completely saturated us; we made our beds in deep mud. About a mile beyond our camping place stood the Huerfano Butte, which is so prominent a landmark. Day's march, 34 miles; total distance from Westport, 642 miles.

June 4. I rode ahead of camp, to Huerfano Butte, a remarkable mound, bearing north from the southernmost Spanish Peak, and about fifty yards from the right bank of the river; its appearance was that of a huge artificial mound of stones, covered half-way up from its base with a dense growth of bushes. It is probably of volcanic origin, and there are many indications in this region of the action of internal fires.

Our ride to-day was full of interest, for we were now approaching the Sangre de Cristo Pass, in the Sangre de Cristo Mountains. We had been travelling for eighteen days, over an uninterrupted plain, until its monotony had become extremely wearisome. The mountain scenery, which we entered soon after raising camp this morning, was of the most picturesque description. We crossed the Huerfano seven miles above the Butte; at this point it issues from a cañon one hundred and fifty yards in length; above it the valley, watered by the Huerfano, forms a beautiful plain of small extent, surrounded by lofty and well-wooded mountains; numerous rills trickle down their sides, irrigate the plain, and join their waters to those of the Huerfano, which are here clear and cold. We did not enter this valley, but left the H. after crossing it, and followed up the bed of one of its tributaries, the Cuchada, a small brook rising near the summit of the Sangre de Cristo Pass. This small valley of the Huerfano contains about six hundred acres, and forms a most ravishing picture; it would be a good place for recruiting cattle after their weary march across the plains, as they would be perfectly secure and sheltered, and the pasturage is excellent. This, however, is the case all through these mountains, for waving grass, gemmed with flowers of every hue, covers them to their summits, except in the region of snow. The Cuchada led us up a succession of valleys of an easy grade. We were now travelling on an Indian trail; for the wagon trail, which I believe was made by Roubideau's wagons, deviated to the right, and went through the pass named after him. This pass is so low that we perceived through it a range of sand hills of moderate height, in San Luis valley; to have gone through it, however, would have occasioned us the loss of a day in reaching Fort Massachusetts, though it is the shortest and most direct route to the Coochatope; and Mr. Beale's views constrained him to take the most direct route to Fort Massachusetts, where he expected to obtain a guide through the unexplored country between New Mexico and Utah, and also to procure some mules. We were therefore very reluctantly compelled to forego the examination of Roubideau's Pass.

Encamped at noon at the foot of a remarkable rock, watered at its base by the Cuchada; it resembled the ruined front of a Gothic church. Encamped for the night six miles farther up the valley, and near the summit of the Sangre de Cristo Pass. An excellent wagon road might be made over these mountains, by the Sangre de Cristo Pass, and a still better one through Roubideau's.

The grass around our encampment was really magnificent; it was in a large mountain meadow, watered by numerous springs and girt in by dark pines. Through an opening in the mountains, to the eastward, we could see the sunny plains of the Arkansas and Huerfano, with its remarkable *butte*, whilst around us heavy clouds were collecting, giving warning of a storm and wet night. We made ourselves shelters and beds of pine boughs. The Delaware had killed a fat antelope, which furnished us a hearty supper; and we sat around our fire, until a late hour, well pleased with having accomplished in such good time and without accident the first stage of our journey, for we expected to reach Fort Massachusetts at an early hour next day. Day's march, 26 miles; total distance, 668 miles.

June 5. The rain fell at intervals all night, but the clouds

Pl. V.

P. 30.

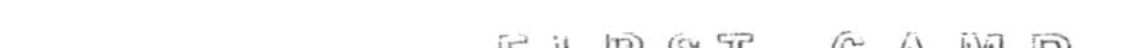

C. H. Heap del.

Lith: of P.S. Duval & Co. Phila

FIRST CAMP.

dispersed before dawn, and the sun rose in a bright and clear sky; the plains, however, were concealed under a sea of snowy mist.

Continued our course to the southwestward through thick pine woods, and in one mile we reached the head waters of Sangre de Cristo Creek, flowing into the Del Norte after its junction with the Trinchera. The Sangre de Cristo mountains, and the Sierras Blanca and Mojada, were covered with snow. We followed down the Sangre de Cristo, which every moment increased in size, its clear and icy waters leaping over rocks, and the mountain sides were covered with tender grass, strawberry blossoms, and violets.

On our maps, the Sangre de Cristo is improperly named Indian Creek, which is a fork of the Sangre de Cristo, and is not named at all on them. Up Indian Creek, I am informed, there exists an excellent pass from San Luis valley to the plains on the eastern side of the mountains.

After crossing Indian Creek, we halted a few minutes to make our toilets previous to our arrival at Fort Massachusetts; and, although our hunter had just ridden into camp with a haunch of fat venison behind his saddle, and our appetites, which were at all times excellent, had been sharpened by a long mountain ride without breakfast, we were too impatient to reach the fort to lose time in camping. We arrived there late in the afternoon, and received a warm and hospitable welcome from Major Blake, the officer in command, Lieutenants Jackson and Johnson, and Dr. Magruder. An incipient rain-storm made us feel sensible that we were still in the vicinity of the Sierra Mojada (or Wet Mountains), which well merit the name, for rain fell every day that we were in or near them; on the highest peaks in the form of snow, and lower down in hazy moisture, alternating with drenching showers. This humidity gives great fertility to this region, and the country bordering on the sides of these mountains, as well as the valleys within their recesses, are unequalled in loveliness and richness of vegetation. To the settler, they offer every inducement; and I have no doubt that in a few years this tract of country will vie with California or Australia in the number of immigrants it will invite to it. It is by far the most beautiful as well as the most fertile portion of New Mexico, and a remarkably level country unites it with the western frontier of the Atlantic States. As soon as this is thrown open to settlement, a continuous line of farms will be established, by which the agricultural and mineral wealth of this region will be developed. Communication will then be more rapid, and instead of the mail being, as it is now, thirty days in reaching Fort Massachusetts, it will be carried through in eight or ten.

Messrs. Beale, Riggs, Rogers, and myself quartered at the Fort; the men encamped two miles below on Utah Creek, in a beautiful grove of cottonwoods. A tent was sent to them, and with fresh bread and meat they were soon rendered perfectly comfortable. There was excellent pasturage around their encampment, on which the mules soon forgot the hard marches they had made since leaving Westport. Day's travel, 25 miles; total distance from Westport to Fort Massachusetts, 693 miles.

June 14. As it was found impossible to obtain here the men and animals that we required, and that it would be necessary to go to Taos, and perhaps to Santa Fé, for this purpose, Mr. Beale and Major Blake left for the former place on the morning after our arrival at the fort. Taos is about eighty, and Santa Fé about one hundred and forty miles to the southward.

During our detention at Fort Massachusetts, I took frequent rides into the mountains on each side of it.

This post is situated in a narrow gorge through which the Utah rushes until it joins the Trinchera, and is a quadrangular stockade of pine log pickets, inclosing comfortable quarters for one hundred and fifty men, cavalry and infantry. Lofty and precipitous mountains surround it on three sides; and although the situation may be suitable for a grazing farm on account of the pasturage, and the abundance of good timber may render this a convenient point for a military station, it is too far removed from the general track of Indians to be of much service in protecting the settlements in San Luis valley from their insults and ravages. The Utahs, who infest the Sahwatch mountains, enter San Luis valley by the Carnero and Coochatope Passes from the westward, and by those of Del Punche, Del Medino, and Del Mosque from the northward and northeastward, and a post established at the head of the valley of San Luis would be much more effective in keeping these marauders in check, as it would there be able to prevent, if necessary, their descending into the valley in large numbers, and completely cut off their retreat with their booty. The valley of the Sahwatch, so rich in pasturage, so well adapted to tillage, and so abundantly watered and timbered, appears to offer the best position for a fort, and it would be as accessible from Taos as the post on the Utah, although the distance would of course be greater.

The cavalry at Fort Massachusetts numbered seventy-five men, of whom forty-five were mounted. Though their horses were excellently groomed and stabled, and kept in high condition on corn, at six dollars a bushel, they would soon break down on a march in pursuit of Indians mounted on horses fed on grass, and accustomed to gallop at half speed up or down the steepest hills. Corn-fed animals lose their strength when they are put on grass, and do not soon get accustomed to the change of diet. Of this fact the officers at the fort were perfectly sensible, and regretted that they were not better prepared for any sudden emergency.

The weather during our stay at the fort was cool and bracing; wind generally from the southwest, with frequent showers of rain.

Mr. Beale returned from the southern country late in the afternoon of this day, and brought with him a guide, and a Mexican *arriero* (muleteer); they were cousins, and both named Felipe Archilete. Jesus Garcia was discharged here, and Patrick Dolan, a soldier who had served out his time, hired in his place. Our party now numbered fourteen.

The guide, Felipe Archilete, or "Peg-Leg," for it was by this *sobriquet* that he was commonly known to Americans, deserves particular mention. He had spent the greater part of his life trading and trapping in the Indian country, and his accurate knowledge of the region between the Arkansas and Sevier River in Utah Territory, as well as his acquaintance with the Utah tongue, promised to render him of great service to us in the absence of Mr. Leroux. A few years ago, in a skirmish with the Utahs, he was wounded in the left ankle with a rifle ball, which completely crippled his foot, and compelled him to use at times a wooden leg, which he carried suspended to his waist. Notwithstanding his lameness, he was one of the most active men of the party, and was always the foremost in times of difficulty and danger.

During Mr. Beale's absence, I replenished our provisions from the sutler's store, and had a small supply of biscuit baked; a bullock which I purchased from the quartermaster, was cut up and jerked by the Delaware, and the mules were reshod, and a supply of spare shoes and nails obtained. They were completely rested, and in even better condition than when we started from Westport; after a general overhauling of the camp equipage by the men, everything was put in order for resuming our journey, as soon as Mr. Beale should return.

June 15. Bidding adieu to our kind friends at the fort, we resumed our journey at noon, and travelled down Utah Creek south-southwest, until it debouched in the valley of San Luis, when we altered our course to west by north. In six miles from Fort Massachusetts, we crossed the trail of Roubideau's wagons from the upper Arkansas settlements; they entered through Roubideau's Pass in the Sierra Mojada. After crossing it, our route led us over a level plain covered with artemisia, cacti, and patches of the nutritious grama. A ride of twenty-five miles brought us at dark to a slough of the Rio del Norte, where we encamped. Day's march, 25 miles; total distance from Westport, 718 miles.

June 16. Our animals were inclined to stray back to the fort, but by constant watchfulness during the night they were prevented from wandering too far from camp. We never hobbled nor picketed our mules, unless compelled to do so by circumstances, for it was noticed that when thus confined they did not eat as heartily as when allowed to range freely in search of the grass they preferred. It was the duty of the men on guard to prevent their straying, and this added much to our fatigue.

Having ascertained that our supply of lead was insufficient, Mr. Rogers and myself started at 4 A. M. to return to Fort Massachusetts to procure more. We crossed a spur of the mountains in a direct line to the fort, instead of going round by their base, thereby saving four or five miles of the distance. The trail was much obstructed by trees and brush; but we reached the fort at an early hour, and also avoided a very troublesome marsh, where some of our mules were mired the day before.

At the fort, we engaged Juan Lente as *arriero* (muleteer), and bought a mule for him. On returning to our last camping place,

Lieut. Johnson gave us an escort of two dragoons. The weather was cool and pleasant in the morning, but warm in the afternoon. Having started from the fort at 2 P. M. we did not reach the slough on the Del Norte until 8½ P. M.

The camp had left in the morning, and had crossed the bottom lands of the Del Norte, eighteen miles in breadth; this crossing is at times difficult and dangerous on account of the numerous sloughs and marshes, which can be altogether avoided, however, by a circuit of a few miles.

Midway to the river they fell in with some Utah Indians, hunting wild horses; the Indians were the first to discover our party, and the foremost stood upright on his horse, in order to obtain a better view; he counted their number, and signalized his discovery with his gun to his comrades, who thereupon approached at full speed. They had their squaws with them and some children, all mounted on good horses, and were quite friendly. In the course of the day they lassoed a mustang, but strangled him in their eagerness to secure their prize. 18 miles; 736 miles.

June 17. Mr. Rogers and myself started at 3 A. M., and overtook our party at 8.30 A. M., as they were preparing to raise camp. We proceeded immediately on our journey, and coasting up the left bank of the Del Norte about ten miles, left it where it made a bend to the westward, directing our course north by west to the Sahwatch valley, the commencement of the Coochatope Pass. Before leaving the Del Norte, the Indians were asked whether there was water in the direction in which we were going; for the commencement of the Sahwatch valley was about thirty miles distant. They replied that we should find water and grass by going around by the foot of the mountains, but none by going direct. The circuitous route they recommended would have occupied us two days, whilst we hoped to accomplish the distance direct before night. Our red friends were unwilling to venture with us, and bade us farewell; we parted with them on friendly terms; they had spent the night in our camp, shared our supper and breakfast, and smoked our pipes.

The plain was as level as the sea to the foot of the mountains, which inclose San Luis valley. A low spur of hills to the northward, indicated the entrance to the valley of the Sahwatch. In fourteen miles from the point where we left the river, we crossed a fine brook of clear and cool water—the Rio de la Garita, which rises in the Sahwatch mountains, and, flowing east, discharges itself into a large lagoon at the base of the Sierra Mojada, in the northern part of the valley of San Luis. Its banks were swampy, and, although later in the season this inconvenience probably does not exist, wagons would do well to cross it nearer to the mountains on the left. Our course was in the face of a breeze which raised clouds of dust wherever the soil was loosened by our animals' feet, and those riding in the rear suffered much inconvenience from it. In ten miles from the Rio Garita, we came to an abundant spring, surrounded by good grass, where we rested but a moment to drink, though we had travelled steadily since morning without eating. Mr. Beale was anxious to reach the entrance of the Sahwatch valley before evening, and to regain some of the time which had been unavoidably lost at Fort Massachusetts. At the spring we found a trail leading to the Sahwatch valley, and as soon as our mules struck it they stepped out with fresh spirit. The valley of San Luis, to the commencement of the Sahwatch is singularly level, the smooth ground seeming only to have the natural curve of the earth. The only vegetation, excepting in the vicinity of water, was artemisia, cactus, and occasionally grama grass.

The valley of the Sahwatch has two entrances from that of San Luis. The one which we selected, on account of its being the nearest, is called by the Spaniards El Rincon del Sahwatch (the corner of the Sahwatch), as it forms a cut-off into Sahwatch valley proper. The main entrance is a few miles farther on. We went three miles up the Rincon, and encamped at sunset at a spring of excellent water, where our mules found fine pasturage. Mr. Rogers and myself rode sixty-eight miles this day, and fifty the day before; which I mention to show the facility of travelling in this region. Day's march, 50 miles; whole distance, 786 miles.

June 18. Mosquitos allowed us little rest. As our animals had had rather a long march the day before, camp was not raised until 8 A. M. For two and a half miles our course was west by north; we then turned to the northward over some steep hills, and, upon reaching their summit, obtained a

UofM

G. H. Heap del.   Lith. of P. S. Duval & Co. Phila.

ENTRANCE OF SAH WATCH VALLEY.

San Luis Valley and the Sierra Blanca in the distance.

UofM

Pl. VII.

P. 37.

G. H. Heap del.

P. S. Duval & Co. Lith. Phil.

SCENERY IN SAHWATCH VALLEY.

glorious view of the valley of the Sahwatch. It was quite level, and from two to five miles in breadth, gradually narrowing to the westward; the rise was imperceptible, appearing like a continuation of the plain of San Luis. An abundant stream, the Sahwatch, nearly as broad as the Huerfano, but deeper, flows through its centre, and empties into the lagoon in San Luis valley. Its surface was clothed with nutritious grasses, and the hills and mountains by which it is hemmed in were covered with a thick growth of firs, aspens, and pines.

We proceeded fourteen miles farther up, and encamped at noon in a small valley running into the main one. There is an abundance of water in all the lateral valleys, as well as grass; in the main one, I noticed a superior quality of sandstone. The weather was clear and pleasant, and wind west.

On resuming our march in the afternoon, we ascended the small valley, as it shortened the distance a couple of miles, and re-entered that of the Sahwatch. After a ride of eight miles we crossed Sahwatch Creek, its waters reaching to our saddles, and encamped, as the sun was setting, at the entrance of the celebrated Coochatope Pass.

Sahwatch valley maintains its level character to this point, and for several miles above, where it was shut from view by a curve. The entrance to the Carnero Pass is about a mile above the Coochatope, and we regretted that we had not time to examine it.

A military post placed in Sahwatch valley, between these two passes, would do important service in holding the Utahs in check. These Indians most frequently enter San Luis valley through these passes, and it is here that a fort would be best placed to prevent their incursions, or to intercept their retreat with booty. The mountains are clothed with timber from their base to their summit, the valley with luxuriant and nutritious grasses, and clear, brawling mountain streams pour into them on every side. The distance to the nearest New Mexican settlements is about one hundred and twenty miles, and the intervening country is a dead level. If undisturbed by the incursions of Indians, these valleys would soon be settled and cultivated; for it is only of late, since the establishment of a military post on Utah Creek, that settlements of any consequence have been made on Costilla and Culebra creeks.

CHAPTER III.

FROM THE COOCHATOPE PASS TO GRAND RIVER—LOSSES ON GRAND RIVER.

COOCHATOPE PASS is a wonderful gap, or, more properly speaking, a natural GATE, as its name denotes in the Utah language. On each side, mountains rise in abrupt and rocky precipices, the one on the eastern side being the highest. We climbed up the one on the left, which is but a confused mass of rocks, but in their crevices were many beautiful and sweet-scented flowers. The bottom of the Pass was level and at right angles with Sahwatch valley; and we had thus far reached twenty-five miles into the mountains, from San Luis valley, without any apparent change of level. Singular as it may appear, it is nevertheless a fact that, notwithstanding the distance that we had penetrated into these mountains, had it not been for the course of the waters, it would have been difficult to have determined whether we were ascending or descending.

A stream issues from Coochatope Pass and joins the Sahwatch; it is called *Coochumpah* by the Utahs, and *Rio de los Cibolos* by the Mexicans: both names have the same signification—*River of buffaloes. Coochatope* signifies, in the Utah language, *Buffalo gate*, and the Mexicans have the same name for it, *El Puerto de los Cibolos.* The pass and creek are so called, from the large herds of these animals which entered Sahwatch and San Luis valleys through this pass, from the Three Parks and Upper Arkansas, before they were destroyed, or the direction of their migration changed, by the constant warfare carried on against them by Indians and New Mexicans. A few still remain in the mountains, and are described as very wild and savage. We saw a great number of elk-horns scattered through these valleys; and, from the comparatively fresh traces of buffaloes, it

G.H.Heap del. P.S.Duval & Co. Lith. Phila.

COOCHATOPE PASS.

"The Gate of Buffaloes," in Sahwatch Mts.

U of M

Pl. IX.

P. 39.

G. H. Heap del.

P. S. Duval & Co. lith. Phila

COOCHATOPE PASS.

was evident that many had visited the pass quite recently. The abundant pasturage and great shelter found here, even in the severest winters, render them a favorite resort at that season for game of every description. Coochatope Pass is travelled at all seasons, and some of our men had repeatedly gone through it in the middle of winter without meeting any serious obstruction from snow. Many Utahs winter in the valleys lying within the Sahwatch mountains, where Mexican traders meet them to barter for buckskins and buffalo robes.

Our Delaware, in commemoration of our arrival at this point, killed a mountain sheep, and soon a dozen sticks were around the fire, on which were roasting pieces of this far-famed meat; but this was a bad specimen, being both old and tough. Day's travel, 22 miles; total distance, 808 miles.

We resumed our journey at 5.30 A. M., and, having travelled two miles, reached the forks of the Coochumpah, taking the west fork up the valley, which here commenced to ascend at an easy grade. The mountain sides were clothed with fine timber, among which were pines, firs, and aspens, and the valley with the most luxuriant grass and clover, this being the first clover we had seen. Around us were scattered numerous elk-horns and buffalo skulls. Eight miles brought us to a remarkable cliff, about one hundred feet in height, which beetled over the trail on our left; nine miles from the "Gate," we saw the last water flowing east to the Atlantic; in five minutes we were on the culminating point of the pass, and in ten more crossed the first stream flowing west to the Pacific. It was almost as if we were standing with one foot in waters which found their way to the Gulf of Mexico, and the other in those losing themselves in the Gulf of California.

In our eagerness to explore this pass to its western outlet, Mr. Beale and I rode far ahead of the remainder of the party. The scenery was grand and beautiful beyond description. Lofty mountains, their summits covered with eternal snows, lifted their heads to the clouds, whilst in our immediate vicinity were softly rounded hills clothed with grass, flowers, and rich meadows, through which numerous rills trickled to join their waters to Coochatope Creek.

At noon we encamped on this stream, where it had already swollen to a considerable size. It is a tributary of Grand River, east fork of the Great Colorado. Near camp was a lofty and steep hill, which I ascended to obtain a better view of the country; one of its principal features was the Coochatope Mountain to the southeast; high, round, and dark with pines.

We were here compelled, by the necessity that we were under of selecting the shortest route, to go by the trail which takes the most direct course to Grand River, though there was a more circuitous route to the right, leading over a level country, but which would have lengthened the journey by two days.

Travelled ten miles in the afternoon over a rich rolling country, well timbered and watered, and covered with luxuriant grasses. Saw many deer, antelopes, and mountain sheep. Day's travel, 34 miles; whole distance, 842 miles.

June 20. The usual cry of "catch up," set the camp in motion at 5.45 A. M. We travelled twenty-two miles over a rolling country, more hilly than our route of the previous day, and encamped on a rivulet at noon. Our course was south by west. The hill-sides and mountains were still covered with a thick growth of pines and aspens; wild flowers adorned the murmuring streams, and beautified the waving grass. Every few hundred yards we came to one of these purling brooks, the haunt of the timid deer, who bounded away at our approach. To the westward, the Eagle Range (La Sierra del Aguila), towered high above the surrounding mountains, its summits capped with snow, some patches of which we passed near our trail. Mr. Beale shot a species of grouse, larger than a prairie hen, and caught one of her young. At 5.30 P. M., in five miles from our noon camp, we crossed the two forks of the Jaroso (Willow Creek), a strong stream running into Grand River, not laid down on any map. At 7 P. M. we rested for the night in a valley watered by a small shallow brook, very marshy, and swarming with mosquitos. Our general course this day was southwest. Numbers of deer and antelopes were seen; indeed, these sheltered valleys seem expressly intended as coverts for these gentle animals.

About a mile before reaching the Jaroso, we crossed a valley where a party of Americans were cruelly murdered by the Utahs, in the spring of this year. Five Americans, and a few Mexicans, were driving sheep to California by this route, and, from some cause which I did not ascertain, a disagree-

UofM

Pl. X.

P. 41.

G. H. Heap del.

Lith: of P. S. Duval & Co. Phil^a

RIO DE LA LAGUNA.

Sierra de la Plata.

ment arose between them and a band of Utahs, who were still here in their winter-quarters. The latter forbade their passing through their country, and, placing a row of elk-horns across the valley, threatened them with instant death if they crossed that line. The whites deeming this a vain threat, attempted to force their way through, were attacked, and all killed. The elk-horns were still in the position in which the Indians had placed them. Our guide, Felipe, had an account of this affair from Utahs who had been actors in the affray. At this point the trail from the Del Norte through the Carnero Pass joins that through the Coochatope. Traders from Abiquiú come by it into these mountains to barter for peltries with the Utahs. Day's travel, 34 miles; total, 876 miles.

June 21. Raised camp at 4.45 A. M. and travelled five miles west by south, crossing a steep and rocky hill covered with pines, and in five miles entered a small valley watered by the Rio de la Laguna (Lake Creek). This creek issues from a lake near the summit of the Sierra de la Plata (Silver Range), about twelve acres in area; we found it unfordable on account of its swollen condition from melting snows. Its current was swift and waters turbid, rolling with a loud roar over a rocky bed. It both enters and leaves this valley through narrow and rocky cañons; above the upper one it flows through another valley of larger extent and of great beauty.

It became a question with us, how our packs were to be transported over the laguna without getting them wet or lost, and we at first attempted to make a bridge by felling a tall pine across the stream, but it fell partly into the water, and the current carried it away, tearing it into pieces. This plan having failed, another was adopted, suggested by what Mr. Beale had seen in his travels in Peru, and the mode of crossing the plunging torrents of the Andes, which was entirely successful.

Mr. Rogers selected a point where the stream was for some distance free from rocks, and succeeded, after a severe struggle, in swimming across; and one of the men mounting a stray Indian pony, which we found quietly grazing in the valley, dashed in after him, and also effected a landing on the opposite side. To them a light line was thrown, and having thus established a communication with the other side, a larger rope was drawn over by them, and tied firmly to a rock near the water's edge.

The end of the rope on our side was made fast to the top of a pine tree; a backstay preventing it from bending to the weight of the loads sent over. An iron hook was now passed over the rope, and by means of a sling our packs were suspended to it. The hook slided freely from the top of the tree down to the rock; and when the load was taken off, we drew the hook and sling back to our side by a string made fast to it. The last load sent over was our wearing apparel, and just after parting with it, a violent hailstorm broke over us, making us glad to seek shelter from its fury under rocks and trees. Most of the day was thus consumed, and it was not until 5 P. M. that we mounted our mules and swam them across. The water was icy cold, and some of the animals had a narrow escape from drowning. We, however, saddled up immediately, and, proceeding four miles from the creek, encamped for the night in a small hollow. On leaving the Rio de la Laguna, the road ascended a high and steep hill. The country travelled over this day was abundantly grassed, the hills timbered with firs, pines, and aspens, and the streams shaded with willows. Day's travel, 9 miles; total, 885 miles.

June 22. We started soon after sunrise and travelled west by south over steep hills, well timbered and covered with rich grasses. The weather was clear and cold, and wind fresh from the west. Crossed three streams swollen by melting snow: the Rio Hondo (Deep River), the Savoya, and the Pentacigo (Leek Creek). At 10 A. M., in twenty miles from the Rio de la Laguna, we crossed the two forks of the Nawaquasitch (Sheep-tail Creek, Utah language). The Mexicans call it Los Riitos Quartos (Twin Creeks), and the Cola del Carnero (Sheep-tail Creek). We forded it immediately above the junction of the forks. Both were much swollen, and we had some difficulty in crossing the packs, some of which got wet. A pair of saddle-bags containing many articles of value to us were lost in this crossing. All these streams are mere rivulets a month or two later. Encamped at noon on the left bank of the western fork of the Nawaquasitch.

Started again an hour before sunset, and following down the left bank of the Nawaquasitch until it turned to the northward through a deep cañon, left it and directed our course to the westward. The Nawaquasitch empties into Grand River (east

P. 42.

G. H. Heap del.

P. S. Duval & Co. lith. Phila.

GROSSING LAGUNA CREEK.

U of M

fork of the Colorado), not far beyond the outlet of this cañon. All the streams that we passed this day are tributaries of Grand River, and are not laid down on any map.

We were now approaching the western limits of the Sahwatch Mountains, and continued down a rivulet until it gave out, as it reached the base of the hills. Upon reaching the plain which extends from the foot of the Sahwatch Range to Grand River, we encamped for the night, having made twenty miles since noon. There was grass in small patches on the brook down which we travelled, and it grew scantier as we approached the plains. This stream dries up entirely in a month or six weeks from this time.

The Pareamoot Mountains (Elk Mountains, Utah tongue), a range of whose unexplored beauties much had been related to us, loomed up darkly between us and the setting sun. Day's march, 38 miles; total distance, 923 miles.

June 23. At an early hour in the morning, Mr. Beale, Felipe Archilete, the Delaware, and I, taking the lead, arrived at the River Uncompagre at 11.10 A. M. We travelled about twelve miles parallel with this river, and found it everywhere a broad rapid stream, entirely too rapid and swift to ford with safety; we therefore continued down its right bank until we reached Grand River.

We had been prepared to find Grand River swollen, for its tributaries which we had crossed were all at their highest stage of water; but we had not anticipated so mighty a stream. It flowed with a loud and angry current, its amber-colored waters roaring sullenly past, laden with the wrecks of trees uprooted by their fury. Sounds like the booming of distant artillery, occasioned by the caving in of its clayey and sandy banks, constantly smote our ears. This fork of the Colorado rises in the Middle Park, and gathers all its head waters in that inclosure, and is described by Frémont, who crossed it there, as being a large river, one hundred and thirty yards wide where it breaks through its mountain rim and flows southwest. Between that point and where we approached it, numerous streams contribute their waters to increase its volume; and where we now stood, anxiously gazing at its flood, it had spread to a breadth of over two hundred and fifty yards.

As it was evident that this river was nowhere fordable, it

was determined to commence at once the construction of a raft. A place where dead wood was found in abundance was selected for our encampment, and to reach it, it was necessary to cross a broad slough, where the mules sank to their bellies in the mud; the packs were carried over on our heads. This brought us to an island of loose, rotten soil, covered with grease wood and some coarse grass. We had no shelter from the sun, which was intensely hot, and the mosquitos and gadflies were perfectly terrific.

From this point, the Pareamoot Mountains were in full view; they ranged from the north, and terminated in an abrupt declivity on the western side of Grand River, opposite to the mouth of the Uncompagre. They were described to me as abounding in game, and well timbered; on their plateaux, are fine lakes filled with excellent fish, rich meadows, abundant streams, every natural attraction, in fact, to induce settlement.

Our guide, Felipe, had spent three years in them, trapping and hunting, and said that there is no richer country on the continent. These mountains are not laid down on any map. Day's travel, 28 miles; total distance, 951 miles.

June 24. Whilst most of the party were busily occupied in collecting and cutting logs, constructing the raft, and transporting the packs, saddles, &c., to the point of embarkation, which had to be done in deep mud, and under a scorching sun, others explored the banks of the river, to ascertain whether a place could be found where the *cavallade* could be crossed over. The river was examined several miles above our encampment, but its banks on our side were everywhere so marshy as to prevent the approach of the mules to the water's edge. At the encampment, the ground was firmer, but we feared to drive them into the river at this point, as it was here not only very rapid and broad, but its opposite banks, as far down as we could see, were marshy and covered with a thick jungle, from which our mules, after the exhaustion of swimming across so swift a current, would have been unable to extricate themselves.

Towards noon the raft was completed, but we were far from feeling confident about crossing at this point. Archilete, who was well acquainted with all the fords and crossing-places, stated that perhaps a better point might be found a few miles below the mouth of the Uncompagre, which flowed into Grand River a short distance below us. As it was evident that it would be risking the entire loss of our animals and packs to attempt to cross them here, it was determined to abandon the raft and to move camp farther down without delay. Everything was again transported to the main shore across the slough. The animals had much difficulty in crossing this place, even without loads; with them, they sank hopelessly into the mud, from which it was very difficult to drag them out.

A more dirty, begrimed, and forlorn looking party was never seen; we were covered with mud to our waists; wherever the mosquitos and gadflies could reach our skin they improved the opportunity most industriously, and most of the men were covered with blisters and welts. All cheerfully took a share in this labor, but a volley of execrations was poured on this quagmire, which was appropriately christened the "Slough of Despond."

Having transported everything to dry land and got the animals through the mud, we once more packed them and resumed our journey down the left bank of Grand River until we came to the Uncompagre, a short distance above its mouth.

The largest animals were here selected to carry the packs across, their feet barely touching the bottom, whilst the strength of the current drove the water over their backs. Some of the men, mounted on horses, led the pack mules, and prevented their being carried down the stream where the water was deeper. One mule, with a valuable pack, having gone in of her own accord, was carried away, lost her foothold and sank, the weight of the pack being too great to allow her to swim; she was swept down the stream with great rapidity, rolling over helplessly until entirely lost to our sight by a bend of the river. Some of the party swam across, and one, benumbed by the coldness of the water, and exhausted by struggling against the stream, would have been drowned had he not been providentially seized just as his strength had entirely failed him.

We encamped a few miles below the Uncompagre, on the left bank of Grand River, upon a bluff from which we had a fine view of its course, and of the Pareamoot Mountains opposite. Our tormentors, the mosquitos, did not fail to welcome us with a loud buzz, whilst the drone of the gadfly, which might with truth be termed the *furia-infernalis* of the plains, gave notice that he was about, thirsting for our blood. Wherever he inserted his proboscis, the sensation was like that of a redhot darning-needle thrust into the flesh, and was followed by a stream of blood. The mules and horses suffered terribly by these flies.

Our provisions, by losses in the river and damage by water, were fast diminishing, and it was deemed prudent at this time to put ourselves on a limited allowance, for it was uncertain how long we might be detained in crossing this river, the Avonkaria, and Upper Colorado.

The pack lost with the mule drowned in the Uncompagre contained many articles of importance to us, besides all our *pinole* (parched cornmeal), and some of the men lost all their clothing.

It was late when we got to camp, and after a day of toil, exposure, and annoyance, nothing more could be done than to select the tree out of which to make a canoe, and the place to launch it; for all idea of crossing on a raft was abandoned. A few miles below the encampment the river was shut in by a cañon, towards which it dove with great swiftness; a raft carried into it would have been torn to pieces in a moment, without a chance for the men on it to save their lives. Day's travel, 5 miles; total, 956 miles.

June 25. At early dawn most of the party commenced working on the canoe; their only tools were two dull axes and two hatchets. A large cottonwood tree was felled for this purpose, and it was hoped to have the canoe finished the next day. The wood, being green and full of sap, was hard to cut, and so heavy that chips of it sank when thrown into the water.

The river still maintained the same level, and the bottom land was overflowed and marshy. The high lands on which we were encamped were composed of a loose, rotten soil, producing no vegetation except stunted sage bushes. The only game we had seen for two days was an occasional sage rabbit, so called from its flesh having a strong flavor of the wild sage (artemisia), on which it feeds. The sun was very hot and mosquitos tormenting; we removed our camp to the bluffs in the hope of avoiding them, but with little success.

At this point, the general course of the river was parallel with the Pareamoot Mountains, from northeast to southwest.

G.H. Heap del.

P.S. Duval & Co. lith. Phil^a

GRAND RIVER,

Below the junction of the Uncompagre.

The latter appeared to rise in terraces, upon which much timber could be seen.

The work on the canoe was continued steadily all day, though some of the party entertained grave doubts about crossing in it; besides, the two rivers beyond Grand River were said to be larger and their current swifter than this. Archilete stated that he had never seen the river so high, and that it was owing to the unusual quantity of snow which had fallen in the mountains during last winter. The wind rose at ten o'clock and blew with violence until sunset, which relieved us in a measure from the torment of mosquitos, but they returned in fresh swarms as soon as it lulled.

June 26. Opposite to our encampment was old "Fort Roubideau," now abandoned and in ruins. It was formerly a trading post belonging to the brothers Roubideau, of St. Louis, Missouri, who carried on a lucrative trade with the Utahs for peltries.

Beavers are quite numerous on all these rivers, and have greatly multiplied of late years since the demand for their furs has diminished.

The canoe was completed at noon, and a fire was kindled in and around it to dry it. At 4 P. M., the first load went over with the Delaware and Archilete. Everything had to be carried to the water's edge through a thick jungle, knee deep in mud, and under a broiling sun.

They reached the opposite side safely, although the current carried them some distance down the stream. The canoe was found to be very heavy, and easy to upset. Archilete, Juan Lente, and myself went with the second load, reached the other side, and, after unloading, dragged the canoe some distance up stream to enable Archilete, who was to take it back, to make a landing at the point where the packs were deposited. Two more of the men crossed with the next load, and Archilete returned in the canoe to the left bank for the night.

We were now four persons on the right bank of the stream, with the prospect of getting the rest of the party and packs across at an early hour the next day. We retired to some dry land about half a mile from the river, and carried to it the few things that had been brought over. Just before dark, Dick, the Delaware, made his appearance in camp, dripping wet, and reported that he had just swam across with some of the mules; that after getting all into the water most of them had turned back, while three mules and one horse, having reached the right bank, had sunk into the mud, from which he had been unable to relieve them. We immediately went down to the water's edge with ropes, and with great difficulty got the horse out of his bed of mud, but found it impossible to extricate the mules. We were compelled to leave the poor animals in their forlorn situation until the morning, when we hoped to get them on dry land.

June 27. Rose at dawn, and our first business was to get the mules out of their dangerous predicament, by cutting bushes and spreading them around the mired animals, thus rendering the ground sufficiently firm to support their weight.

At an early hour, a signal was made to us from the other side that the canoe was about starting to cross. We therefore went down to the river side to receive its load. In a few minutes she made her appearance, driving rapidly down the stream. She was heavily loaded, barely four inches of her gunwale being above the water's edge. Felipe Archilete, a strong and active fellow, was paddling, whilst George Simms was crouched in the bow of the boat. They were unable to reach the point where previous landings had been effected, and were soon shut from our sight by trees and tangled bushes, growing close to the water. In a few seconds we heard the most alarming cries for help, and upon rushing to the spot from which these cries proceeded, found Archilete and George just emerging from the water, nearly exhausted with their struggles.

It appears that upon approaching the bank and grasping some small limbs of trees overhanging the water, the latter broke, whereupon one of the men, becoming alarmed, attempted to jump from the boat to the shore, causing it immediately to upset. They were both thrown into the stream, which here ran with a strong current, and it was with difficulty that they reached the shore. I immediately called to one of the men who was standing near the horse, to gallop down the river's edge, and by swimming him into the middle of the stream to endeavor to reach the canoe should it make its appearance. But it was never seen again, nor did we recover any of the articles with which it was loaded. We lost by this accident seven rifles, nearly all our ammunition, pistols, saddles, corn-meal, coffee, sugar, blankets, &c.

With broken axes and dull hatchets it would have been difficult if not impossible to have constructed another canoe; and, besides, the men were too much discouraged by this loss to undertake the labor with the spirit necessary to carry it through.

Our party was equally divided; we were seven on each side. Some of the gentlemen on the left bank were now anxious to return to New Mexico to proceed to California by some other route; but Mr. Beale would not listen for a moment to such proposition. He hailed me at eight o'clock, and told me that as soon as he could construct a raft, and get the few remaining things and the animals over, we would push on for the Mormon settlements near the Vegas de Santa Clara. Expedition was necessary, for we had provisions for only four or five days.

The Delaware swam back to Mr. Beale's side to assist him to construct a raft or canoe. He was a splendid swimmer, and went through the water like an otter. They immediately commenced the construction of another canoe, but both axes being broken, they soon had to relinquish the task as hopeless.

An inventory was made of the provisions, and it was found that we had twenty-five pounds of biscuit, mostly in dust, twenty-five pounds of dried venison, and ten pounds of bacon. Although this was but slender provision for fourteen hungry men, we had no fear of starvation, or even of suffering, as long as we had the mules. I also discovered in an old bag a small supply of powder and lead, and some chocolate and tobacco. A canister of *meat-biscuit*, upon which we had depended in case of an emergency of this sort, had unfortunately gone down with the canoe.

At an early hour in the morning, we saw flying from a tree on the left bank, the preconcerted signal to "come down for a talk." To reach the river, we had to wade for half a mile through a deep marsh, into which we sank to our knees, and the air was thick with mosquitos.

Mr. Beale informed me that it had been decided to return to Taos for supplies, and inquired whether we could get back to the left bank. As two of the men on my side stated that they could not swim, it was decided to make a raft, and, if possible, to save the articles we had with us. Before this was determined upon, however, Mr. Beale ordered Archilete to swim over to his side, which the latter did at once, taking his timber leg under his arm; and in the afternoon they made another ineffectual attempt to get the animals across. There was but one point where it was possible to drive them into the river, and here they crowded in on each other until those underneath were near drowning. Mr. Beale and one of the men, who were riding, went into the river to lead the band across. The mules fell on them from the bank, which was at this place about three feet high, and for a moment they were in imminent danger of being crushed. An old horse alone struck boldly over, but none of the other animals followed his example. They all got out on the same side, and could not be again driven into the water.

Mr. Beale now desired me to make arrangements for returning to his side of the river, and while preparing the animals to move down to our camping ground, I thought I heard a faint shout, and at the same time perceiving two dark objects moving in the water, some distance up the stream, I suspected that they were men from the opposite shore endeavoring to reach land on our side. The current was carrying them swiftly on towards a high bank overhanging the stream, where, without help, to have effected a landing would have been impossible.

Hastily seizing a rope, and calling to the men to follow, I ran to the top of the cliff. In fact, they were our two best swimmers, Dick and Felipe, who were scarcely able to keep their hold until ropes could be led down to them. We drew them up half perished, and it required a good fire and something stimulating to restore circulation to their limbs, benumbed by the icy coldness of the water. Although we had no sugar, some coffee, that the Delaware had brought, tied in a handkerchief on his head, cheered the men, and we passed a good night, happy in any rest after such a day of toil.

June 29. At an early hour in the morning, I commenced throwing into the river everything that we could possibly dispense with, such as clothing, &c. I allowed each man to select sufficient clothes from the general stock to make up one suit, and it was singular how soon their wants increased. Some of the Mexicans, who heretofore had been satisfied with one shirt and a pair of pants, now arrayed themselves in as many breeches, drawers, shirts, and stockings as they could force themselves into. I *cachèd*, under a thick bush, a few Indian goods that we had brought with us as presents.

The three mules and two horses were passed over to the left shore without much difficulty by pushing them into the water from a bank, whence the eddy immediately carried them into the middle of the stream. They got out safely on the other side, and we at once commenced constructing the raft.

It was completed at 1 P. M., and, although it was twelve feet in length by eight in breadth, the weight of seven men, with the saddles, arms, and provisions we had saved, caused it to sink eighteen inches under water. It drifted rapidly down the stream, the men whooping and yelling, until one struck up the old song of "O Susannah!" when the rest sang the chorus. In this style, we fell upwards of two miles down the river, propelling ourselves with rough paddles. Mr. Beale and others of the party stood on a hill on the opposite side cheering and waving their hats. Having approached within ten yards of the left bank, our tritons, Dick and Archilete, sprang into the water, with ropes in their teeth, and reaching the shore soon dragged the raft to the bank, upon which the remainder of the crew landed.

CHAPTER IV.

JOURNEY OF MR. HEAP TO NEW MEXICO AND BACK.
MR. BEALE'S SEPARATE JOURNAL.

No time was lost in collecting and saddling the animals, and our packs being reduced from eleven to three, they were soon loaded. Those whose saddles went down with the canoe used their blankets instead, and at four P. M. we started to return to New Mexico. The defeat which we had sustained at Grand River, and the consequent delay, caused some of the party to be in low spirits; but regrets were useless; we determined to return again, and so well provided as to prevent a second failure. We now measure back. Day's travel, 8 miles; distance from Grand River, 8 miles.

June 30. We were in our saddles at sunrise, for the lightness of our baggage occasioned no waste of time in packing. Those of the party who had lost their blankets passed a cold night under their saddle-cloths. Our breakfast consisted of a few spoonfuls of *atole* (cornmeal mush), washed down with coffee without sugar; and although the repast was far from palatable, we found it wholesome and *filling*, a property which was to us of much importance. The mules had been much harassed by the various attempts made to drive them across the river, and by the mosquitos and gadflies; yet they had picked up both flesh and spirit, and appeared happy to be treading once more on dry land, where they were not exposed to the momentary danger of sinking into a mudhole. We therefore travelled rapidly, and at 3.30 P. M. reached the Nawaquasitch, forty-three miles from our last encampment. It was here that we had previously experienced some difficulty in crossing, and where a pair of saddle-bags, containing many articles of value to us, were lost. The road during the day was the same which we had before travelled in going to Grand River; the face of the country was generally perfectly level, offering to our view but little of interest until we reached the foot-hills of the Sahwatch range, which we entered by a narrow valley, watered by a small rivulet. This we followed up about twenty miles, the country rapidly improving in beauty and fertility as we advanced into the mountains. We this time crossed the Nawaquasitch below the forks, and followed up its right bank about two miles. All around us the hills and mountains were covered with rich verdure; beautiful copses and groups of trees diversified the scenery, giving it the appearance of a settled country, only wanting dwellings to render it a perfect picture of rural beauty.

As the grass at this place was rich and nutritious, timber abundant, and fine streams irrigated every valley, it was selected by Mr. Beale for an encampment, where he would await my return from New Mexico with fresh supplies. Wagner, Young, Dick Brown (the Delaware), and Felipe Archilete, Jr., would remain with him, and I was to take Felipe Archilete, Sr. (Pegleg,) as guide; and was also accompanied by those of the party who preferred going the longer route to California, *via* Fort Laramie and Great Salt Lake, to risking another encounter with Grand River and the unknown hardships beyond. Day's travel, 43 miles; distance from Grand River, 51 miles.

July 1. It was not until eight o'clock that I started from Mr. Beale's camp on the Nawaquasitch. He and the men who remained with him had many letters to write, which caused some detention. We left them with regret, for who could foresee what might happen to their little party in this lonely region, particularly as the season was approaching when the Indians would be returning here from buffalo-hunting? In addition to other causes for anxiety, we had but a small store of provisions, consisting of sour cornmeal and coffee, which, when divided between the two parties, gave to each barely enough for three days' subsistence. The Delaware had gone out hunting at an early hour, and, as we lost sight of the camp, we saw him descending a mountain at some distance with a deer behind his saddle, which he was carrying into Mr. Beale's camp.

The Rio de la Laguna (Willow Creek), where we had lost nearly a day in crossing our packs, had fallen slightly, and, as we had now but little that could be injured by water, we rode our mules across without stopping. At 6 P. M. we reached Rio Jaroso (Willow Creek), where the trail leading to the Puerto del Carnero (Mountain-sheep Pass) branches off to the southward from that to the Coochatope Pass.

This trail leads into San Luis valley by a shorter route than that by the Coochatope, and as it would give me the opportunity of examining a region and pass entirely unknown except to Indians, and Mexicans trading with them, I selected it for our passage through the Sahwatch range. I consider it a fortunate circumstance that I came to this determination, for the pass through which we went proved to be, in many respects, superior even to the Coochatope.

When we diverged to the right to take this trail, we commenced ascending a long and narrow gorge, which led us by an easy grade to the summit of a hill, where we encamped at 7 P. M. near an abundant spring. It would be needless repetition to mention again the luxuriance of the grass which covered the valleys, hill-sides, and mountains, for all through the Sahwatch range the country maintains the same rich and fertile character.

Our last meal was in the morning, and consisted of a ball of dough, which to some bore a fancied resemblance to the old Virginia hoe-cake. The soothing effects of this delicious morsel on our stomachs had for many hours passed away and been forgotten, so that when we gathered around the camp-fire to partake of a soup of grouse shot by Peg-leg, nine men more hungry it would have been difficult to find. We saw during the day many deer and antelopes, but the only rifle in the company was Peg-leg's, and it had been so much damaged as to render it almost useless for a long shot. Day's travel, 40 miles; distance from Grand River, 91 miles.

July 2. I passed a miserable night; it was cold and frosty, with a piercing north wind. My saddle-blanket was the only covering I had, and it was worn so thin and threadbare that it imparted scarcely any warmth. We saddled up and started at sunrise, directing our course nearly due east. The trail led over a mountain covered with thick pine forests, interspersed with rich meadows, and watered by numerous clear rills, until we reached a portion of the range where a hurricane or whirlwind had, some years ago, uprooted and strewed in every direction a forest of tall pine trees. Through this tangled mass we forced our way with difficulty, but finally got through and commenced a gradual descent on the eastern side of the range.

Peg-leg and myself were riding at a distance in advance of the rest of the party, when, upon crossing the summit of a hill, we suddenly found ourselves in the midst of a large flock of tame goats, behind which was a band of fifty mounted Utahs, to whom they belonged. The Indians immediately gathered around us and overwhelmed us with questions; but were civil, and seemed light-hearted and merry. Most of the men had good rifles, and their horses were all in fine condition. My first thought upon meeting these Indians was the possibility of replenishing our exhausted larder with dried meat, and Peg-leg no sooner informed them that we had been on short commons for several days than they dismounted, unpacked their animals, and from their store presented me with a plentiful supply of dried buffalo, deer, and antelope flesh. Men, women, and children crowded around my mule, each handing me a parcel of meat; and, although it was apparent that they expected nothing in return, I gave them as good a supply of tobacco, powder, lead, and percussion caps as I could spare; but nothing delighted them so much as a box of lucifer matches; for, having shown them that by a simple friction they might produce a blaze, their joy was great, and each member of the band was eager to perform the feat of kindling a fire.

A garrulous old Indian, who wore, by way of distinction, a "Genin" hat, sorely battered and bruised, and which had become the property of this venerable Utah by one of those reverses of fortune to which hats are so liable, addressed us a harangue accompanied by many gestures. Peg-leg translated his meaning to me, which was to the effect, that they had been unsuccessful in the buffalo hunt, on which they depended in a great measure for their subsistence; that they had been many months in the buffalo country, but the treacherous Cheyennes and Arapahoes, had driven them off, and had killed some of their young men. He added, that of dried antelope and deer meat they had a plenty, and that we were welcome to as much as we needed. This unexpected generosity made me regret that it was out of my power to make them a suitable return, and I explained to them, that our losses in Grand River had deprived us of the means of making them presents. He replied that what I had already given was quite sufficient.

Our party had by this time overtaken us, but fearing that the "amicable relations so happily existing" might be disturbed, I desired them not to stop, retaining only a pack animal to load with the meat which I had obtained.

With these Indians were many squaws and children. The former rode astride of the packs, and the boys, some of whom were not more than five years of age, were mounted on spirited horses, which they managed with much dexterity and grace, and were armed with small bows and arrows, two of which they held with the bow in their left hand ready for service. The chiefs invited us to encamp with them, that they might treat us with goats' milk and have a "talk;" but I considered it most prudent to separate from them before any cause of disagreement should arise to mar the good understanding that existed between us; besides, it was too early in the day for us to stop. I told them that, in the direction in which they were going, they would meet some of our friends whom we had left for a short time, and that on our return we would bring them tobacco and other presents. They promised to treat our friends well, and, after a general shaking of hands, we parted mutually pleased with each other.

We encamped at noon on a fork of Sahwatch Creek, running to the eastward through a broad grassy valley, and after a rest of two hours resumed our journey. We had not proceeded far when we noticed at a short distance to our right a singular-looking object, which appeared to be rolling rather than walking over the ground. On approaching it, it proved to be a decrepit Utah squaw, bending under the weight of two packs of buffalo robes, one of which she bore on her shoulders, whilst the other was suspended in front. She was much terrified when we galloped towards her, and, although she made a feeble attempt to fly, her shaking limbs bent under her, and she sank to the ground paralyzed with fear. We, however, reassured her, and got her to explain to us the cause of her being in this lonely region by herself, Archilete being interpreter. She told us that, three moons previous, a party of her people going to hunt buffaloes, had left her and another old woman in the mountains; as neither had horses, and they were unable to keep up with the band on foot. She said that they had subsisted on meat left them by their tribe, and ended by telling us that she had just buried her companion, who had died the previous night, and that she was now on her way to the summer rendezvous of her people, ladened with her own and her companion's packs. We informed her that she would probably overtake a band of Utahs that night or the next day, and placed her on their trail. She seemed glad to receive this news, and still more so when we turned our mules' heads to leave her, though we had shown her all possible kindness—so hard is it in them to believe in the sincerity of white people.

The trail led over low hills and down a succession of beautiful slopes, running mostly in a southerly direction, until we entered a narrow winding valley two and a half miles in length by one hundred to two hundred yards in breadth. It was shut in on each side by perpendicular walls of rock rising from fifty to seventy-five feet above the level of the valley, whose surface was flat and carpeted with tender grass. A stream of clear water meandered through its centre, and the grade was so slight that the stream, overflowing its banks in many places, moistened the whole surface.

As we descended this beautiful and singular valley, we occasionally passed others of a similar character opening into it. It ends in Sahwatch valley, which we entered about an hour before sunset.

We had here the choice of two routes: the first was down Sahwatch valley to its outlet near the head of the valley of San Luis, which would have taken us over the same ground that we had traversed in coming from Fort Massachusetts; the second crossed Sahwatch valley here, passed over a shorter and as good a route, and entered San Luis valley near where the Garita leaves the mountains. We selected the last route.

Coochatope Pass enters Sahwatch Valley a mile below Carnero Pass. Crossing Sahwatch valley, here half a mile broad, and the creek about ten yards in breadth and three feet in depth, we travelled up a narrow valley for a short distance into the hills, and encamped at dark. Day's travel, 47 miles; distance from Grand River, 138 miles.

July 3. During the early part of the night the mosquitos swarmed around us, but it soon became cold, which drove them away. We were delayed some time after sunrise in consequence of most of the mules having gone astray; they were not recovered until near seven o'clock, when we resumed our journey. Our course was generally east, down a succession of valleys, whose surface was level and moist, with hills rising abruptly on either side. We saw a great abundance of game, but killed nothing but a grouse. These mountains teem with antelope, deer, and mountain sheep.

The valleys down which we travelled, and which opened into each other with the regularity of streets, grew gradually broader as we descended. We finally entered one watered by Carnero Creek, which joins the Garita in San Luis valley, and at noon encamped a short distance above a gate or gap through which the stream passes. Half a mile below this gap there is another, and a quarter of a mile farther a third; the passage through them is level, whilst the trail around them is steep and stony. In the afternoon, we went through the first gap, made a circuit around the second, as it was much obstructed with trees and bushes, and, leaving the third on our left, rode over some low hills, and five miles from camp crossed the Garita. We were once more in San Luis valley, and all before us was a perfect level, as far as the sight could reach. We encamped on the Rio Grande del Norte, as the sun was setting behind the pass in the Sierra de San Juan, at the head of the Del Norte. This pass was in sight of us, and is the one in which Colonel Frémont met with so terrible a disaster in the winter of 1848–49, so near was he to the object of his search, the Coochatope.

From the plains this pass appears to be more practicable than either the Carnero or the Coochatope; but it can be traversed only by mules, and by them only from the middle of August until the first snows fall, early in December. In winter it is impassable, and in spring, and until August, the River Del Norte, which flows through part of it, and is swollen with melting snows, is the principal obstruction. This pass is known to the Mexicans as the Puerto del Rio Del Norte (the Pass of the River Del Norte), but Americans call it *Williams's Pass*, in honor of "Old Bill Williams," who discovered it, and was Colonel Frémont's guide. Through it is the shortest road to Grand River, it being one day shorter than by the Carnero, and nearly two days shorter than by the Coochatope. The hills, for, as they appeared to us, from the plains they cannot be called mountains, seem broken and rugged, and appear to have numerous passages between them, whilst the mountains, in which are found the Carnero and Coochatope Passes, exhibit from the plains no point where a pass might be supposed to exist. Day's travel, 48 miles; distance from Grand River, 186 miles.

Fourth of July. We built large fires during the night, hoping to drive away the mosquitos by the smoke; but, the wind being from the river, as fast as we got rid of one swarm another made its appearance. Notwithstanding our long ride of the preceding day, we got but little sleep, and were glad to catch up at early dawn. We followed down the left bank of the Rio del Norte, crossing numerous *esteros* (sloughs), until 1 P. M., when we encamped at the same spot where we had passed the first night out from Fort Massachusetts. We had made forty-five miles since morning, and had travelled so rapidly that the pack animals did not get into camp until an hour later.

This being the anniversary of our country's birthday, and not having sufficient food for more than one scanty meal, we had dispensed with breakfast in order to celebrate the occasion at noon with all the proper honors. Some bitter cornmeal and a few scraps of antelope meat, which had been so often culled that what remained consisted of the shreds of sinews, constituted our bill of fare. As soon as the banquet was ended, I started with the intention of reaching the settlements on the Culebra, a distance of about forty miles, that night. As a distinct trail led to these hamlets, the party could follow without a guide, and I therefore took Peg-leg with me. They were to encamp that night on Trinchera Creek, a pretty brook five miles from our noon camp, fringed with willows, and where they would find abundant pasturage.

After riding eight hours at a steady pace over a plain, I arrived at midnight at a small village on the Culebra, inhabited by Mexicans. The night was warm and calm, and from the Trinchera clouds of mosquitos filled the air. Both we and our mules were much fatigued, having travelled eighty-five miles since morning, after a ride of four days through the mountains at the rate of from forty to forty-eight miles each day.

I was invited into one of the huts, where a couple of women commenced at once baking *tortillas* (thin cakes of dough baked on a piece of sheet-iron) and boiling goats' milk with salt. A sheep was killed, and a plentiful supply of *tortillas* baked to be ready for our party in the morning, and I directed one of the Mexicans to start at early dawn to meet and guide them in.

My blanket was spread on the floor near the fireplace, though I was invited to share a bed made of hides stretched on a rough frame, and filling two-thirds of the room, already occupied by three men, two women, two girls, and four children, all more or less *en déshabille.* Day's travel, 85 miles; total from Grand River, 271 miles.

July 5. Before daybreak the house was invaded by lambs, kids, and pigs, and all farther attempts at sleep were vain. Glad to escape from their noise, I got a horse and rode to the upper hamlets on the Culebra. The valley here spreads out in a meadow, a perfect sea of verdure, several thousand acres in extent, on which were numerous herds of cattle and horses. The whole valley of the Culebra is at times rendered almost uninhabitable by the mosquitos, which are particularly troublesome around the lower settlements, and the natives keep up constant fires, in the smoke of which both they and their cattle seek protection against the common enemy.

Having concluded the necessary arrangements for leaving at this pasturage the animals we had brought with us from the Nawaquasitch, I started with Felipe, on hired horses, for the Costilla, twenty miles distant, where we passed the night. Costilla Creek has its source in the Sangre de Cristo Mountains, on the east of the valley of the Rio del Norte, into which its waters flow. On its banks are numerous farms, which are skilfully irrigated, but in other respects are cultivated very carelessly by the Mexicans; however, their crops, consisting of wheat, corn, beans, and peas, gave promise of better results than those on the Culebra. These settlements are new; the houses, although of *adobes*, are well built, and the people quiet and industrious. They are mostly *peons* (bondsmen) to wealthy landowners residing in Taos, and but few own the soil they cultivate. They enjoy the blessing denied their neighbors, of being entirely exempt from the annoyance of mosquitos, for those exposed constantly to this evil can alone form a conception of the misery it occasions. Day's travel, 20 miles; total distance, 291 miles.

July 6. To secure an early start, and to prevent our animals from trespassing upon the cultivated fields, none of which are inclosed, a man was engaged to watch them whilst at pasture during the night; but my horse having been allowed to escape, it was not until after sunrise that I could procure another. A ride of twenty-two miles brought us to the Colorado (Red River), our road taking us across three small streams (Las Ladillas), on the borders of which were extensive sheep *ranchos*. The Colorado is formed by the junction of two abundant streams, which issue from deep cañons in lofty and abruptly rising mountains. The valley of the Colorado is about three miles in length by one in breadth, and the Colorado River, having passed it, flows through a deep channel in the plain, and unites its waters to those of the Del Norte. The valley presents a beautiful view, and, being abundantly irrigated by means of *acequias* (canals), every acre of it is under cultivation. The village of the Colorado consists of one hundred *adobe* houses, built to form a quadrangle, with their doors and windows presenting upon the square inside.

Mr. Charles Otterby, a Missourian, long domiciliated in New Mexico, invited me to his house and procured me a fresh horse, as the one I had ridden from the Costilla (a distance of twenty-two miles) in two hours and a half, had broken down. I left Colorado at noon, and, travelling twelve miles across a mountain, over a rough and stony road, I reached the Rio Hondo (Deep Creek), which is so called from its channel being sunk in many places far below the level of the plain; for the stream itself is neither deep nor broad. I here engaged a young American, Thomas Otterby, to go with us to California, he having a reputation almost equal to Kit Carson's for bravery, dexterity with his rifle, and skill in mountain life. I also purchased a mule to replace my unshod and sore-footed horse, and rode to Taos, nine miles beyond, across a level plain, arriving there at 3 P. M.

Mr. St. Vrain, for whom I had a letter, being absent from Taos, I was hospitably received by his lady. I immediately called on Mr. Leroux, who had a few days previous returned from Fort Atkinson in improved health. Making known to him the accident which had befallen us at Grand River, and stating our wants, I obtained, with his assistance, the supplies we needed. Raw hides were procured and sewed together, to be used as boats for crossing rivers. Corn was parched to make *pinole* (parched and pounded cornmeal, sweetened), coffee roasted, &c.

San Fernando de Taos is situated in the centre of a broad plain, watered by two or three small brooks, whose waters are entirely absorbed in the irrigation of the lands around the town. It presents, both within and without, a poor appearance; its low earth-colored houses, scattered irregularly about, look dingy and squalid, though within many of them are comfortable; and they are all well adapted to the climate. The town is surrounded with uninclosed fields, very fertile when irrigated, and the Taos wheat, originally obtained from the wild wheat growing spontaneously on the Santa Clara and the Rio de la Virgen, has obtained a wide reputation. In the vicinity of San Fernando de Taos are several hamlets—the Pueblo de Taos, inhabited by the Taos Indians, a quiet and inoffensive race, and good field laborers; La Placita de Taos, El Rancho, El Ranchito, &c. Six miles to the southwest was a United States dragoon camp, from which the troops were absent, they having marched to Abiquiú in consequence of troubles with the Navajo Indians. Day's travel, 43 miles; total distance from Grand River to Taos, 333 miles.

Return from Taos to Grand River; and we now measure the distance back from Taos.

July 11. Having concluded my purchases, which delayed me longer than had been anticipated (for everything had to be made or prepared for our use), I sent off late on the 8th a wagon containing the supplies, and two men with the mules, to meet me at the Culebra, where I would overtake them. Starting the next day I passed them at Rio Colorado on the 10th, and arrived at the Culebra a day ahead of my party. From the time of our arrival in Taos, Peg-leg had been surrounded by his friends and boon companions, relating to them his late exploits on Grand River, and his frequent libations to Bacchus, in wretched Taos brandy, had rendered him incapable of keeping his seat on horseback. I left him practising the Apache warwhoop in the square of Taos, and I did not see him again until the wagon and men had arrived at the Culebra, and I was prepared to depart. He then made his appearance, looking very sick, unhappy, and repentant.

The men I had hired were Thomas Otterby, José Galliego, an old mountaineer who had been to California with Colonel Frémont, and was well recommended as guide and *bull-hide boat builder*, and Juan Cordova, a Mexican *arriero* (muleteer). We numbered in all five.

Messrs. Riggs and Rogers with their party remained at Taos, intending to pursue their journey to California *via* Fort Laramie and Great Salt Lake.

We saddled up shortly before sunset, and encamped nine miles below on the Culebra, to get our packs in order for an early start on the morrow. The first day with a train of pack mules is always a troublesome one; the animals are new, the men have not learned their dispositions and qualities, the harness does not fit, and it is necessary to make many changes, which occasion delay. My day's ride was 61 miles, back from Taos.

July 12. Raised camp at five and travelled until noon, when we encamped on the slough of the Del Norte, where we had already been three times. We fortunately had filled our leather canteens at the Trinchera, for we found the water here no longer drinkable. The sun was intensely hot, and our old friends, the mosquitos, did not fail to find us out. We stopped for the night on the Del Norte, eighteen miles farther on, where we shot several wild geese, which we found here in great numbers. Day's travel, 40 miles; distance from Taos, 101 miles.

July 13. Although I was up many times during the night, looking after the mules, and had them all picketed in thick grass, three succeeded in drawing their picket-pins and went off in the direction of Fort Massachusetts. After a chase of ten miles they were brought back, and we started at 6 30 A. M. Encamped on the Garita, where I had only intended to rest the animals for a couple of hours; but as it commenced to rain, and I feared that the packs might get damaged, I concluded to pass the night here, and housed everything under the ox-hides. A party of Mexican Ciboleros (buffalo hunters), going to hunt buffalo on the Upper Arkansas, encamped near us. Day's travel, 41 miles; distance from Taos, 142.

July 14. We kept guard during the night, as we saw fresh signs of Indians, and our animals were inclined to stray. It rained most of the night. Raised camp at sunrise, and, without stopping, travelled through the Carnero Pass to Sahwatch valley, near which we encamped before sunset. Day's travel, 49 miles; distance from Taos, 191.

July 15. Travelled steadily all day, with the exception of a short rest at noon, and encamped at night on a small rill running into the Jaroso (Willow Creek). Day's travel, 43 miles; from Taos, 234 miles.

July 16. We started at dawn, crossed the Rio de la Laguna without unpacking, as its waters had fallen, and at 2 P. M. I met Harry Young, whom Mr. Beale had sent to guide us to his camp on the Savoya Creek, to which he had moved during my absence. We found Mr. Beale and his small party all well, and anxiously expecting us. Their camp was surrounded by a considerable number of Utahs, some of whom I recognized as the same we had met near the Sahwatch, on the 2d of July.

Soon after we got into camp, Mr. Beale dispatched Wagner and Galliego to Grand River with the bull-hides, directing them to make a boat should they fail in finding a ford; and a little later we proceeded to the Nawaquasitch, so as to make an early start on the morrow and reach Grand River before night. Day's travel, 42 miles; distance from Taos, 276 miles.

MR. BEALE'S SEPARATE JOURNAL DURING MY VOYAGE TO TAOS AND BACK.

Mr. Beale commences his journal on the day that we parted; with the reasons for sending back, and the names of those who went, and of those who remained with him.

July 1, 1853. Rogers, Riggs, Cosgrove, George, Dolan, Juan, and Gregorio left us to return to the settlements, and go thence by Salt Lake to California. This was on account of one of our party, whom I did not think could stand the farther hardships of the journey. Harris Heap and Felipe Archilete went in also to show them the nearest road, and to guide them to Taos, and get supplies. Remained in camp to await the return of Heap, with provisions, &c. Remained with me the Delaware (Dick Brown), Felipe Archilete, Jr., Harry Young, and Wagner. Nothing to eat in camp; sent the Delaware out to hunt, and we commenced a house. About nine, Dick returned with a buck; finished the house; sick with dysentery. We find the venison good, it being the first meat or food of any kind, except cornmeal and water, we have had for a week.

July 2. Weather pleasant; mosquitos abundant, but not troublesome; washed the two dirty shirts which composed my wardrobe. No signs of Indians, and begin to hope we shall not be troubled with them. Nevertheless, keep the *fright medicine** at hand, and the guns ready. Grass abundant and good, animals thriving; the Delaware killed an elk; dried some meat; still sick.

July 3. Employed the day in drying the meat killed yesterday. Weather very hot; but for the sunshine one would suppose it to be snowing, the air being filled with light fleeces like snow-flakes from the cottonwood. The creek is falling, but slowly. Time drags very heavily; three days gone, however, and nine remain; twelve days being the time allotted to go and return from Taos.

July 4. Celebrated the day by eating our last two cups of pinole; felt highly excited by it. Henceforth we go it on tobacco and dried meat. The Delaware killed a doe, tolerably fat; dried the meat; still sick; bathed in creek; found the water excessively cold, but felt much refreshed and better after the bath, besides having killed an hour by it—a very important item.

July 5. To-day we killed only a rabbit. The day has been somewhat cool, though the evening is dry and sultry, and the mosquitos much more troublesome than usual. Took a bath, which seems to give me relief from my malady, which, thank God, is no worse. We hope that our men have reached Taos this evening.

July 6. To-day has been cloudy, with rain in the mountains all around us, though but a few scattering drops have reached the valley. We all complain this evening of great weakness and entire lack of energy, with dizziness in the head, and do not know from what cause it proceeds. The bath in the creek has not had its usual invigorating effect; mosquitos very troublesome; made a little soup in a tin box and found it tolerable.

* Our medicine chest had been intended for a lady's use, and contained a bottle of anodyne drops, labelled with the following directions: "Three drops, to allay palpitations of the heart occasioned by fright."

July 7. For the last two days we have killed nothing. This evening we had quite a shower of rain; started to take a long walk, but broke down very soon, being too weak to go far. I find my sickness worse to-day, but it is the least of my anxieties. Would to God I had none other! Took the usual evening bath in the creek, which has slightly fallen during the day, and the water not quite so cold, which encourages me to hope that the supply of snow in the mountains is nearly exhausted.

July 8. This morning our anxieties from Indians have commenced. At ten o'clock three of them rode into camp, and shortly afterwards some dozen more.

July 9. Yesterday, after the Indians arrived, I gave them what little tobacco we could spare and some of our small stock of dried elk meat. After eating and smoking for awhile they insisted on my accompanying them to their camp, which was some ten miles off. I explained to them as well as I could who I was.

Knowing that it is best always to act boldly with Indians, as if you felt no fear whatever, I armed myself and started with them. Our road for a mile or two led over a barren plain, thickly covered with grease wood, but we soon struck the base of the mountain, where the firm rich mountain grass swept our saddle-girths as we cantered over it. We crossed a considerable mountain covered with timber and grass, and near the summit of which was quite a cluster of small, but very clear and apparently deep lakes. They were not more than an acre or two in size, and some not even that, but surrounded by luxuriant grass, and perched away up on the mountain, with fine timber quite near them. It was the most beautiful scenery in the world; it formed quite a hunter's paradise, for deer and elk bounded off from us as we approached, and then stood within rifle-shot, looking back in astonishment. A few hours' ride brought us to the Indian camp; and I wish here I could describe the beauty of the charming valley in which they lived. It was small, probably not more than five miles wide by fifteen long, but surrounded on all sides by the boldest mountains, covered to their summits with alternate patches of timber and grass, giving it the appearance of having been regularly laid off in small farms. Through the centre a fine bold stream, probably three feet deep by forty wide, watered the meadow land, and gave the last touch which the valley required to make it the most beautiful I had ever seen. Hundreds of horses and goats were feeding on the meadows and hill-sides, and the Indian lodges, with the women and children standing in front of them to look at the approaching stranger, strongly reminded me of the old patriarchal times, when flocks and herds made the wealth and happiness of the people, and a tent was as good as a palace. I was conducted to the lodge of the chief, an old and infirm man, who welcomed me kindly, and told me his young men had told him I had given of my small store to them, and to "sit in peace."

I brought out my pipe, filled it, and we smoked together. In about fifteen minutes a squaw brought in two large wooden platters, containing some very fat deer meat and some boiled corn, to which I did ample justice. After this followed a dish which one must have been two weeks without bread to have appreciated as I did. Never, at the tables of the wealthiest in Washington, did I find a dish which appeared to me so perfectly without a parallel. It was some cornmeal boiled in goats' milk, with a little elk fat. I think I certainly ate near half a peck of this delicious atole, and then stopped, not because I had enough, but because I had scraped the dish dry with my fingers, and licked them as long as the smallest particle remained, which is "manners" among Indians, and also among Arabs. Eat all they give you, or get somebody to do it for you, is to honor the hospitality you receive. To leave any is a slight. I needed not the rule to make me eat all.

After this we smoked again, and when about to start I found a large bag of dried meat and a peck of corn put up for me to take to my people.

Bidding a friendly good-by to my hosts, and dividing among them about a pound of tobacco and two handkerchiefs, and giving the old chief the battered remains of a small leaden picayune looking-glass, I mounted my mule to return. The sun was just setting when I started, and before reaching the summit of the mountain it was quite dark. As there was no road, and the creeks very dark in the bottoms, I had a most toilsome time of it. At one creek, which I reached after very great difficulty in getting through the thick and almost impenetrable undergrowth, it was so dark that I could see nothing; but, trusting to luck, I jumped my mule off the bank and brought up in water nearly covering my saddle. Getting in was bad enough, but coming out was worse; for, finding the banks high on the other side, I was obliged to follow down the stream for half a mile or more, not knowing when I should be swimming, until I succeeded with great difficulty in getting out through the tangled brushwood on the opposite side. I arrived at camp late at night, and found my men very anxiously awaiting my return, having almost concluded to give me up, and to think I had lost my "hair." A little rain.

July 11. To-day I raised camp, and went over to the valley of the Savoya, near my Indian neighbors. The more I see of this valley the more I am delighted with it. I cannot say how it may be in winter, but at this time it is certainly the most beautiful valley, and the richest in grass, wood, soil, and water, I have ever seen. The Delaware brought into camp last evening a small deer, alive, which he had caught in the mountains. It was a beautiful creature, but escaped in the night.

July 12. Went out this morning with the Indians to hunt. They lent me a fine horse; but God forbid that I should ever hunt with such Indians again! I thought I had seen something of rough riding before; but all my experience faded before that of the feats of to-day. Some places which we ascended and descended it seemed to me that even a wild-cat could hardly have passed over; and yet their active and thoroughly well-trained horses took them as part of the sport, and never made a misstep or blunder during the entire day. We killed three antelopes and a young deer. Yesterday an Indian, while sitting at our camp, broke the mainspring of his rifle lock. His distress was beyond anything within the power of description. To him it was everything. The "corn, wine, and oil" of his family depended on it, and he sat for an hour looking upon the wreck of his fortune in perfect despair. He appeared so much cast down by it that at last I went into our lodge and brought my rifle, which I gave him to replace the broken one. At first he could not realize it, but as the truth gradually broke upon him, his joy became so great that he could scarce control himself; and when he returned that night he was the happiest man I have seen for many a day.

These Indians are all well armed and mounted, and the very

best shots and hunters. Our revolvers seem, however, to be a never-failing source of astonishment to them, and they are never tired of examining them. Yesterday, I allowed them to fire two of ours at a mark, at thirty paces. They shot admirably well, putting all the shots within a space of the small mark (size of a half dollar), and hitting it several times. A rainy day.

July 13. To-day has been showery, and the evening still cloudy, and promising more rain during the night. Our eyes are now turned constantly to the opposite side of the valley, down which the road winds by which we expect our companions from Taos.

These days have been the most weary and anxious of my whole life. Sometimes I am almost crazy with thinking constantly on one subject, and the probable disastrous result which this delay may have on my business in California.

> "Stone walls do not a prison make,
> Nor iron bars a cage;
> The heart that is content will take
> These for a hermitage."

God knows I have done all for the best, and with the best intentions. A great many Indians came into the valley this evening. Ten lodges in all, which, with the fifteen already here, and more on the road, make up a pretty large band. Dick killed an antelope. Last two nights have slept in wet blankets, and expect the same to-night. Last night it rained all night. The Spanish boy has been quite ill for two days past.

July 14. This morning I explored the mountain lying to the north of our camp, forming a picturesque portion of our front view. After ascending the mountain and reaching the summit, I found it a vast plateau of rolling prairie land, covered with the most beautiful grass, and heavily timbered. At some places the growth of timber would be so dense as to render riding through it impossible without great difficulty; while at others it would break into beautiful open glades, leaving spaces of a hundred acres or more of open prairie, with groups of trees, looking precisely as if some wealthy planter had amused himself by planting them expressly to beautify his grounds. Springs were abundant, and small streams intersected the whole plateau. In fact, it was an immense natural park, already stocked with deer and elk, and only requiring a fence to make it an estate for a king. Directly opposite, to the south, is another mountain, in every respect similar, and our valley, more beautiful to me than either, lies between them. In the evening took a long ride on the trail to meet our long-expected companions. I did not meet them, and returned disappointed, worried, and more anxious than ever.

July 15. This has been a great day for our Indian neighbors. Two different bands of the same tribe have met, and a great contest is going on to prove which has the best horses. They have been at it since the morning, and many a buckskin has changed hands. The horses are all handsome, and run remarkably well. We have had more than fifty races; a surfeit of them, if such a thing as a surfeit of horseracing is possible.

July 16. Here at last. This morning I saddled my mule to go and hunt up our expected companions. I had not gone far before I met about fifty Indians, from whom I could learn nothing of them, and was beginning to despair, when I met a loose mule, and, as I knew it was not one of the Indians', I concluded it must belong to some of our companions. Going on a mile or two farther, I met Felipe, who told me that Heap and the others were just behind. I immediately returned to camp to get dinner ready for them, so that we might go on this evening to the Uncompagre. Here terminates the most unpleasant sixteen days of my life; but for this beautiful country, to look at and explore, I think I should have gone crazy. The time seemed endless to me, but my zealous comrades had not unnecessarily lengthened it, for they had averaged 45 miles a day during the double journey (going and coming), and that through the whole mass of mountains which lie between the Upper Del Norte and the Grand River Fork of the great Colorado (Red River) of the Gulf of California.

Here ends Mr. BEALE'S separate journal.

CHAPTER V.

JOURNEY TO THE MORMON SETTLEMENTS NEAR LAS VEGAS DE SANTA CLARA.

July 17. We were now again united, and freed from the anxiety for each other's safety which had been weighing on us since the day of our separation. We resumed our journey at sunrise, with the hope of soon overcoming all difficulties. Although the sun rose in a cloudless sky, yet before noon the rain commenced falling in heavy showers. Mr. Beale and myself, having much to relate to each other, rode several miles ahead of the men. We descended to the plain at the foot of the Sahwatch mountains by the same trail over which we had already twice travelled, and which was now familiar to us. On approaching the Uncompagre, we travelled parallel with its course towards Grand River, keeping on the trail of the two men sent ahead the day before with the hides to construct the boat. At noon, we noticed two recumbent figures on a distant butte, with horses standing near them; when we had approached within a mile they sprang to their saddles and galloped towards us at full speed. They were Utah Indians, on a scout, and evinced no fear of us, but, approaching, frankly offered us their hands. We conversed with them partly by signs and partly by means of the few Utah words which we had picked up, and their scanty knowledge of Spanish, which extended only to the names of a few objects and animals. They told us that large numbers of their tribe were encamped a few miles below, on the Uncompagre, and, bidding them farewell, we went on to meet our train.

Soon after parting with them, we saw on the hill-sides and river bottom, a vast number of gayly-colored lodges, and numerous bands of Indians arriving from the northward. Upon approaching, we were received by a number of the oldest men, who invited us to ascend a low, but steep hill, where most of the chiefs were seated. From this point we had a view of an animated and interesting scene. On every side fresh bands of Indians were pouring in, and the women were kept busy in erecting their lodges in the bottom near the Uncompagre, as well as on the higher land nearer to us. Horses harnessed to lodge poles, on which were packed their various property, and in many cases their children, were arriving, and large bands of loose horses and mules were being driven to the river side to drink or to pasture. Squaws were going to the stream for water, whilst others were returning with their osier jars filled, and poised on their heads. Some of the young men were galloping around on their high-mettled horses, and others, stretched lazily on the grass, were patiently waiting until their better halves had completed the construction of their lodges, and announced that the evening meal was prepared. All the males, from the old man to the stripling of four years, were armed with bows and arrows, and most of the men had serviceable rifles. We almost fancied that we had before us a predatory tribe of Scythians or Numidians, so similar are these Indians in their dress, accoutrements, and habits, to what we have learned of those people.

An old chief, who, we were told, was one of their great men, addressed us a discourse, which very soon went beyond the limits of our knowledge of the Utah tongue, but we listened to it with the appearance of not only understanding the subject, but also of being highly interested with it. Our men, with Felipe Archilete, the guide and interpreter, were many miles in the rear, and we waited until their arrival, for Mr. Beale wished to take advantage of this opportunity to have a conversation with these chiefs, two of whom were the highest in the nation.

When Felipe came up, Mr. Beale and the capitanos, as they styled themselves, engaged in a long "talk." Mr. Beale told them that many Americans would be soon passing through their country on their way to the Mormon settlements and California, with wagons and herds, and that, if they treated the whites well, either by aiding them when in difficulty, guiding them through the mountains, and across the rivers, or by furnishing them with food when they needed it, they would always be amply rewarded. They appeared much gratified to hear this, and by way, no doubt, of testing whether his practice coincided with his preaching, intimated that they would be well pleased to receive, then, some of the presents of which he spoke; remarking, that as we had passed through their country, used their pasturage, lived among their people, and had even been fed by them, it was but proper that some small return should be made for so many favors. This was an argument which Mr. Beale had not foreseen; but having no presents to give them, he explained how it was; that, having lost everything we possessed in Grand River, it was out of his power to gratify them. This explanation did not appear at all satisfactory, nor did they seem altogether to credit him. They were very covetous of our rifles, but we could not, of course, part with them. The old chief became taciturn and sulky, and glanced towards us occasionally with a malignant expression.

We took no notice of his ill-temper, but lit our pipes and passed them around. In the meanwhile, our men had, in accordance with Mr. Beale's directions, proceeded to Grand River, where they were to seek for Wagner and Galliego, and encamp with them. Felipe, whose quick and restless eye was always on the watch, dropped us a hint, in a few words, that it was becoming unsafe to remain longer in the midst of these savages, for he had noticed symptoms of very unfriendly feelings.

We were seated in a semicircle on the brow of a steep hill, and a large crowd had collected around us. Rising without exhibiting any haste, we adjusted our saddles, relit our pipes, and shaking hands with the chiefs who were nearest to us, mounted and rode slowly down the hill, followed by a large number of Utahs, who, upon our rising to leave them, had sprung to their saddles. The older men remained seated, and our escort consisted almost entirely of young warriors. They galloped around us in every direction; occasionally, a squad of four or five would charge upon us at full speed, reining up suddenly, barely avoiding riding over us and our mules. They did this to try our mettle, but as we took little notice of them, and affected perfect unconcern, they finally desisted from their dangerous sport. At one time, the conduct of a young chief, the son of El Capitan Grande, was near occasioning serious consequences. He charged upon Felipe with a savage yell, every feature apparently distorted with rage; his horse struck Felipe's mule, and very nearly threw them both to the ground. The Indian then seizing Felipe's rifle, endeavored to wrench it from his hands, but the latter held firmly to his gun, telling us at the same time not to interfere. We and the Indians formed a circle around them, as they sat in their saddles, each holding on to the gun, whose muzzle was pointed full at the Indian's breast. He uttered many imprecations, and urged his followers to lend him their assistance. They looked at us inquiringly, and we cocked our rifles—the hint was sufficient—they declined interfering. For some minutes the Utah and Felipe remained motionless, glaring at each other like two game-cocks, each watching with flashing eyes for an opportunity to assail his rival. Seeing that to trifle longer would be folly, Felipe, who held the butt-end of the rifle, deliberately placed his thumb on the hammer, and raising it slowly, gave warning to the young chief, by two ominous clicks, that his life was in danger. For a moment longer, the Utah eyed Felipe, and then, with an indescribable grunt, pushed the rifle from him, and lashing his horse furiously, rode away from us at full speed. Felipe gave us a sly wink, and uttered the highly original ejaculation—"Carajo!"

We crossed the Uncompagre about twelve miles above our former fording-place. The rain, which had been falling at intervals all day, now descended in torrents, and the river soon became so deep and rapid, that our return was entirely cut off. Our object in crossing it was to ascertain the condition of Grand River, where we had previously been balked by the loss of the canoe. We travelled until nine o'clock, when we met some Utahs sent by Wagner to inform us that he had found a ford, which would dispense with the necessity of building a boat. The rain not abating, and having ridden since morning upwards of fifty miles, we concluded to accept the hospitality of our Indian friends, who offered us a lodge in an encampment, which we soon after reached. It consisted of six large deer-skin lodges on the brow of a hill overlooking in front the angry current of the Uncompagre, whilst on the left was Grand River, about a mile distant. From this point we saw numerous fires dotting the opposite shores of the Uncompagre, amongst which shone a larger one lit by our men, for the purpose of guiding us through the storm to their encampment. Before we entered the lodge, a number of squaws and children issued from it, to make room for us, and scattered themselves among the other lodges; the men remained, squatting closely together on one side, while Mr. Beale, myself, and Felipe, spreading our saddle-blankets near the fire, threw ourselves, in utter weariness, upon them. At this moment we would willingly have sold our birth-rights for a mess of pottage, for we had tasted nothing since dawn.

We soon lit and passed around the friendly pipe, and made ourselves as comfortable and as much "at home" as circumstances would permit. The flickering blaze of the fire fell on the wrinkled visages of two or three old squaws, who had quietly crept near the door for a view of the "Mericanos," while outside, and peering over each other's shoulders, were a group of girls, whose bright eyes and laughing faces disclosing their pearly teeth, formed an agreeable contrast with the serious and even surly countenances of the men, and haggard appearance of the older squaws. Knowing that our men would feel anxious on account of our prolonged absence (for having left us in the midst of the Indian encampment they had good reason to fear for our safety), Mr. Beale inquired whether there was any one who would undertake to carry a message to them across the river. A handsome young Indian volunteered to go, and Mr. Beale liberally promised to reward him on his return with a plug of tobacco, which he exhibited, to prove that he was in earnest. This generosity was duly appreciated; and it is probable that, with the offer of a few more plugs, the whole band might have been sent over as attachés to the embassy. Mr. Beale wrote to Young, to send us coffee, sugar, and biscuit; and our messenger, having stripped to the buff, rolled the paper up, and carefully thrust it through the lobe of his ear, which was pierced with large holes. Mounting a powerful horse, he disappeared in the darkness, towards the Uncompagre.

Much sooner than we had anticipated, he returned—his horse as well as himself—dripping with moisture, and brought, safely tied on the top of his head, the articles Mr. Beale had written for. He also carried in his ear a note from Young, stating that the Indians were quite peaceable and well-disposed, and had indicated a ford near which our men were encamped.

All uneasiness, on their account, being set at rest, we gave ourselves up entirely to the enjoyment of our novel situation. Knowing that nothing, not excepting music, "hath such charms to soothe the savage breast" as a good *feed*, Felipe asked for a large kettle, which was soon produced, and suspended from three sticks, over the fire. This he filled with coffee, well sweetened, and threw in also the biscuit. Affairs were now assuming an aspect which our hosts appeared to consider of intense interest. Their eyes did not wander for a moment from the magic kettle; and their half-opened mouths actually watered as the delicious aroma of the coffee filled the lodge. Felipe now called for our cups, which we carried suspended to our saddles, and for every other utensil in the camp, and served the delicious beverage around. The redskins sipped it scalding hot, accompanying each sip with a deep *ugh!* signifying their great enjoyment; and, having drained their cups to the dregs, they rubbed their stomachs, in token of its having done them infinite good. Fatigued as we were we soon stretched ourselves out to sleep, and though the wind howled around us, and the rain fell all night, we slept soundly and comfortably, the fire in the centre keeping the lodge quite warm, whilst an aperture in the top allowed the smoke to escape freely. Days travel, 50 miles; distance from Taos, 326 miles.

July 18. We saddled up at early dawn, swam our mules across the Uncompagre, and rejoined our men. They informed us that Juan Cordova had deserted the day before, and returned to Mr. Beale's encampment on the Savoya in company with the two Indians we had met in the morning, and who were going that way.

We found camp filled with Indians, who, however, behaved in a friendly manner, and had even supplied the men with a bucket-full of goat's milk. No time was lost in preparing to ford Grand River, and some Indians went ahead to show us the way. On reaching the stream we found that it had fallen about six feet, and under the guidance of the Indians had no difficulty in getting over. The water reached nearly to the mules' backs, but the packs had been secured so high as to prevent their getting wet.

The Indians followed us across in large numbers, and at times tried our patience to the utmost. They numbered about two hundred and fifty warriors, and were all mounted on fine horses, and well armed with bows and arrows, having laid aside their rifles, which Felipe considered a sign that their designs were unfriendly, as they never carry them when they intend to fight on horseback. Their appearance, as they whirled around us at full speed, clothed in bright colors, and occasionally charging upon us with a loud yell, made a striking contrast with that of our party, mounted as we were upon mules, in the half-naked condition in which we had crossed the river (for it was dangerous to stop for a moment to dress). They enjoyed many laughs at our expense, taunting us, and comparing us, from our bearded appearance, to goats, and calling us beggarly cowards and women. Most of these compliments were lost to us at the time, but Felipe afterwards explained them. The old chief, the same who had given us such a surly reception on the preceding day, and his son, who had made a trial of strength with Felipe for his rifle, soon joined us, and behaved with much insolence, demanding presents in an imperious manner, and even endeavored to wrench our guns from our hands, threatening to "wipe us out" if we refused to comply with their wishes. They frequently harangued the young men, and abused us violently for traversing their country, using their grass and timber without making them any acknowledgment for the obligation. The latter listened in silence, but most of them remained calm and unmoved, and evinced no disposition to molest us. The chiefs then changed their tactics, and endeavored to provoke us to commence hostilities. Mr. Beale calmly explained to them that, having lost everything in the river, he was unable to make them such presents as he would have desired, and added (addressing himself to the chiefs) that he clearly saw that they were evil-hearted men; for, after treating us as brothers and friends, they were now endeavoring to make bad blood between us and their people. He ended by telling them that we had a few articles which he would have distributed to them, had they not behaved in so unfriendly a manner; but that now, the only terms upon which they could obtain them was by giving a horse in exchange. Mr. Beale's motive for not giving them presents was our inability to satisfy the whole party, for all we possessed was a piece of cloth, a calico shirt, and some brass wire, and these articles, valueless as they were, if given to a few, would have excited the jealousy and ill-will of the less fortunate, and thus made them our enemies. The Indians, however, declined giving a horse in exchange for what we offered, saying that it would not be a fair bargain. Mr. Beale then said: "If you want to trade, we will trade; if you want to fight, we will fight;" requesting those who were not inclined to hostilities, to stand aside, as we had no wish to injure our friends.

The chiefs, finding themselves in the minority as regarded fighting, finally consented to give us a mare for our goods; and after the trade was made we parted, much relieved at getting rid of such ugly customers.

The Utahs had been in company with us for several hours, and had often separated our party. During all this time our rifles were held ready for use, not knowing at what moment the conflict might commence. Had we come to blows, there is no doubt that we should have been instantly overwhelmed. The Delaware had kept constantly aloof from the party, never allowing an Indian to get behind him; and although he silently, but sullenly, resisted the attempts that were made to snatch his rifle from his grasp, he never for a moment removed his eyes from the old chief, but glared at him with a ferocity so peculiar, that it was evident that feelings even stronger than any that could arise from his present proceedings, prompted the Delaware's ire against the rascally Utah. Dick subsequently told us that, when he was a boy, he had fallen into the hands of this same old chief, who had been urgent to put him to death. Dick had nursed his revenge with an Indian's constancy, and, upon the first blow, intended to send a rifle ball through his skull.

Several times Felipe warned us to be on our guard, as the attack was about to commence, and Mr. Beale directed all to dismount upon the first unequivocal act of hostility, to stand each man behind his mule, and to take deliberate aim before firing.

Travelling down Grand River, at some distance from its right bank, we came to where it flowed through a cañon. The ground on either side of the river was much broken by ravines. The country, about a mile from the river, was barren and level, producing nothing but wild sage and prickly pear. After a harassing day we encamped on a rapid, clear and cool brook, with good pasturage on its banks, called in the

Utah language, the Cerenoquinti; it issues from the Pareamoot Mountains and flows into Grand River. Day's travel, 25 miles; whole distance from Westport, computed from June 23, 976 miles.

July 19. Resumed our journey at 5.30 A. M., and travelling twelve miles southwest over a level and barren country, encamped on the Avonkarea (Blue River, Utah tongue). Our encampment was on a high rocky bluff overhanging the stream, and offering a beautiful view of its course. The scenery was grand beyond description; the fantastic shapes of the mountains to the northward resembled in some places interminable ranges of fortifications, battlements, and towers, and in others immense Gothic cathedrals; the whole was bathed in the beautiful colors thrown over the sky and mountains, and reflected in the stream by a glowing sunset.

This river was broader and more rapid than Grand River, and, as we had anticipated, entirely too deep to ford. At the point where we encamped, it was about three hundred yards in breadth, and it had evidently recently been much wider. It frothed and foamed as it rushed impetuously past the rocks, bearing on its bosom huge trees, which rolled and writhed like drowning giants. The men immediately commenced making a frame for the boat, the qualities of which we were about to test. The keel and longitudinal ribs were made with saplings, and the transverse ribs with small limbs of willow, which bent easily to any shape required. The hides—two of which had been closely sewed together—were softened by soaking in the river, spread under the frame; and the edges, perforated with holes, were brought up its sides and tightly laced to them with thongs. The boat was finished by sunset, and, although neither as light nor as graceful as a birch-bark canoe, it promised to carry us and our packs over safely.

Soon after arriving at the Avonkarea, we were hailed from the opposite shore by a Mexican, who informed us that he and his party had been waiting twenty days for the waters to fall, being unable to cross over.

He stated that they had left the Mormon settlements at the Vegas de Santa Clara on the 20th of June, and had lost two of their men by drowning in Green River. Mr. Beale promised to assist them over.—12 miles; 988 miles.

July 20. Commenced crossing at an early hour. The boat answered admirably; it was buoyant, easily managed, and safe. Before sunset most of the train had crossed, and the Delaware had succeeded in swimming the mules over, by following in their wake, and heading off those that tried to turn back. It took us longer than we had anticipated, to get our effects across, as it was necessary at each trip to tow the boat some distance up the right bank, in order to make our encampment on the left, without drifting below it. The current was very rapid, and the work of towing the boat up through the bushes which overhung the stream, very laborious. Some of the Mexicans and a few of their packs were carried in safety to the left bank. It rained heavily during the afternoon, and we passed a wet night under our blankets. The camp was crowded with Indians, who were anxious to trade, but were not troublesome. As some of them passed the night with us, we allowed our animals to run with theirs.

Henry Young was at one time in a very precarious position, from which he was relieved with difficulty. One of the mules had stubbornly resisted every effort to get her over, and had finally made a landing under a high precipice on the left shore, from which it was impossible to dislodge her, without going into the water and swimming to the spot. This was attempted by Young, and as the current here swept down with tremendous velocity, he was on the point of drowning, when fortunately he seized a rock, upon which he landed. It was now dark, the rain falling fast, and to have passed the night in this situation was certain destruction, for he was under a precipice, and in front of him roared the Avonkarea. No one knew that he had gone into the water, and we were not aware of his distress until he had attracted our attention by his shouts, and a flash of lightning revealed him to us. The boat was got down to him after more than an hour's work, and he was finally brought into camp nearly frozen.

July 21. The remainder of the packs and men crossed in the morning, and the day was consumed in sending the rest of the Mexicans and their luggage to the opposite side. They were also assisted in crossing over their animals. These men reported that they had been badly treated by the Mormons at the Vegas de Santa Clara, and that two of their number had been put in jail. They warned us to be on our guard, when we arrived in Utah Territory, as they (the Mormons) had threatened to shoot or imprison all Americans passing through their country. Notwithstanding their plausible story, the Mexicans only impressed us with the belief that, having misbehaved, they had received the chastisement they deserved, for it was well known to us that the Mormons strictly prohibited the practice of the natives of New Mexico of bartering firearms and ammunition with the Indians for their children.

We wrote many letters by these men, which they promised to deliver to Mr. Leroux, in Taos.

The hides were removed from the frame of the boat and reserved for future use, and having got our animals together we resumed our march at 7 P. M.

The Avonkarea joins Grand River five or six miles below where we crossed it. We travelled down the last-mentioned stream, our course being southwest, and encamped at 11 P. M. at Camp L'Amoureux, so called after a French trapper who trapped here for several years, until drowned in Grand River. Our road lay over a level plain, whose loose, rotten soil was covered with a thick growth of artemisia, cactus, and greasewood. At this camp, both grass and timber were abundant, but the mosquitos allowed no rest to man or beast. A plain extends on this side of the river about twelve miles in breadth, bounded on the northwest by a range of steep, bald, and deeply furrowed mountains. Day's travel, 16 miles; total distance from Westport, 1,004 miles.

July 22. We were in the saddle at 7.30 A. M., and in ten miles reached the Rio Salado (Salt Creek), and following down its bed, which only contained water in holes, encamped on Grand River, near where it (Salt Creek) discharges itself. This creek is a running stream in winter, and its water is then drinkable; but it ceases to run in summer, and its water, which is then only found in hollows, is very brackish. Wherever the main river (Grand River) can be reached, which is practicable at some points, there are good camping places, where grass and timber are abundant.

The face of the country, as on the previous day, was an arid plain, with scanty vegetation. To the northwest, at a distance of eight miles, was a range of steep bluffs, and Grand River, on our left, was shut from view by naked hills.

A few Indians visited camp, and partook of our dinner. We obtained from them some beautiful buckskins, which the Utahs have a skilful mode of preparing. They told us that the river abounded with large fish, and one of the men immediately manufactured a hook with a horseshoe nail. We had satisfactory evidence of the weight of the fish, for the first that bit carried away "hook and line, bob and sinker."

Travelled twenty miles in the afternoon, and encamped again late at night on Grand River. To avoid the mosquitos, some slept on the top of a lofty rock, and were tolerably free from their annoyance; but those who made their beds below were allowed no rest. From the Rio Salado, our route lay over arid hills of sand and sandstone. 30 miles; 1,034 miles.

July 23. Raised camp at sunrise, travelling over rough and barren hills near the river, and at 10 A. M. rested for the last time on its banks. The scenery here was picturesque. On our side, the stream was overhung by high cliffs of dazzlingly white sandstone, against which it dashed with violence; whilst on the left shore were extensive meadows, ornamented with numerous clusters of trees. All hands bathed in the river, and found its waters cool and refreshing. The heat of the weather was intense, until a distant thunderstorm refreshed the air.

Resuming our journey, we left Grand River, and, directing our course west-southwest across a sandy and parched plain towards Green River, stopped for the night at 10 P. M., at a place where there was scanty grass and no water; but we had brought a supply for our own use, and had watered the mules before starting. Day's travel, 36 miles; total distance, 1,070 miles.

July 24. The men passed a refreshing night, perfectly free from the mosquitos, which had been a source of such serious annoyance since leaving the settlements in New Mexico. Started at 5 A. M., and, travelling thirty-five miles, encamped on Green River Fork of the Great Colorado at 1 P. M.

The country we traversed was stony and broken by dry watercourses. On every side, and principally to the north and northeast, extended ranges of rugged hills, bare of vegetation, and seamed with ravines. On their summits were rocks of fantastic

G. H. Heap del. P. S. Duval & Co. lith. Phil.ª

VIEW ON GREEN RIVER.

shapes, resembling pyramids, obelisks, churches, and towers, and having all the appearance of a vast city in the distance. The only vegetation was a scanty growth of stunted wild sage and cacti, except at a point known as the Hole in the Rock, where there were willows and other plants denoting the vicinity of water, but we found none on our route. The sun was exceedingly hot, and we, as well as our mules, were glad to reach the river, where we could relieve our thirst. Saw four antelopes near Green River, to which the Delaware immediately gave chase, but was unable to get within gunshot.

Green River was broader and deeper than either Grand River or the Avonkarea, but its current was neither so rapid nor so turbulent. The scenery on its banks was grand and solemn, and we had an excellent view of it from our camping place on a high bluff.

The frame of the boat was commenced at once. Some Indians made their appearance on the opposite shore, and one of them swam over to our side, assisted by a log, on which he occasionally rested. Day's travel, 35 miles; total distance, 1,105 miles.

July 25. At an early hour the men resumed their work on the boat; the hides were found to be rotten and full of holes, as we had neglected to dry them after crossing the Avonkarea; but by dint of patching with pieces of India-rubber blankets and sheepskins, and smearing the seams with a mixture of tallow, flour, soap, and pulverized charcoal, the boat was made sufficiently tight, that, with constant bailing, all the men and packs were carried over in four trips. I went with the first load to guard our packs, as Indians were on the left bank watching our proceedings.

Mr. Beale made great exertions to hurry the train over this river. He went across at every trip, jumping into the river where it was shallow, and taking the boat in tow until he was beyond his depth. He was thus for many hours in the water, encouraging the men by his example. We had now an excellent party; the men were daring and adroit; they exhibited no fear when we were so hard pressed by the Utahs, and when exposure or toil was required of them, not one flinched from his duty. Some appeared almost to rejoice whenever there was a difficulty to overcome, and we never heard the Delaware's wild shout and laugh without suspecting that either he or his mule had got into some predicament, either by sliding down a bank, or getting into the mire, or entangled in a jungle. He never asked for help, and rejected all assistance, relying on himself in every emergency.

At sunset, the crossing of Green River was effected, and we gladly gave the boat to the Indians, who ripped it to pieces to make moccasson soles of the hides. We proceeded a mile up the stream, and encamped in the midst of luxuriant grass. A band of twenty-five mounted Utahs accompanied us and passed the night in our camp; we gave them to eat, and they seemed quite friendly. Their accounts of the Mormons corroborated what the Indians and Mexicans on the Avonkarea had told us. Day's travel, 1 mile; whole distance, 1,106 miles.

July 26. In the morning the Utahs, who, the night before, were apparently so friendly, showed a disposition to be insolent, but our party keeping close together, they did not dare to commence hostilities; most of them had rifles, and all had bows and quivers full of arrows with obsidian heads. They accompanied us for some miles, importuning us for presents, and finally left us in a bad humor. Had we been able to conciliate these Indians with a few gifts, such as blankets, beads, tobacco, brass wire, &c., we should not have had the least trouble with them. We parted on friendly terms with those on the Savoya, where Mr. Beale had remained during my journey to Taos; for, on leaving, he distributed a variety of small articles which I had brought for them, and with which they were entirely satisfied.

Started at five, and at noon encamped at Green River Spring. The water here was cool, but not abundant; it is, however, constant, and good grass and some cottonwoods and willows are found around it.

The character of the country and soil continued unchanged, rocky ridges worn into fantastic shapes, and soil loose, dry, and barren. The trail led through rocky ravines of red sandstone. Day's travel, 18 miles; whole distance, 1,124 miles.

July 27. We were on the road before daylight, and travelled thirty-eight miles west by south; crossing the east fork of San Rafael Creek, we halted at 8 P. M. on the west fork, a few miles above their junction, and twenty from where this creek flows into Green River. At our encampment, the creek was seven yards in breadth and eighteen inches deep. The water was cool and sweet, and good pasturage on its banks.

The trail led us over low hills much cut up by dry and rocky ravines, and on our right were sandstone bluffs. Vegetation was scanty, principally dwarf cedars, artemisia, and cactus, and occasionally patches of grama grass. We found no water from camp to camp. A longer trail than the one we took leads through a level valley. About twelve miles from Green River Spring, the country opened to the north and northwest, showing a level plain to the foot of the Wahsatch Mountains. These mountains extended north, west, and southwest as far as our sight could reach, and some of the loftiest were capped with snow. The heat of the sun was tempered by a pleasant westerly breeze. Day's travel, 38 miles; whole distance, 1,164.

July 28. Travelled twenty miles south by west, and halted at noon on the Rio del Moro (Castle Creek, so called on account of buttes near it resembling fortifications). In ten miles from the San Rafael, crossed a broad brook of clear and cool water, running into Green River. Between the streams vegetation was scanty and stunted, and the soil clayey, dry, and barren; to the westward were steep hills, beyond which could be seen the green and wooded slopes of the Wahsatch range.

Noticed fresh tracks of animals going north, evidently those of cattle stolen by Indians, from the Mormons.

Our noon camp was near the point where Moro Creek issued from the mountains. The clayey soil of which they are composed had been washed by rains, into the strangest shapes. At times, long lines of battlements presented themselves; at others, immense Gothic cathedrals, with all their quaint pinnacles and turrets, which reminded us of the ruined castles and churches that we had seen in our travels in the old world. The different colors of the clay added to the singularity of the scenery, and strengthened the resemblance.

In the afternoon, we continued to travel parallel to the hills in a south by west course, and in seven miles came to a gap, giving issue to a small stream, which we ascended three miles. The aridity of the country continued unchanged; the looseness of the soil, constantly kept shifting by rains, prevented much vegetation except in bottom lands; there was a scanty growth of some of the hardier plants, such as dwarf cedars. In the valley in which we encamped was good grass, which increased in quantity and improved in quality as we ascended it. Day's travel, 30 miles; whole distance, 1,192 miles.

July 29. Resumed our journey before sunrise, and went up the creek seven miles. This gorge, for it is almost too narrow to be called a valley, affords a good pass through the range. It narrows from one hundred yards to thirty-five feet, with lofty and perpendicular rocks on each side, and the ascent is very gradual. The hills were clothed, from their summits to their base, with a thick growth of pine trees, cedars, and aspens, and the brook was swarming with trout. The *divide* is broad, level, and smooth, and the descent on the western side easy; the trail, as is generally the case with Indian paths, went over a steep hill, which shortened the distance; but this ascent could easily have been avoided by going a couple of miles round to the left. Since leaving Green River, the duties of guide had devolved on José Galliego, but we found him far from efficient, and greatly missed the accurate knowledge that Felipe had of the country before we reached that river.

Our noon halt was on the Rio Salado (Salt Creek), a name which it obtains from flowing past some mines of rock-salt, for its waters are pure and sweet. We were now in the Great Salt Lake Basin, Salt Creek flowing to the northward and discharging into Sevier (Nicollet) River, which empties into a lake of the same name in the Basin.

We here found an abundance of good grass, which was not unwelcome to the mules, the rapid rate at which we travelled requiring that they should feed well to retain their strength. Thus far, none of our animals had shown signs of failing, and most of them were in excellent travelling condition. Since leaving the Savoya, we had met but little game; an antelope, shot by the Delaware on the banks of the Avonkarea, and four to which he had given chase near Green River, being all that we had seen.

On the summit of the divide, and before descending into the valley of the Rio Salado, I took a careful survey of the surrounding country, which offered many new and interesting features.

The Wahsatch Mountains are composed of several parallel ranges running from the north to the south, with fine well-watered valleys between them. They are short, and between the valleys are numerous passes. We here discovered our guide's error in leaving an excellent pass through the range, on the summit of which we were standing, to follow a mountain trail, which soon gave out, and left us to struggle through the brush, greatly fatiguing our pack animals.

We encamped for the night, on the Salado, in a broad and level valley. Throughout the mountains the pasturage reminded us of that in the Sahwatch range, although in the valley it was less luxuriant.

Soon after guard was set for the night, an attempt was made by Indians to *stampede* our animals. The watchfulness of the man on guard, however, defeated their purpose; he fired, but missed them. One of the mules was slightly wounded by an arrow. Day's travel, 30 miles; whole distance 1,222 miles.

July 30. Directing our course west, we entered a chasm or cañon in the hills six miles in length, and quite level and smooth. This brought us again to the Salado, at the point where it flows past the mines of rock-salt, from which it derives its name. The course of the creek is here southwest, and it joins Sevier or Nicollet River about three miles below the mines. At the mines, we found a wagon-trail leading to Mormon settlements, which our guide informed us were about a day's journey distant to the northward. We followed this trail to Sevier River, where it turned to the northward; and crossing the Salado near its mouth, travelled south up the left bank of the Sevier, on which we encamped at noon.

The course of the river in this valley is from south to north; it is about twelve yards in breadth and from three to four feet in depth. Sevier valley is perfectly level, and three miles in breadth; for many miles above and below the junction of the Salado it is arid and destitute of timber; there was good grass, however, in the river bottom. The mountains which inclose the valley east and west are apparently sterile, but their recesses are well timbered; for during the morning's march we crossed two small streams flowing from the westward, near which were vast quantities of drift-wood.

The weather was exceedingly hot, without a breath of air; and the dust raised by the animals, in travelling over the loose and dry soil, hung over us in clouds.

In the afternoon, continued up the valley; four miles brought us to beautiful meadows, which extend for several miles along Sevier River, and are caused by the overflow of several small streams from the westward. The grass was of the most luxuriant description, and reached above our saddle-girths. Ascended the river twelve miles farther, and encamped after dark on its banks. Day's travel, 37 miles; whole distance, 1,259 miles.

July 31. We saddled up before sunrise, and travelling north, reached at eight o'clock the head of the valley where Sevier River from the southwest, and Beaver Creek from the west, both issuing from deep cañons, join their waters. We here came to a stand, it being evident that farther progress in the direction we were travelling was impossible. The guide insisted that our road was through one of the cañons, but before proceeding it was deemed advisable to make a reconnoissance, when both were found equally impracticable, even for men on foot. After losing two hours in an ineffectual search, we turned our mules' heads to the northward, and, travelling three miles down the left bank of Sevier River, we crossed it, passed over a steep hill, and descended into another valley, watered by the same stream; when, too late for the discovery to be useful to us, we perceived a level wagon road, made by the Mormons, leading into it. Sevier is the corruption of Severo, and is called on Colonel Frémont's map Nicollet.

This valley lies north and south, and surpassed in beauty and fertility anything we had yet seen. It is about thirty miles in length by four in breadth, surrounded by mountains, down whose sides trickled numberless cool and limpid brooks, fringed with willows and cottonwoods. Sevier River flows through its centre, and it abounds in its entire breadth in rich pasturage. The mountains which inclose it were clothed, from summit to base, with oaks and pines.

After a short rest we proceeded south up this valley, and at dark stopped on a brook running from the westward into Sevier River. In riding through the grass we heard numerous rattlesnakes, and killed several; they sprang at some of the men and animals, but none were bitten. Day's march, 18 miles; whole distance, 1,277 miles.

August 1. We travelled until noon up the left bank of Sevier

River, and halted near its junction with the San Pasqual (its main fork), where the latter issues from a cañon at the head of the valley. The San Pasqual, above the cañon, flows through a valley of great beauty.

At our noon halt, we struck a trail which we supposed to be the old trail from Abiquiú to California; but it has been so long disused that it is now almost obliterated.

In the afternoon, we travelled about four miles up a ravine bearing a little to the west of south, and which took us to the summit of a steep mountain. We had left the wagon trail which we had found in the valley, as it took a long circuit to avoid this ascent. The summit of the mountain was broad and flat, and clothed with grass. Day's march, 36 miles; whole distance, 1,313 miles.

August 2. We were now approaching another stage in our journey which we were impatient to reach. The Mormon settlements near Las Vegas de Santa Clara were at a short distance, and we made an early start in the hope of reaching them before dark. We descended the mountains in a westerly direction through abundantly-watered valleys, everywhere covered with grass. I found wild rye growing in great abundance, the seed quite large and full.

At dusk, on the previous day, we had discovered a party of mounted Indians examining us from a neighboring ridge, and were on the lookout for them all the morning. Soon after sunrise a few Pah-Utahs, the first of that tribe which we had seen, came running down a hill-side to meet us, and, accosting us in a friendly manner, asked whether we were Mormons or *Swaps* (Americans). They informed us that a Mormon village was not far off, and Mr. Beale and I, riding in advance of our party, in a few hours, arrived at the town of Paragoona, in Little Salt Lake Valley, near Las Vegas de Santa Clara.

Paragoona is situated in the valley of the Little Salt Lake, and lies near the foot of the mountains which form its eastern boundary, at four miles from the lake. It contains about thirty houses, which, although built of adobes, present a neat and comfortable appearance. The adobes are small and well pressed, and are made of a pink-colored clay. The houses are built to form a quadrangle, the spaces between them being protected by a strong stockade of pine pickets. Outside of the village is an area of fifty acres inclosed within a single fence, and cultivated in common by the inhabitants. It is called The Field, and a stream from the Wahsatch Mountains irrigates it, after supplying the town with water.

The Mormons have found iron ore in the mountains, where they have established several smelting furnaces; they stated that it was of an excellent quality, and that the mines were inexhaustible.

Shortly before our arrival in the Territory, hostilities had broken out between Walkah, a Utah chief, and the Mormons, and we found them in a state of great alarm and excitement, in consequence of some of his recent acts.

We did not remain long at Paragoona; for soon after our arrival, the inhabitants, in obedience to a mandate from Governor Brigham Young, commenced removing to the town of Parawan, four miles to the southward, as he considered it unsafe, with the smallness of their number, for them to remain at Paragoona. It was to us a strange sight to witness the alacrity with which these people obeyed an order which compelled them to destroy in an instant, the fruits of two years' labor; and no time was lost in commencing the work of destruction. Their houses were demolished, the doors, windows, and all portable wood-work being reserved for future dwellings; and wagons were soon on the road to Parawan, loaded with their furniture and other property.

We left Paragoona in the afternoon, and rode to Parawan over an excellent wagon-road, made and kept in repair, and bridged in many places, by the Mormons. We passed, at a mile on our left, a large grist and saw mill worked by water power.

This ride to Parawan formed a strange contrast to our late journeying through the wilderness. At all the cross-roads were finger-posts, and mile-stones measured the distance.

Parawan is situated at the base of the mountains, and contains about one hundred houses, built in a square, and facing inwards. In their rear, and outside of the town, are vegetable gardens, each dwelling having a lot running back about one hundred yards. By an excellent system of irrigation, water is brought to the front and rear of each house, and through the centre and outside boundary of each garden lot. The houses are ornamented in front with small flower-gardens, which are fenced off from the square, and shaded with trees. The Field covers about four hundred acres, and was in a high state of cultivation, the wheat and corn being as fine as any that we had seen in the States; the people took a laudable pride in showing us what they had accomplished in so short a time, and against so many obstacles. Day's travel, 32 miles; whole distance, 1,345 miles.

August 3. Most of the day was spent in having the animals shod, and in getting extra shoes made to replace those which might be lost in crossing the desert region between the Vegas de Santa Clara, and Mohaveh River. An American blacksmith, assisted by a couple of Pah-Utah youths, did this work, and we were surprised to see what skilful workmen these Indians made. Most of the Mormon families have one or more Pah-Utah children, whom they had bought from their parents; they were treated with kindness, and even tenderness; were taught to call their protectors "father" and "mother," and instructed in the rudiments of education. The Mormon rulers encourage a system which ameliorates the condition of these children by removing them from the influence of their savage parents, but their laws forbid their being taken out of the Territory. The children are not interdicted from intercourse with their people, who are allowed freely to enter the town; but the latter evince very little interest in their offspring, for, having sold them to the whites, they no longer consider them their kith or kin.

The water of Little Salt Lake is as briny, we were told, as that of Great Salt Lake, and we noticed that its shores were covered with saline incrustations for a mile or more from the water's edge; but the Mormons stated that the salt was of little value, being impregnated with saleratus and other alkaline matter, which rendered it unfit for use. They obtain their supplies of this article from mines of rock-salt in the mountains.

The excitement occasioned by the threats of Walkah, the Utah chief, continued to increase during the day we spent at Parawan. Families flocked in from Paragoona, and other small settlements and farms, bringing with them their movables, and their flocks and herds. Parties of mounted men, well armed, patrolled the country; expresses came in from different quarters, bringing accounts of attacks by the Indians, on small parties and unprotected farms and houses. During our stay, Walkah sent in a polite message to Colonel G. A. Smith, who had military command of the district, and governed it by martial law, telling him that "the Mormons were d——d fools for abandoning their houses and towns, for he did not intend to molest them there, as it was his intention to confine his depredations to their cattle, and that he advised them to return and mind their crops, for, if they neglected them, they would starve, and be obliged to leave the country, which was not what he desired, for then there would be no cattle for him to take." He ended by declaring war for *four* years. This message did not tend to allay the fears of the Mormons, who, in this district, were mostly foreigners, and stood in great awe of Indians.

The Utah chieftain who occasioned all this panic and excitement, is a man of great subtlety, and indomitable energy. He is not a Utah by birth, but has acquired such an extraordinary ascendency over that tribe by his daring exploits, that all the restless spirits and ambitious young warriors in it have joined his standard. Having an unlimited supply of fine horses, and being inured to every fatigue and privation, he keeps the territories of New Mexico and Utah, the provinces of Chihuahua and Sonora, and the southern portion of California, in constant alarm. His movements are so rapid, and his plans so skilfully and so secretly laid, that he has never once failed in any enterprise, and has scarcely disappeared from one district before he is heard of in another. He frequently divides his men into two or more bands, which, making their appearance at different points at the same time, each headed, it is given out, by the dreaded Walkah in person, has given him with the ignorant Mexicans, the attribute of ubiquity. The principal object of his forays is to drive off horses and cattle, but more particularly the first; and among the Utahs we noticed horses with brands familiar to us in New Mexico and California.

He has adopted the name of Walker (corrupted to Walkah), on account of the close intimacy and friendship which in former days united him to Joe Walker, an old mountaineer, and the same who discovered Walker's Pass in the Sierra Nevada.

This chief had a brother as valiant and crafty as himself, to whom he was greatly attached. Both speaking Spanish and broken English, they were enabled to maintain intercourse with the whites without the aid of an interpreter. This brother the Mormons thought they had killed, for, having repelled a night attack on a mill, which was led by him, on the next morning they found a rifle and a hatchet which they recognized as his, and also traces of blood and tracks of men apparently carrying a heavy body. Although rejoicing at the death of one of their most implacable enemies, the Mormons dreaded the wrath of the great chieftain, which they felt would not be appeased until he had avenged his brother's blood in their own. The Mormons were surprised at our having passed in safety through Walkah's territory, and they did not know to what they were to attribute our escape from destruction. They told us that the cattle tracks which we had seen a few days previous were those of a portion of a large drove *lifted* by Walkah, and that the mounted men we had noticed in the mountains in the evening of August 1, were scouts sent out by him to watch our movements. They endeavored to dissuade us from prosecuting our journey, for they stated that it was unsafe to travel even between their towns without an escort of from twenty-five to thirty men.

The Mormons had published a reward of fifteen thousand dollars for Walkah's head, but it was a serious question among them who should "bell the cat."

We procured at Parawan a small supply of flour and some beef, which we *buccanée'd.*

The kind reception that we received from the inhabitants of these settlements, during our short sojourn among them, strongly contrasted with what we had been led to anticipate from the reports of the Mexicans and Indians whom we had met on the road. On our arrival, Colonel G. A. Smith sent an officer to inquire who we were, our business, destination, &c., at the same time apologizing for the inquiries, by stating that the disturbed condition of the country rendered it necessary to exercise a strict vigilance over all strangers, particularly over those who came from the direction of their enemy's territory. Mr. Beale's replies being, of course, satisfactory, we were treated as friends, and received every mark of cordiality. We spent the evening of our arrival in Parawan at the house of Col. Smith, who was in command of this portion of the territory, and was organizing a military force for its protection. He related to us the origin of these southern settlements, the many difficulties and hardships that they had to contend with, and gave us much interesting information of the geography of the surrounding country. He also stated that furnaces for smelting iron ore were already in operation in the vicinity of Paragoona and Parawan, and that the metal, which was obtained in sufficient quantity to supply any demand, was also of an excellent quality; and that veins of coal had been found near Cedar City, on Coal Creek, eighteen miles south of Parawan, one of which was fifteen feet in thickness, and apparently inexhaustible. A large force of English miners was employed in working these mines, and pronounced the coal to be equal to the best English coal. I saw it used in the forges; it is bituminous, and burns with a bright flame.

As regards the odious practice of polygamy which these people have engrafted on their religion, it is not to be supposed that we could learn much about it during our short stay, and its existence would even have been unobserved by us, had not a "Saint" voluntarily informed us that he was "one of those Mormons who believed in a plurality of wives," and added, "for my part I have six, and this is one of them," pointing to a female who was present. Taking this subject for his text, he delivered a discourse highly eulogistic of the institution of marriage, as seen in a Mormon point of view; of the antiquity of polygamy, its advantages, the evils it prevents, quoting the example of the patriarchs, and of eastern nations, and backing his argument with statistics of the relative number of males and females born, obtained no doubt from the same source as the Book of Mormon. This discourse did not increase our respect for the tenets he advocated, but we deemed it useless to engage in a controversy with one who made use of such sophistry. From what he said, I inferred that a large number of Mormons do not entirely approve of the "spiritual wife" system, and, judging from some of the households, it was evident that the weaker vessel has in many instances here, as elsewhere, the control of the *ménage.*

We left Parawan at dusk, having sent most of the party in advance, with directions to await our arrival at the nearest of those rich meadows known as Las Vegas de Santa Clara, about eighteen miles distant.

On entering the valley of the Little Salt Lake, we came upon the line surveyed by Col. Frémont, and described in his report published in 1846. It was our intention to follow this line until we reached Mohaveh River, where we intended to take two or three men and enter Tulare Valley through Walker's Pass in the Sierra Nevada, allowing the remainder to pursue their journey up the Mohaveh, through the Cajon Pass, to Los Angeles. As the Mormons had opened a wagon-road all the way, we anticipated no difficulty in getting to our journey's end in good time.

The party arrived at Cedar City about midnight, but indisposition prevented me from keeping up with them, and I was finally compelled to spread my blanket near the roadside and rest until morning. Day's travel, 18 miles; whole distance, 1,363 miles.

Aug. 4. I saddled my mule at daylight, and in a few hours reached Cedar City. I was informed here that the party had already left, but that I could overtake the camp a few miles from the town.

Cedar City is a place of more importance than either Parawan or Paragoona, but is built on a similar plan. Around it are extensive fields, abundantly irrigated, giving promise of a rich harvest; the hills in the rear of the town are well timbered, and it is in this vicinity that the Mormons have discovered the coal veins destined to form the wealth of the region. The inhabitants are principally foreigners, and mostly Englishmen from the coal districts of Great Britain. At the time of our visit, the place was crowded with the people of the surrounding country seeking refuge from the Indians, and its square was blocked up with wagons, furniture, tents, farming implements, &c., in the midst of which were men, women, and children, together with every description of cattle, creating a scene of confusion difficult to describe.

I overtook the camp in a large grove of cottonwoods, and we immediately resumed our journey.

It is here that we saw the first of the meadows of Santa Clara, which give some celebrity to this region. They are embraced between 37° and 38° north latitude. This vega was covered with tender grass and watered by numerous streams, which preserve its freshness even during the most sultry seasons. To travellers from the south, coming off the desert lying between the Mohaveh and these vegas, they certainly offer a delightful relief; and, although our animals had only recently been luxuriating in the rich mountain pastures of the Wahsatch, their uniform verdure and level surface, shaded in many places by extensive glades of cottonwoods, offered a delightful feeling of security, as though we were once more within the confines of civilization.

We now travelled on the Mormon wagon-trail leading to San Bernardino, in the south of California. We had heard of another route leading west to Owen's River, thence through a pass in the Sierra Nevada, which leads into the Tulare Valley near the head of the Four Creeks; but unfortunately we were unable to take this route, for we could neither obtain a guide nor even information on the subject; and, moreover, it would have been departing from his views of examining the country on the Mohaveh, for the purpose of locating Indians there, for Mr. Beale to have altered his course. The route by Owen's River shortens the distance nearly two hundred miles, cutting off the large elbow to the southwest, and, according to the accounts we had received, it conducts over a tolerably level, well watered, and grassy country.

We rested for a short time at noon, and then travelled until 10 P. M. over a level plain and good wagon-road, on each side of which was much dry grass; but we saw no water until encamping on a *vega* (meadow) which we reached through a gap in the mountains on our left. This meadow was about seven miles in length, penetrating deep into the mountains, and, although there was little running water, yet the grass was everywhere green and tender. Day's travel, 38 miles; whole distance, 1,401 miles.

Aug. 5. We returned to the plain, and continued to travel south by west until noon, when we encamped in the most southern of the vegas, which was more beautiful than any we had yet seen—rich in waving grass, and watered by numerous rills. It is inclosed by a low ridge of hills; its declivity is mostly to the northward; being on the rim of the Great Salt Lake Basin, in fact, on the divide, a portion of its waters run into the Basin, whilst the Rio de Santa Clara, which runs into the Rio de la Virgen, a tributary of the Great Colorado, takes its rise here.

These vegas are called by the Mormons Mountain Meadows.

In the afternoon, travelling south, we descended a slope, which brought us after dark to Santa Clara Creek, near which we encamped. Day's travel, 28 miles; whole distance, 1,429 miles.

CHAPTER VI.

DEPARTURE FROM LAS VEGAS DE SANTA CLARA. PASSAGE OF THE DESERT. ARRIVAL AT LOS ANGELES, CALIFORNIA.

August 6. The Santa Clara at our encampment was a slender rill; but a few miles lower down, its volume was considerably increased by the accession of several streams.

We were now approaching the desert, and we this day travelled only ten miles, to allow our animals to recruit by rest and food. The road followed down the stream, and although level, was much overgrown with bushes.

After travelling a few miles, we met a small party of Pah-Utah Indians, who evinced great joy at seeing us, accosting us without fear. On approaching their village, a collection of miserable bush huts, we were met by an aged Indian, apparently their chief, holding in his hand a pipe, the stem of which was a reed and the bowl a piece of tin. With much gravity, he bade us welcome to his village, and after blowing three wreaths of smoke towards the sun, he offered us their symbol of friendship, with which we imitated his example. As soon as we had dismounted, a venerable squaw, laboring under great excitement, rushed towards Mr. Beale, and seizing his hands, forced into them a couple of green *tunias* (prickly pears), which she invited him to eat, a ceremony, I have no doubt, having a meaning as mystical as the first. And having thus entered into bonds to keep the peace and complied with all the exigencies of etiquette, we were considered the guests of the nation.

Among these Indians we witnessed one of the benefits which they have derived from their intercourse with the Mormons, who take every opportunity to ameliorate the condition of this wretched tribe. Near their village was a large and well-irrigated field, cultivated with care, and planted with corn, pumpkins, squashes, and melons.

The Pah-Utah Indians are the greatest horse thieves on the continent. Rarely attempting the bold *coups-de-main* of the Utahs, they dog travellers during their march and follow on their trail like jackals, cutting off any stragglers whom they can surprise and overpower, and pick up such animals as stray from the band or lag behind from fatigue. At night, lurking around the camp, and concealing themselves behind rocks and bushes, they communicate with each other by imitating the sounds of birds and animals. They never ride, but use as food the horses and mules that they steal, and, if within arrow-shot of one of these animals, a poisoned shaft secures him as their prize. Their arms are bows and arrows tipped with obsidian, and lances sometimes pointed with iron, which they obtain from the wrecks of wagons found along the road; they also use a pronged stick to drag lizards from their holes.

The Indians being apprehensive that our animals might trespass on their field, which was without inclosure, we permitted them to drive the band several miles up the stream, where we had noticed an abundance of white clover; and, whilst thus confiding in them, we had security for their honesty by several Indians passing the night in our camp, where they laid near the fire, coiled up like dogs; besides which, their women and children, and entire crops, on which they depended for their subsistence during the approaching winter, were also in our power.

In the afternoon we visited their huts, which presented a squalid scene of dirt and wretchedness. When the women saw us approaching they concealed their children, fearing that we might wish to carry them off. Noticing that something moved under a large wicker basket, one of us examined its contents, which were found to be a little naked fellow, his teeth chattering with fear.

Yearly expeditions are fitted out in New Mexico to trade with the Pah-Utahs for their children, and recourse is often had to foul means to force their parents to part with them. So common is it to make a *raid* for this purpose, that it is considered as no more objectionable than to go on a buffalo or a mustang hunt. One of our men, José Galliego, who was an old hand at this species of man-hunting, related to us, with evident *gusto*, numerous anecdotes on this subject; and as we

approached the village, he rode up to Mr. Beale, and eagerly proposed to him that we should "charge on it like h—l, kill the *mans*, and may-be catch some of the little boys and *gals*."

Camp was all day crowded with men and squaws; the former had reduced their costume to first principles, and even the latter were attired in a style of the most primitive simplicity. They spoke with great volubility and vehemence, using many gesticulations, regardless of the common usage of other Indians, of speaking but one at a time. It appeared as though they thought aloud, and were not addressing any one in particular. Our ragged and forlorn appearance, unshaven chins, and sun-scarred visages, excited great merriment, and they used no ceremony in pointing and laughing at us. Day's travel, 10 miles; whole distance, 1,439 miles.

August 7. The Indians drove our animals into camp before dawn, and we were on the road at sunrise, travelling down the Santa Clara. In ten miles the road diverged to the right from the creek, and for eight miles passed through a region of rugged and arid hills and cañons, when it issued upon an inclined plane leading to the Rio de la Virgen. Although generally level, it was a rough road for wagons, and with the exception of one good spring, four miles from the Santa Clara, we saw no water until we encamped on the Virgen. A scanty growth of cactus, agave americana, greasewood, and small cedars, was the only vegetation after leaving the creek. A Pah-Utah handed me some ears of wheat, the grains of which I preserved, and he stated that it grows spontaneously near the Santa Clara. It is from this stock that the New Mexicans have obtained the seed which they call Payute wheat, and the Mormons, Taos wheat. It has been much improved by cultivation, and is considered the best in New Mexico and Utah. A party of Indians accompanied us for twelve miles, begging for *tabac*, and we noticed several *smokes* during the day, and fires after dark, made by the natives on the Virgen, to warn the country of our approach. We set double guard at night, and the mules evinced by their restlessness and uneasiness the vicinity of Pah-Utahs. Day's travel, 35 miles; whole distance, 1,474 miles.

August 8. The Rio de la Virgen is a turbid and shallow stream, about twelve yards in breadth. It flows with a rapid current over a sandy bed, and as we descended it, the growth

of cottonwood gave place to mesquit trees and willows. The mesquit tree bears in some localities an abundance of sweet pods, on which mules feed greedily, and they are a good substitute for corn, being almost as nutritious. We crossed scanty patches of wiry salt grass, which affords but little nourishment.

The river bottom was hemmed in by bluffs, beyond which, on the right, was an extensive plain much cut up by gullies, and on the left a range of dark mountains, which in many places came down to the river's edge. The road which followed down the bottom, was at times through deep sand, as was mostly the case since leaving the Vegas de Santa Clara. The scenery was gloomy and forbidding, and gave indication that we were approaching a wild and desolate region. We noticed during the day many fresh Indian tracks, and at times caught glimpses of dark forms gliding through the bushes on either side. Day's march, 29 miles; whole distance, 1,503 miles.

August 9. By keeping a watchful guard, our animals were saved from the Pah-Utahs, who hovered around us all night.

We rode down the Virgen ten miles farther, when we left it to cross the hot and sterile plain, eight miles broad, extending between the Virgen and the Rio Atascoso (Muddy Creek). It was thickly covered with sharp flints, and bore a scanty growth of stunted mesquit bushes, which on the dry plains bear few pods; for a couple of miles from each stream the country was much broken by ravines.

Rio Atascoso is a narrow stream, but in many places quite deep; its water is clear, and it derives its name from the slimy and miry nature of its banks and bed. Day's march, 18 miles; whole distance, 1,521 miles.

August 10. We again had Indians around us all night, making their usual signals, but by keeping a strict double guard they were prevented from stealing or wounding our animals. Soon after sunrise, a party of Pah-Utahs showed their heads from behind some rocks near camp, and shouted to us; finding that we did not attempt to molest them, they cautiously exposed more of their persons, and finally dropped among us by twos and threes, until they numbered fifteen. They professed entire innocence of being concerned in the proceedings of the previous night, laying them all to the charge of other Pah-Utahs, and expressed for us the warmest attachment. At this time a strange figure, entirely divested of clothing, suddenly made his appearance on the summit of a rock thirty yards from us; his face was covered with a thick coating of crimson paint, a slender bone, eight inches in length, was thrust through the septum of his nose, and in his left hand he carried a bow and a bunch of arrows. This worthy addressed us a long speech, introducing himself as *the* great chief of all the Pah-Utahs (which was false, as they recognize no chief), intimating that the monotonous existence which he had hitherto been leading had become irksome to him, that he wished to travel and see the white man's world, and that, if we consented to admit him into our company, he would endeavor to "make himself generally useful." He ended by offering to give himself away to any one who would accept of him. Although any accession to our number was not at all desirable, to have refused his request would have nipped in the bud the aspirations of this ambitious youth, Mr. Beale therefore allowed him to join our party, handing him a pair of old buckskin pants and a woollen shirt, which he at once donned, feeling very proud, but very uncomfortable.

The first *jornada* (long distance between waters) across the desert commences at the Muddy; and to avoid the heat which at this season is very oppressive during the day, we did not resume our journey until the afternoon. The road led us for six miles up a broad and sandy ravine, issuing from which we entered upon an extensive and undulating plain, whose sandy and stony soil produced no vegetation except artemisia. We travelled all night, during which a hot wind blew from the southward.

August 11. Dawn found us still on the jornada, between Muddy Creek and the Ojo del Gaetan (Spring of Gaetan) or Vega Quintana, as this meadow is sometimes called, which we reached at 8 A. M. without the loss of an animal. Thus far we had lost three mules; one was drowned in the Uncompagre, another was left on the Virgen, and the third at the Muddy. Both of the latter were animals that we had obtained on the journey, and, being unshod, became tender-footed and were unable to keep up with the train.

The Vega Quintana is a meadow of several thousand acres in extent, watered through its centre by two deep but narrow streams of clear and icy cold water.* It is shaded in many places with mesquit trees, willows, and vines covered with clusters of small but sweet grapes. Two Pah-Utahs, who were gathering mesquit beans, fled in alarm at our approach, and we saw numerous coveys of the California partridge. This oasis deserves the name of The Diamond of the Desert, so beautiful and bright does it appear in the centre of the dreary waste that surrounds it. Dusty and weary as we were, after our long and toilsome ride, a bath in the brook was a luxury in which we indulged more than once during the day that we spent here. Day's march, 45 miles; whole distance, 1,566 miles.

August 12. We reached the second vega, Quintana, at 11 A. M., after riding seventeen miles southwest by west; the road passed over a stony desert, which produced no other vegetation than stunted artemisia and an occasional cactus and mesquit bush. The rivulet which here fertilizes the ground and produces some verdure issues from the mountains through a bald and rugged gap.

This vega is a favorite camping place of the Mormons, and is covered with the wrecks of wagons and of stoves and other iron work.

All our provisions, except pinole, were now exhausted; and as this was our only dependence, we made a division of what remained between the ten persons who now (since the Pah-Utah had joined us) composed our party. We found that by using only six table-spoonfuls each per day, the pinole might be made to last until our arrival in the settlements of California. We had seen no game for many days, nor did we expect to meet any until we reached the Mohaveh. Day's march, 17 miles; whole distance, 1,583 miles.

August 13. Wearied with watching all night, we resumed our journey at dawn. Indians were around us as usual, and many signs of their vicinity, which would have escaped our notice, were pointed out to us by "Pite," as we had christened our new follower. We had scarcely started, before a torrent of yells and abuse was poured upon us from every side. No one could be perceived, but every rock and bush apparently con-

* In May, 1844, Colonel Frémont ascertained the temperature of these springs as being 71° and 73° respectively. We found them so cold that it required some resolution to bathe in them.

cealed an Indian. Pite was not slow in replying to them, and for a moment they were silent with astonishment at receiving, in such pure vernacular, a reply to their insults. Soon, however, the war of words was renewed with fresh fury, and had we understood them, we should doubtless have enjoyed a very choice specimen of Pah-Utah billingsgate. Pite prudently kept close among us; brave as he was with his tongue, he entertained a wholesome fear of falling into the hands of his fellow-countrymen, for they would soon have brought his travels to a close.

Our road led us through a cañon or chasm which we had entered the previous day; it followed the bed of the stream, and was much obstructed by heavy sand and scattered rocks. We passed two singular caves, one of which presented a close resemblance to the cyclopean order of architecture, with the principle of the arch and keystone admirably preserved. The other forcibly reminded us of the façade of an old Catholic church, such as is often seen in Italy.

After travelling ten miles through rocky ravines, with bald and furrowed mountains on either side, we ascended a ridge which brought in view an extensive and barren plain, bounded on all sides by lofty mountains. To the westward we perceived a range which extended from north to south, and which appeared to have frequent breaks in it.

In the afternoon, we arrived at the Aqua Escarbada, where we expected to have to dig for water; but the ground had been so deeply excavated, that a running spring had been reached.

Shortly before reaching this place, we found on the road-side the remains of an American, with the mark of a rifle-ball in his skull. From papers which were scattered around, we ascertained that he was a Mormon on an exploring expedition, and his buckskin garments not having been wet by rain, proved that he had been killed this season. Day's travel, 25 miles; total, 1,608 miles.

August 14. Twelve miles from the Escarbada, the road makes a sudden bend to the westward, and ascends a steep ridge, from the top of which a magnificent, but solemn and dreary view presented itself. Four ranges of mountains, overtopping each other, extended from north to south, and bounded the western horizon; to the eastward was spread a wide extent of country, which offered, in every direction, the same absence of timber, and of almost all vegetation. The solitude was unrelieved by the song of bird or the chirp of insect; the mournful murmur of the breeze, as it swept over the desert, was the only sound that broke the silence. In many places, a deceptive mirage spread fictitious lakes and spectral groves to our view, which a puff of wind, or a change in our position, suddenly dissolved.

A rapid descent down a sinuous ravine, from two to three miles in length, brought us to the sink in the plain, where is found the Ojo de Archilète (Archilete's Spring), at some distance from which are many small willows, but in its immediate vicinity there is a total absence of shade; the water is clear and cool, but slightly brackish. A cruel tragedy, heroically avenged by Kit Carson and Alexander Godey, and recorded by Frémont, occurred here in 1844, and has rendered this spot memorable; we found near the spring the skull of an Indian, killed perhaps in that affray. Day's travel, 22 miles; whole distance, 1,630 miles.

August 15. A ride of five miles brought us to the Amargosa (Bitter Creek), a ravine containing a scanty supply of warm, fetid, and nauseating water, in a succession of holes. We encamped at the foot of a rock on its eastern side, where a slender brackish spring barely supplied our wants. The valley, or broad ravine, through which the Amargosa, during the rainy season, is for a few miles a running stream, winds with a general course from southeast to northwest, and is hemmed in by steep black and rocky hills.

The second jornada across the desert commences at the Amargosa, and ends at the Agua del Tio Meso (the Spring of Uncle Meso). It is fifty miles in length, and we anticipated much toil and suffering in crossing it. We endeavored to guard against the loss of our mules from hunger, by laying in a small supply of green reeds and mesquit beans, the only forage, except salt grass, that could be obtained here; and, not expecting to find water the whole distance, all our canteens were filled.

We commenced this dreary journey at 2 P. M. The heat was intense, and, instead of diminishing as the sun descended, it became more oppressive. For twelve miles the road was over deep sand, into which the mules sank above their fetlocks.

8

In fifteen miles, we diverged to the left across a spur of rocky hills, the road leading through a ravine, where, much to our surprise, we discovered the remains of houses, *rastres* (Mexican quartz crushers), and all the appliances of gold mining. These we subsequently ascertained were the Salt Spring Gold Mines, where a fortune had been sunk by men who were sufficiently deluded or sanguine to abandon the rich mines of California, travel across one hundred and fifty miles of desert, and live upwards of twelve months in a spot so desolate and forlorn that there is actually not sufficient vegetation to keep a goat from starvation. We here found two springs, one sulphurous and nauseating, the other brackish. The canteens were replenished, but it was impossible to water the mules.

August 16. The heat increased as we advanced into the desert, and most of the party had divested themselves of the greater part of their clothing. The guns, which we carried across the pummels of our saddles, were hot to the touch; and, to add to our annoyance and suffering, the wind, ladened with an impalpable sand, blew fiercely from the southward, feeling as if issuing from the mouth of a furnace, and obliterating in many places all traces of the road. The mules, already jaded by travelling across the sandy plain, went slowly along, their heads drooping to the ground. The pale moon, occasionally overshadowed by clouds, threw a ghastly light over the desert, and skeletons of animals glistening in her beams, strewed the way, adding horror to the scene.

Shortly before dawn we entered some hills to the westward, where the heat was less intense. Three of the mules were unable to go farther, and their saddles and packs were placed on other animals, and men left with them, together with some reeds and beans and a small supply of water. We were now all on foot, our animals having barely sufficient strength to carry their saddles. At daylight we began to scatter, and those who could go in advance did so, for our thirst was beginning to be intolerable. It was not until 10 A. M., after twenty hours of continuous march, completely prostrated with heat, toil, hunger, and thirst, that we reached the Agua del Tio Meso.

This camping ground (which is called on the maps Agua del Tomaso) has two small pools fed by tiny springs. The water in the pools is only fit for animals, and that in the springs we found barely drinkable; the grass was scanty and salt; but when mules are starving, they are not particular in their choice of food.

The men who had been left with the mules joined us late in the afternoon; they had suffered much, but brought in all the animals. Poor Pite was not the last one in; his thirst was dreadful, and when he reached the spring he threw himself on the ground and drank to repletion.

This spring is named after an old Mexican called Meso, who was styled *Tio*, or uncle, on account of his age. He discovered it when he and his party were nearly perishing with thirst. Their happy deliverance was celebrated by a great feast; he washed and dressed himself, and rambled about the place singing until he fell dead, killed by a stroke of apoplexy. Two peons, abandoned on the desert by their master, reached this spring after their party had left for the Mohaveh. Unable to proceed farther, they both died of starvation, and the next travellers who encamped here, found their skeletons locked in each other's embrace, as if they had expired in the act of devouring one another.

These painful associations, together with the utterly desolate appearance of all around, cast a gloom over our spirits; and we could not raise them, as old Tio Meso did, by a feast; for all we had that day was a couple of spoonsful of boiled pinole. The road across the jornada is good, with the exception of the first twelve miles, where it is sandy. The only vegetation that I noticed was artemisia, on the plains, and mesquit and dry greasewood among the hills. Day's march, 55 miles; whole distance, 1,685 miles.

August 17. During the night we had a heavy storm; the howling wind, blowing from the desert, was hot and filled with sand, and the rain fell in large drops, without refreshing the air.

The Agua del Tio Meso is an oasis; for, although a wretched spot, it is the only resting-place in the desert between the Amargosa and the River Mohaveh. We were glad to leave it, at 4 A.M. Two of the mules soon showed signs of failing, and remained on the road in charge of one of the Mexicans. We rested for a few minutes at 10 A. M. to breakfast, having filled our canteens at Tio Meso's spring. The Delaware had killed a rabbit, the first of any game that we had seen for a long time; but we left it on the road, with some water, for the Mexican, as we feared that he might be delayed until late.

The desert retained its level and monotonous character until we reached Mohaveh River, at 7 P. M., our animals almost perishing from hunger and thirst.

The sandy soil through which the Mohaveh flows absorbs nearly all its water, and where we struck it it was no longer a running stream. Grass, however, was everywhere abundant, together with a thick growth of willows, reeds, and mesquit bushes, interlaced with grape-vines; and in some places there were beautiful groves of cottonwoods.

All our troubles as regarded a scarcity of water and grass were now at an end, and from this point our journey was over a level country, offering no impediment whatever to a good road as far as the settlements in California. Except on the edge of the river, however, the land was barren and unproductive, offering no point fit for settlement.

Mr. Beale and myself had intended on reaching the Mohaveh to have gone in advance of our people; but we could not leave them in their starving condition. It was also our intention to have selected two or three of the men to accompany us across the desert between the Mohaveh and Walker's Pass, in the Sierra Nevada; but we found that of all our animals there were not five that could travel over twenty miles a day; and, as the intervening country was entirely destitute of water and grass, we were compelled reluctantly to relinquish this object.

The Mexican left with the mules arrived at 11 P. M., having remained faithfully by them until he brought them in. We thus crossed this desert without abandoning a single animal, which is, I believe, almost unprecedented. Day's travel, 30 miles; whole distance, 1,715 miles.

August 18. We allowed our mules to rest until the afternoon before we proceeded up the Mohaveh. Its course is from the west through a broad level plain, bounded on either side by lofty mountains. Its water increased as we ascended it, and we found several large ponds well stocked with fish. Day's travel, 8 miles; total, 1,723 miles.

August 19. The road was through heavy sand, and often left the river at a distance of two miles. We encamped at noon near a large and deep pond of very cool and clear water, alive with fish, principally mullets, some of which were large. We had just finished our allowance of pinole, when the Delaware rode into camp with a splendid antelope lashed behind his saddle, and reported that he had shot another, which was immediately sent for. As the question of starvation was now set at rest, it was determined that Mr. Beale and myself and two of the men should proceed as rapidly as our mules could travel, whilst the remainder of the party were to follow us by easy stages to the settlements. Day's travel, 19 miles; whole distance, 1,742 miles.

August 20. Accompanied by the Delaware and Harry Young, we started in advance of the party, and before noon had ridden twenty miles up the right bank of the Mohaveh. Its bottom was covered in many places with a thick undergrowth, and occasionally by large groves of cottonwood, and bounded on the south by high and rugged hills. The weather was pleasant, with a breeze from the westward.

Where we crossed the Mohaveh it was a rapid stream, twenty-five yards in breadth and one foot in depth, but its water was too warm to be drinkable. Passed several fine meadows near the river, and saw bands of antelopes, also hares and partridges. After a rest of seven hours we resumed our journey, the road leading up to an extensive plain, thickly covered with cedars and pines, intermingled with palmyra cactus and aloes. It forks about ten miles from the river. The lefthand fork, which we took, follows the old Spanish trail, whilst the other, which had been recently opened by the Mormons, makes a bend to avoid a rough portion of country. They both join again in the Cajon Pass. We travelled until 11 P. M., when we rested under the cedars on the plain, where we found dry bunch grass, but no water. Day's travel, 40 miles; whole distance, 1,782 miles.

August 21. For the last time the cry of "catch up" was heard, and we saddled our mules before dawn, impatient to reach our journey's end. On approaching the mountains, which extended between us and the valley of Los Angeles, the country presented a more broken appearance. After travelling six miles, we commenced descending the Pacific slope, and soon after reached the head waters of the Santa Anna, a creek rising to the eastward of the mountains, and which finds its way through the Cajon Pass to the Pacific Ocean, south of San Pedro.

We entered this pass, and the most magnificent scenery presented itself to our eyes. Around us were lofty mountains, their summits clothed with pines and their base with chimsal, mansanita, dwarf oaks, and aloes. In the valley were numerous clusters of sycamore, which attains here a large size, and is one of the most beautiful trees in the country. The ground was covered with innumerable tracks of grizzly bears, and the Delaware kept a keen lookout for the rough-coated gentry. During our journey, he had killed at least one specimen of each species of game to be found in the region which we had traversed, and he was anxious to have an encounter with the largest and fiercest of them all, the mighty grizzly of California; but he was disappointed; although our men, in coming through this pass a few days later, had a desperate fight with a bear, which they finally overcame.

We issued from the mountains at noon, when the beautiful valley of San Bernardino, with its stupendous mountain, broke upon our view. Never did so beautiful a sight gladden the eyes of weary travellers; and, having been in the saddle since dawn, we turned our jaded mules into a rich meadow, where the grass reached to their knees, and we rested under the shade of a grove of sycamores.

Leaving the valley of San Bernardino behind us, we directed our course northwest in the direction of Los Angeles. We travelled steadily until nightfall without perceiving any signs of habitations, though our hopes were constantly kept alive by fresh tracks of men and cattle; finally, at nine o'clock, when we were on the point of dismounting, our weary beasts being scarcely able to lift their feet, we were saluted by the cheering bark of a dog, and in a few minutes found ourselves in the centre of a large cluster of buildings, and welcomed in the most friendly manner to Cocomongo Ranchio, by the Mexican proprietor. Day's travel, 35 miles; whole distance, 1,817 miles.

August 22. Our arrival at the Ranchio de Cocomongo will long be a green spot in our memories; and it was a pleasant sight to us to witness the satisfaction of our travel-worn mules, in passing from unremitting toil and scanty food to complete rest and abundant nourishment.

We obtained fresh horses, and a gallop of thirty-five miles through a rich and settled country brought us to the city of Los Angeles, where every kindness and attention was shown to us by Mr. Wilson, Indian Agent, and his accomplished lady.

We had been given up for lost, and several parties had gone in search of us. Some of our friends had spent six weeks in Walker's Pass, where they expected us to arrive, and had kept up fires by night and smokes by day on a point visible at a long distance in the desert, to guide us in case we should have lost our way. Day's march, 35 miles; total distance from Westport, Missouri, to Los Angeles, California, 1,852 miles.

The remainder of our party arrived two days later, and thus, without serious accident to any of the men, and with the loss of only three of the mules, we accomplished the distance from Westport to Los Angeles in exactly one hundred days. Some of the party, however, had travelled seven hundred and fifteen miles more, in going to Taos from Grand River and in returning.

RÉSUMÉ.

CENTRAL ROUTE FROM WESTPORT, MISSOURI, TO LOS ANGELES, CALIFORNIA.

SECTION I.

From Westport, Missouri, to Council Grove, 122 *miles.*

THIS portion of the route is over a broad wagon-road, excellent in summer, but heavy rains render it impassable at certain points, where slight bridges would obviate all difficulties.

Bridges are required at Bull Creek, One Hundred and Ten, Dragoon Creek, Council Grove, and two other points. Trains are sometimes detained at these runs for weeks by heavy rains. A few thousand dollars ($3,000) would be sufficient to render this road as good as any in the States, at all seasons.

Grass along this section is abundant, and camping places frequent.

At Council Grove, there is a large, well-furnished store, where a constant supply of everything required for the road is kept. Also, a good farrier and blacksmith. Parties from New Mexico can here obtain a refit at prices much under those they have to pay in New Mexico.

The country around Council Grove is rich in pasturage, and well timbered. When the Indian titles are extinguished, and a territorial government established, this country will be immediately and thickly settled.

SECTION II.

From Council Grove to Fort Atkinson, Arkansas River, 239 *miles.*

The face of the country is level. It is all prairie, gently undulating. Cottonwood Creek, Little Arkansas, and Pawnee Fork, require bridging; with these exceptions, the road is firm and good.

Except at three or four points, the country is destitute of timber. Pasturage good.

SECTION III.

From Fort Atkinson (Arkansas River) to mouth of Huerfano River, 247 *miles.*

The country is a rolling prairie, and its surface more uneven, with a gradual ascent to the westward of about seven feet to the mile.

No timber on the left bank of the Arkansas (it having all been destroyed) until we reach the Big Timbers, where there is an extensive grove of cottonwoods. From thence to the Huerfano there is an abundance of timber.

The soil is dry and hard, and the road excellent. The grass is more rank in the river bottom, and scantier on the plains. Good camping grounds are to be found every few miles.

SECTION IV.

From the mouth of the Huerfano to Fort Massachusetts, 85 *miles.*

A gently undulating plain leads from the Arkansas to the foot of the Sangre de Cristo Mountains and the Sierra Mojada, from which the Huerfano issues. It is covered with good bunch grass, and the river bottom is well timbered, and affords excellent pasturage.

The Huerfano, at the season that we crossed it (early in June), was swollen by melting snows, but we had no difficulty in finding a good ford.

These plains abound with game—deer, antelopes, and hares; and, near the river, wild turkeys.

The Huerfano enters a cañon about thirty-four miles from its mouth, through which it runs for about ten miles; and both sides of the river are here much broken by gullies. These may be avoided by keeping at a distance of from two to three miles from it. After passing the cañon, the best road is near the stream.

Following the river, the road enters the Sangre de Cristo Mountains, about forty-three miles above its mouth.

The best pass through these mountains is Roubideau's. Its elevation is so moderate, that some sandhills in San Luis Valley, of moderate elevation, can be perceived some time before reaching the pass. It is obstructed with dead timber, which is the principal difficulty to overcome. Another pass, traversed by travellers on horseback, crosses an elevated ridge near the head waters of Sangre de Cristo, which flows west into San Luis Valley, and down this to Utah Creek.

Rich pasturage, timber, and water abound all through these mountains, and they teem with game.

SECTION V.

From Fort Massachusetts to Coochatope Pass, 124 *miles.*

Eighty-one miles of this distance is over a perfectly level country. The road leaves Utah Creek, and in twenty-five miles, course N. W., descends into the bottom lands of the Del Norte. It then crosses numerous sloughs, until it reaches a point 30 miles beyond, where it leaves the river, and goes in a N. by W. course for the entrance of Sahwatch Valley, and up that to the entrance of Coochatope Pass. After entering this pass, for seven miles the ascent is very gradual; it then becomes more rapid until the dividing ridge is crossed. The sloughs of the Del Norte can be avoided by a detour to the right.

San Luis Valley is quite level, and from twenty to twenty-five miles in breadth. Sahwatch Valley is five miles broad at its entrance, and gradually narrows to one mile, and is also perfectly level. The valley of the Coochumpah, in which is the Puerto de los Cibolas (Coochatope), is closely hemmed in by hills, and its ascent is scarcely perceptible until we reach within a couple of miles of the divide.

Good pasturage is found on numerous points on the Del

Norte; scanty grass in San Luis Valley, except at the crossing of Garita Creek, fourteen miles from the Del Norte, and at a spring, about ten miles north of the Garita, at both of which good pasturage is abundant. Throughout Sawatch and Coochumpah valleys, abundant grass, timber, and water are found.

Coochatope Pass is much obstructed by trees and underwood, and it had only been travelled by Indians and Indian traders with pack mules, at the time of our passing through; since then two wagon trains have gone through.

The Carnero Pass leads from San Luis Valley to Grand River. Its principal obstruction is a quantity of dead timber in one of the valleys, which might soon be removed by burning. Grass, wood, and water as abundant as in the Coochatope Pass. The trail to the Carnero leaves the Del Norte about eighteen miles above where that to the Coochatope leaves it, and joins the trail through the latter, near the Rio Jaroso (Willow Creek).

SECTION VI.

From Coochatope Pass to Grand River, 134 *miles.*

This section passes over the mountainous country comprised within the Sahwatch range. The road is entirely practicable for wagons. A more level road makes a detour of eighty miles.

Early in summer, the Coochatope, Estrendoso, Jaroso, Rio de la Laguna, and the Nawaquasitch, all except the first, rising in the Sierra de la Plata, and crossing the road at right angles, are so swollen, as to be impassable for wagons without much trouble; bridges, for which abundant timber grows on their banks, are required over them.

Timber, grass, and water are abundant all through this range; about twenty miles from Grand River, the country becomes level, and is destitute of pasturage, except near the River Uncompagre, down which the road goes until reaching Grand River.

SECTION VII.

From Grand River to Green River, 154 *miles.*

All level country, and many good camping grounds at easy distances. Timber near the streams.

Grand River is fordable from August till April; at other times it is swollen by melting snows. The same may be said of the Avonkarea, though in some years its waters do not fall sufficiently to be fordable. I was told that Green River is never fordable, but doubt the correctness of this information, and believe that in most years, from August to early in the spring, animals can wade across it. But for wagons, these three streams should have ferry boats.

SECTION VIII.

From Green River to Mormon Settlements near Las Vegas de Santa Clara, Utah Territory, 242 *miles.*

Eighty-six miles are across barren plains, occasionally seamed with dry watercourses. Good camping places are found at easy distances, with grass, water, and wood.

For one hundred and fifty-six miles the trail leads through successive ranges of the Wahsatch Mountains. All these ranges are separated by broad valleys, watered by abundant streams, and smaller ones give access to and unite the larger ones.

Throughout these mountains grass, water, and timber are abundant; game is scanty.

SECTION IX.

From Settlements near Las Vegas de Santa Clara to Mohaveh River, 374 *miles.*

This section is over a part of or near the Great Salt Lake Basin; and in it are two *jornadas* (long distance between waters); the first is 45, the second 55 miles in length.

At the Mormon settlements, beef, flour, and cornmeal can be purchased at reasonable rates. Groceries are scarce and dear.

With the exception of the jornadas, camping grounds are found along this route at short distances, on the Vegas de Santa Clara, Rio Santa Clara, Rio de la Virgen, Muddy Creek, Vegas del Gaetan, Ojo de Archilete, and Amargosa Creek.

In some of these places the grass is salt and wiry, and affords little nourishment. Mesquit bushes, which grow on all the waters of the desert, bear a nutritious bean on which animals feed greedily.

The only game is sage rabbits.

SECTION X.

From Mohaveh River to Los Angeles, 137 *miles.*

The road now follows up the Mohaveh, and near it is good pasturage, and timber. Water is first found in holes; higher up there is running water.

After leaving the river, the road crosses an elevated plain covered with small trees and good bunch grass, but no water is found until arriving on the head waters of the Santa Anna, a creek flowing into the Pacific, a distance of about 25 miles. A rough wagon-road leads down this creek, through the Cajon Pass into the valley of San Bernardino, from which a broad, well-beaten track leads to Los Angeles.

ITINERARY OF THE CENTRAL ROUTE.

From Westport, Missouri, to Los Angeles, California.

DATE.	CAMPS.	DISTANCE.	DISTANCE FROM W.	REMARKS.
May 15	Ind. Creek		12	Cottonwoods, willows, good grass.
" 16	Bull Creek	23	35	Some timber; good grass and water.
" 16	Garfish Creek	22	57	Nearest wood, half mile; water and grass.
" 17	"110"	23	80	Running stream; timber, good grass.
" 17	Dragoon Creek	12	92	" fine timber and grass.
" 18	Stream	10	102	Good water; timber and grass.
" 18	"	4	106	" " "
" 18	Hollow	6	112	Water in holes; grass.
" 18	COUNCIL GROVE	10	122	Settlement; abundant timber; grass; water.
" 19	Hollow	17	139	Water; grass and timber abundant.
" 19	Lost Spring	15	154	Good water, not abundant; grass; no wood.
" 20	Cottonwood Creek	16	170	Large timber; running water; good pasturage.
" 20	Turkey Creek	19	189	Plenty of water and grass; no wood.
" 21	Pool	12	201	Grass and water; small bushes.
" 21	Little Arkansas	18	219	Good timber; grass and water.
" 21	Owl Creek	10	229	Timber and grass; no water, except after rains.
" 22	Great Bend of Ark.	35	264	Wood; grass and water.
" 22	Walnut Creek	7	271	" "
" 23	Pawnee Fork	31	302	Well wooded; grass and water.
" 23	Pond	9	311	Good pasturage; water; no wood; plenty "buffalo chips."
" 24	"	25	336	Water; grass.
" 24	Arkansas River	20	356	Water; grass; small bushes.
" 25	FORT ATKINSON	5	361	" " "
" 26	1st Crossing of S. Fé trail	10	371	" " "
" 26	2d " "	5	376	" " "
" 26	Camp on Ark.	20	396	" " "
" 27	"	20	416	" coarse grass; no wood.
" 28	Island on Ark.	19	435	" " little wood.
" 28	Chouteau's Island	12	447	" coarse rank grass; drift-wood.
" 29	Slough of Ark.	28	475	" wiry grass; no wood.
" 29	Arkansas River	8	483	" " "
" 30	Big Timbers	20	503	" coarse grass; large timber.
" 30	Arkansas River	12	515	Good water; abundant bottom grass; timber.
" 31	Lower Dry Creek	25	540	Scanty dry grass; water in pools, warm; wood.
" 31	BENT'S FORT	7	547	Bottom grass; river Arkansas; wood.
" 31	Upper Dry Creek	7	554	" " "
" 31	Pond	6	560	Dry bunch grass; water; wood near river.

ITINERARY OF THE CENTRAL ROUTE—CONTINUED.

DATE.		CAMPS.	DISTANCE.	DISTANCE FROM W.	REMARKS.
June	1	Below mouth of Timpas	15	575	Bottom grass; water; wood.
"	1	Timpas Creek	5	580	Water in holes, slightly brackish; good grass; wood.
"	2	HUERFANO RIVER	18	598	Water; rich grass; timber.
"	2	"	10	608	" " "
"	3	Pool	24	632	Water holes; grass; bushes.
"	3	Huerfano River	10	642	Water; luxuriant grass; timber.
"	4	Rock on Cuchada in Sangre de Cristo	20	662	" " "
"	4	SUMMIT OF SANGRE DE CRISTO	6	668	Water in springs; luxuriant grass; large pines.
"	5	FORT MASSACHUSETTS	25	693	Excellent water; abundant good pasturage; timber.
"	15	Slough on Rio del Norte	25	718	Stagnant water; coarse grass; bushes
"	16	Rio del Norte	18	736	Good water; abundant bottom grass; trees.
"	17	"	10	746	Good water; good grass; trees.
"	17	Rio de la Garita	14	760	" " willows.
"	17	Spring	10	770	" " bushes.
"	17	Rincon del Sahwatch	16	786	" " trees.
"	18	Sahwatch Valley	16	802	" " timber.
"	18	COOCHATOPE GATE	6	808	" " wood.
"	19	Summit of Pass	9	817	" " large timber.
"	19	Coochatope Creek	15	832	" " trees.
"	19	Spring	10	842	" " "
"	20	Rivulet	22	864	" " "
"	20	Rio Jaroso (Willow Creek)	5	869	" " "
"	20	Spring	7	876	" " "
"	21	Rio de la Laguna (Lake Creek)	5	881	" " large timber.
"	21	Spring	4	885	" " "
"	22	Rio Nawaquasitch (Sheep-tail Creek)	18	903	" " "
"	22	Creek	20	923	Water in holes; scanty grass; small trees.
"	23	Rio Uncompâgre	16	939	Water; coarse grass; trees.
"	23	Mouth of the Uncompagre	12	951	" " "
July	18	Cerenoquinti Creek	25	976	" good grass; wood.
"	19	River Avonkaria	12	988	Coarse grass; timber.
"	21	Camp l'Amoureux, on Grand River	16	1004	Abundant grass; timber; river water.
"	24	Rio Salado, Grand River	10	1014	" " "
"	24	Grand River	20	1034	" " "
"	23	"	15	1049	" " "
"	23	Plain betw'n Grand and Green Rivers	21	1070	Scanty grass; no wood; no water.
"	24	Green River, left shore	35	1105	Abundant grass; wood; river water.
"	25	Green River, right shore	1	1106	" " "

ITINERARY OF THE CENTRAL ROUTE—CONTINUED.

DATE.		CAMPS.	DIST-ANCE.	DISTANCE FROM W.	REMARKS.
July	26	Green River Spring	18	1124	Some good grass; small spring; good timber.
"	27	San Rafael Creek	38	1162	Good pasturage; small trees; good water.
"	28	Brook	10	1172	" " "
"	28	Rio del Moro	10	1182	" " "
"	28	Creek in Wahsatch Mountains	10	1192	" " "
"	29	Rio Salado	15	1207	" " "
"	29	"	15	1222	Coarse grass; " "
"	30	Sevier (Nicollet) River	21	1243	" " "
"	30	Meadows	4	1247	Luxuriant grass; bushes; good water.
"	30	Sevier River	12	1259	Good grass; small trees; good water.
"	31	"	10	1269	Excellent grass; " "
"	31	Rivulet, affluent to Sevier	8	1277	" large trees; "
Aug.	1	Junction of Sevier and San Pasqual Rivers	20	1297	" small trees; "
"	1	Summit of last range of Sahwatch Mts.	16	1313	Excellent grass; bushes; no water near.
"	2	PARAGOONA (Mormon settlement)	28	1341	Excellent grass; no wood near except bushes; good water.
"	2	PARAWAN "	4	1345	" " "
"	3	CEDAR CITY, 1st, Vega de Santa Clara	18	1363	Excellent grass; large timber; good water.
"	4	2d, Vega de Santa Clara	38	1401	Excellent grass; small trees; water in holes.
"	5	3d, " "	12	1413	Excellent grass; small trees; running water.
"	5	Santa Clara Creek	16	1429	Good grass; large trees; running water.
"	6	" "	10	1439	Grass and clover; large trees; running water.
"	7	Spring	14	1453	Grass; small trees; good water.
"	7	Rio de la Virgen	21	1474	Salt grass; trees; warm, turbid water.
"	8	"	14	1488	Salt grass; mesquit beans; trees; turbid water.
"	8	"	15	1503	" " "
"	9	"	10	1513	" " "
"	9	Rio Atascoso (Muddy Creek)	8	1521	" " "
"	11	Ojo del Gaetan (Jornada)	45	1566	Good pasturage; bushes; cool, running water.
"	12	Vega Quintana	17	1583	Good pasturage; trees; spring.
"	13	Agua Escarbada	25	1608	Grass and mesquit beans; small trees; water to be dug for.
"	14	Ojo de Archilete	22	1630	Good pasturage; bushes; cool water.
"	15	Amargosa	5	1635	Salt grass; mesquit beans; water in pools, bad; small spring, brackish water, under rock.

ITINERARY OF THE CENTRAL ROUTE—CONTINUED.

DATE.	CAMPS.	DIST-ANCE.	DISTANCE FROM W.	REMARKS.
Aug. 16	Agua del Tio Meso (Jornada)	50	1685	Scanty salt grass; small bushes; bad, scanty water.
" 17	Mohaveh River	30	1715	Good grass; abundant wood; water in holes.
" 18	"	8	1723	Good grass; large trees; water in holes.
" 19	"	19	1742	" " "
" 20	"	20	1762	" " running water.
" 20	Plain	20	1782	Dry bunch grass; cedars; no water.
" 21	Santa Anna Creek	8	1790	Good grass; timber; running water.
" 21	Sycamore Camp	12	1802	Fine grass; large timber; springs.
" 21	Cocomongo Ranch	15	1817	" " running water.
" 22	LOS ANGELES	35	1852	

APPENDIX.

LETTER FROM MR. CHARLES W. McCLANAHAN,

Published in the National Intelligencer (Washington), Nov. 7, 1853.

FORT MASSACHUSETTS (N. M.), Aug. 28, 1853.

HON. T. H. BENTON:—

DEAR SIR: Knowing that you feel interested in the middle route for the great Pacific Railroad, and believing that any information in regard to it would be acceptable, no matter how humble the source from which it comes, I have determined to state what I know about it. This information is from travelling the route just behind Captain Gunnison. I left Virginia the first of April, went to Missouri and Illinois to purchase sheep for the California market. After purchasing, I started to take them by Salt Lake, the Humboldt River, &c., feeling assured that I would have to winter at Salt Lake. I had gotten the sheep as far as St. Joseph's, (Mo.) Having some business in St. Louis, I met with Captain Gunnison, and learned from him that there was a better route by way of Utah Lake, and that he was going to open it, and that, from what he knew about it, it would be much better for me to take it. After thinking a good deal over it, I determined to take it, as there was a very large number of stock on the old route, and a good prospect of getting to California this season. I read your address with a great deal of interest; and, feeling assured these statements about the route could be relied on, I left Missouri at Westport, on the 18th of June, with a large number of sheep and some cows—Mr. Crockett, of Virginia, a partner with me. At Westport, I met with the two Mr. Ross's, of Iowa, with their families, going the old route; they also determined to accompany me the new route. After travelling a few days, I fell in with the two Mr. Burwells, of Franklin City, Virginia, with a large number of cattle, who also were persuaded to join me. We travelled the Santa Fé road twenty-five miles above Fort Atkinson, keeping on the well-beaten track to thirty miles above Bent's Old Fort, and crossed the Arkansas River at the mouth of Apispah Creek, crossed over to the Huerfano, up that stream about twenty miles, and crossed the Sierra Blanca Mountains through Captain Gunnison's Pass, about twelve miles south of Leroux's Pass to this fort. The distance given by Captain Gunnison is 693 miles from Westport, Missouri.

I have travelled over the mountains of Virginia, Pennsylvania, and Tennessee, over several of the passes of the Sierra Nevada in California, and I have never seen a better or more easy Pass for carriages and wagons than the one found by Captain Gunnison, through the Sierra Blanca [Sangre de Cristo] just opposite to Fort Massachusetts, and distant from it fifteen miles. I travelled the old route to California in 1849, and can speak of the two routes from actual experience, having gone over both with wagons. I look upon this route as far superior, and feel confident that as soon as it is known it will and must be the great thoroughfare from the Atlantic to the Pacific. On this route, there is an abundance of grass and water, so much that stock will travel and keep fat; the large majority of our sheep are as fat as any mutton in the Philadelphia or Baltimore market, and a very large number of Mr. Burwell's cattle are fine beef; and I have never seen any stock, after having travelled so far, look half as well. Both of the Mr. Ross's have carriages, and as yet nothing has in the least given way. I can say without fear of contradiction that this is one of the finest natural roads in the world, combining everything necessary to sustain stock; and I am confident that, if its advantages are fully made known to Congress, it will be adopted for the great Pacific Railroad. On this line, almost the entire route can be settled; as all the land from Missouri to Bent's Fort is rich and very fertile, equal to the best lands of Missouri and Illinois, and no land can beat the Sierra Blanca [Sangre de Cristo ?] for grass; even to the very summit it stands as thick as the best meadows; many acres would mow at least four tons per acre. Then comes the large and beautiful valley of San Luis, said to be one of the most fertile in New Mexico; indeed, fine land is upon the whole route, and the climate such that stock can live all winter upon the grass. I will here state the route I think best for emigrants to travel: Leave Westport, Missouri, take the road to Uniontown, then to Fort Centre, then take Captain Gunnison's trail, which leads from the Kansas to the Arkansas, near the mouth of Walnut Creek, up the Arkansas above Bent's Old Fort, thirty-two miles; then up the Huerfano, through Captain Gunnison's Pass to Fort Massachusetts; then to Little Salt Lake, Walker's Pass, Sierra Nevada; then down the valley of the San Joaquin to Stockton or San Francisco. There are settlements at different points all along this route, where emigrants can get supplies, none farther apart than two hundred miles. After leaving Missouri, you pass first Council Grove, next the Fort on Walnut Creek, next Green Horn, next Fort Massachusetts, Little Salt Lake, Santa Clara, Vegas de Santa Clara; at each of these supplies can be had. I feel confident, when Captain Gunnison makes out his report, that this route will be adopted. The pass through the Sierra Blanca [Sangre de Cristo?] is so low and gradual that a railroad can be made over it, and the grade will not exceed fifty feet to the mile. Captain Gunnison is doing his whole duty, and well deserves the thanks of the whole country, for the very well laid out road through this almost unexplored country. I will write you again after getting through to California, and describe the rest of the way.

Yours respectfully,

CHARLES W. McCLANAHAN.

EXTRACT OF A LETTER FROM MR. R. S. WOOTTON,

Published in the Missouri Democrat.

DON FERNANDEZ DE TAOS, NEW MEXICO, October 22, 1853.

EDITOR MISSOURI DEMOCRAT:—

Having passed several years in the mountains and in this country, and having some knowledge of the same, I propose giving, through your valuable columns, to the emigrants, some information as regards the Central Route to California. During the last year, I have taken a drove of sheep from this place to California, over the route Colonel Frémont intended to have gone in the winter of '48, '49, at the time of his disaster. I made the trip through to California in ninety days, arriving there with my sheep in good order, having passed through some of the finest country I ever saw, had good camps, and plenty of wood, water, and grass every night during the whole trip. This route is at least 450 miles nearer than the route by Fort Laramie and South Pass. I recommend to emigrants by all means to take this route in preference to any other. Start from Kansas or any town on the western frontier of Missouri, come up the north side of the Arkansas River to the mouth of the Huerfano River, about forty-five miles above Bent's Fort, up the Huerfano River to Roubideau's Pass, or the Pass El Sangre de Cristo, either of them practicable for wagons, the ascent and descent being narrow valleys made by small mountain streams, and so gradual as to offer no obstruction to wagons. Both these passes lead into the valley of San Luis, one of the finest valleys in the world; follow up the valley to the Coochatope Pass, in the Grand River Mountain; down the Coochatope River, to the valleys of Grand and Green Rivers, until you strike the Great Spanish trail; then follow the trail to the Little Salt Lake and to the St. Clara Springs; at both of these places there are flourishing towns built by the Mormons, where emigrants can procure such things as they want at fair prices. I was offered flour at $2 50 per 100 pounds, and groceries at fair prices. From St. Clara Springs to San Francisco, by Walker's Pass, there is a good wagon-road, and settlements all the way. Captain Gunnison with his party left the Pass El Sangre de Cristo about the 16th August, and made the journey through to Green River in twenty-four days, with twenty wagons. A few days behind Captain Gunnison was a party of emigrants, who had made up their minds to pass the winter at Salt Lake, in consequence of being so late in the season; after being informed of this route, they determined to try the road; the party was conducted by Captain McClanahan, of Virginia; with the party was Colonel Ross and brother, from Iowa, with their families, with several other gentlemen. They had 2,000 sheep, and from 3 to 400 head of cattle. Mr. Leroux, the guide of Captain Gunnison, met the emigrants on his return to this place on Grand River, and reports that they were very much pleased with the route, their stock being in excellent condition. Captain McClanahan, who has been several times to California with stock by the South Pass route, says there is no comparison between the routes; that he would sooner pass five times from the Arkansas to Grand River, than pass through the Black Hills on the Laramie route once. There is now being commenced a settlement on the Arkansas River at the mouth of the Huerfano, at which place emigrants can also procure such necessaries as they may be in want of; also information as to the route, or guides if they wish. There is also a good ferry at the mouth of the Huerfano, and ferries will also be established during the coming summer on Grand and Green Rivers. There is also another great advantage that this route has over a more northern one, as emigrants can leave Missouri as late as the 1st August, and be in no danger of being stopped by snow. After reaching the Great Spanish trail in the valley of Green River, from thence to California there is never any snow, and the months of October and November are more pleasant to travellers, and better for stock, than the summer months.

* * * * * * *

I am, sir, respectfully,

Your obedient servant,

R. S. WOOTTON.

CAMELS, AS A SUBSTITUTE FOR HORSES, MULES, ETC.

During our journey across the continent, I took particular note of the country, with reference to its adaptation to the use of camels and dromedaries, and to ascertain whether these animals might be introduced with advantage on our extensive plains.

Having, by a residence of many years in Asia and Africa, become well acquainted with their qualities and powers of endurance, I am now convinced that they would be of inestimable value in traversing the dry and barren regions between the Colorado and the Sierra Nevada; and I am glad to see that the Secretary at War has, in his late report to Congress, asked for an appropriation for the purpose of importing a certain number, in order to test their usefulness.

I will now state a few facts which will show the valuable qualities that these animals possess, the manner in which they may be rendered serviceable, and the facility with which they might be domesticated on our continent.

In enumerating the qualities which render the camel and dromedary so well suited to our western waters, I will quote from several travellers, whose statements will corroborate my own:—

1. *Their power to endure hunger and thirst.*—Tavernier, the great Eastern traveller, states that his camels, in going from Aleppo to Ispahan, by the Great Desert, went nine days without drinking.

The French missionary, Huc, who travelled in Tartary, Thibet, &c. in the years 1844, '45, '46, gives some interesting information in relation to this animal. Speaking of the Desert of Ortos, on the northern border of China, he says: "Everywhere the waters are brackish, the soil arid, and covered with saline efflorescences. This sterility is very injurious to cattle; the camel, however, whose robust and hardy nature adapts itself to the most barren regions, is a substitute with the Tartars for all other animals. The camel, which they with truth style 'the treasure of the desert,' can abstain from food and drink for fifteen days, and sometimes for a month. However poor the country, he always finds sufficient food to satisfy his hunger. In the most sterile plains, the herbs which other animals will not touch, and even bushes and dry wood, will serve him for food." In Barbary, they can remain five days without drinking during the summer when the heat is intolerable, and there is little or no herbage; but when there is grass, and particularly in spring, they require no water for three weeks.

2. *Their strength, speed, and endurance.*—No animal can compete with the camel for strength and endurance. The African traveller, Shaw, relates that on his journey to Mount Sinaï, which was over a very hot and stony region, though each of his camels carried seven *quintals* (784 pounds), he travelled ten, and sometimes fifteen hours a day, at the rate of three miles an hour.

Another traveller (F. A. Neale, *Eight Years in Syria*) states: "The Turcoman camel, a much finer animal than the Syrian, will carry, equally poised, two bales, weighing together half a ton."

Huc remarks: "Although he costs so little to nourish, the camel can be properly appreciated in those countries only where he is in constant use. His ordinary load is from seven to eight hundred pounds, and with this burden he can travel about ten leagues a day."

In Barbary, they carry from 550 to 600 pounds, and travel forty miles a day.

3. *The longevity of the camel.*—The naturalist, Buffon, states that camels live from forty to fifty years. In Tunis, where I had daily opportunities of seeing them, they live fully fifty years. Mr. Huc says that they retain their vigor for many years, and if they are allowed a short period of rest in the spring, to pasture, they are of good service for fifty years.

The camel, therefore, possesses more useful qualities than any other animal subjected to the use of man. His strength is such that he can carry more than three mule loads, though he requires as little nourishment as the ass.

In Asia and Africa, the journeys of the caravans are often from two thousand to three thousand miles in length, during which they average from thirty to thirty-five miles a day.

They are remarkably docile and obedient to their masters; lie down to be loaded and unloaded; at night sleep crouched in a circle around the encampment. They rarely stray away, nor are they, as mules, liable to be frightened; it would be difficult—nay, impossible—to stampede a caravan of camels. When turned out to pasture, they eat in an hour as much as serves them to ruminate the whole night, and to nourish them during twenty-four hours.

The female camel furnishes excellent milk longer than the cow, upon which the Arabs often subsist during their long journeys. Their hair, which is renewed annually, is more in request than the finest wool; the fleece weighs about ten pounds.

The dromedary possesses the same qualities as the camel, as regards abstemiousness, docility, &c., to which he adds much greater speed and endurance.

The dromedary is a much taller and finer-shaped animal than the camel. The Arabs assert that he can travel as far in one day as one of their best horses can in four. They are so hardy that they travel in the desert for eight or ten days at the rate of from one hundred and twenty-five to one hundred and fifty miles per day, during which time they require very little food or water. I saw a party of Arabs, mounted on dromedaries, arrive in Tunis in four days from Tripoli, a distance of six hundred miles.

In these journeys they do not bear heavy loads, but carry a man, with his arms and provisions, which are equivalent to about two hundred and fifty pounds.

General Yusuf, of the French army, travelled from Blidah, a town in the interior of Algeria, to the city of Algiers, in a carriage drawn by dromedaries. Though these animals had a few days before made a journey from Medeah to Boghar, a distance of one hundred and eighty miles, in twenty-four hours, the General drove them at the rate of ten miles the hour.

Huc remarks: "Those that are employed to carry dispatches are made to travel eighty leagues in a day; but they only carry a rider."

The same author observes: "When their fur is long, camels can endure the most severe frosts. Naturalists have stated that camels could not live in cold climates; they probably had reference to those of Arabia."

In Turkey in Europe, where the winters are very severe, camels are in common use at all seasons. They are also used in winter as well as summer, on the elevated steppes of Tartary as far north as 50°.

APPENDIX.

(II.)

ROUTE FROM LAS VEGAS DE SANTA CLARA TO WALKER'S PASS, BY THE WAY OF OWEN'S RIVER AND OWEN'S LAKE.

It is seen by the Journal that it was the wish of Col. Benton that we should have gone nearly due west from Santa Clara Meadows to Owen's River, and also the reason why we followed the old Spanish trail by the Mohaveh, and thence to Los Angeles. His reason was, that the Spanish trail went too far to the south, and over the desert, while it was believed there would be a more direct way, and over a better country, by keeping west to Owen's River, at the eastern base of the Sierra Nevada. This was the belief of Col. Frémont, who had examined Owen's River and Lake, and laid them down in his map of 1848, and also sketched a mountain running east and west, about latitude 38, along the southern base of which he judged (from the nature of mountains and valleys in that region) there must be a belt of fertile land, with wood, water, and grass, making a valley east and west; which was the course that the route for the road required. His views have been subsequently verified, and as early as 1849–50, by a party of emigrants, headed by the Rev. J. W. Brier, who has published an account of it in the *Christian Advocate*, a religious paper in San Francisco.

REVEREND MR. BRIER'S STATEMENT.

"In September, of 1849, we left Salt Lake, in Hunt's large wagon train, for Los Angeles. We travelled nearly south to a point on the old Spanish trail, called 'The Divide,' about 75 miles southwest of Little Salt Lake.* Near this point we were overtaken by some Mormons, who brought with them a way-bill of a new and better route from the Divide to the southern mines, *via* Owen's Lake, Walker's Pass, and Tulare Valley. This way-bill was given by a hunter, named Ward, who had assumed the habits and intermarried with the Utahs, and was one of Walker's band. The way-bill stated that we should find a succession of fertile valleys, and plenty of grass and water, in a direct line to Owen's Lake and Walker's Pass.

"This way-bill, and other causes, induced that part of the company to which I belonged to take the cut-off. Leaving the Spanish trail, we travelled west 25 miles, through an opening in the mountains, having an excellent and almost level road. We then turned south, through a long, narrow valley, which brought us up on some table-lands, near the head waters of the Santa Clara. At this point we should have turned to the west, and would thereby have reached the first Muddy by a more direct line and by a much better road. But, bearing off too far south, a few hours brought us to the Santa Clara, in the vicinity of deep and impassable cañons. After three days of fruitless explorations in a southerly course, most of the company returned to the Spanish trail. But the company to which I was attached, discovering an open country to the west, and, believing we had gone too far south, resolved on a western course. Twenty miles brought us to the first Muddy. In travelling this twenty miles, we found no serious obstacles, excepting a cedar forest, through which we cut a road. By bearing to the south, in this instance, we lost about ten miles and found a rougher road. Still, we found nothing difficult or serious even by this route. This region abounds in spruce and cedar.

"From the first to the second Muddy is about 50 miles. The country over which we passed was a succession of valleys, separated by low dividing ridges. About 10 miles north, the country seemed a continuous plain nearly the entire distance. This part of the road can boast of nothing but a good solid foundation for a road, being rather sterile. From the second

* **This is the third Vegas de Santa Clara, in which the Rio de Santa Clara running south, and a stream discharging into Sevier or Nicollet Lake, head. H.**

Muddy, we took a southwest direction, through a valley 60 miles in length, some parts of which were very fertile, having an extraordinary growth of bunch grass. On the north side of the valley there is a high mountain range nearly 100 miles long; in this mountain we discovered creeks large enough to turn a mill. Leaving this valley, we descended by a long slope into what seemed to be a lower region of country and entirely different, being more desert, yet better adapted to a road than the former, having a more solid foundation. The mountains in this region are so isolated as to admit of a passage through them in almost any direction. From our descent into this part of the route to Owen's Mountains it is about 50 miles, and presents no obstacle in the way of the erection of a road, and needs but little grading. When within 25 or 30 miles of the pass in Owen's Mountains to which the way-bill directed us, most of the company, becoming alarmed at the prospects, and being deceived by the gestures of two Indian captives, took a south course for 100 miles, or near that, and were then compelled to leave their wagons and cross Owen's Mountains on foot, and that, too, over its very highest summits, and where it spreads itself into four distinct ranges, which, however, terminate a little further south.

"From these heights, a depression could be seen to the north. where we should have crossed. The distance from the desert, east of Owen's Mountains, to Owen's River, I suppose is about 50 miles; from Owen's Lake to Walker's Pass is about 50 miles; and all that distance, or most of it, is an open valley, from five to ten miles wide, lying between the Sierra Nevada and Owen's Mountains. The ascent from the eastern side to the summit of Sierra, in Walker's Pass, is gradual and easy; and the descent down Kern River is still more so. A part of our company passed through in January, 1849, and found no snow. The entire distance from the Divide on the Spanish trail to Walker's Pass I estimate at about 350 miles. In all this distance, Owen's Mountain is the only impediment, and, from all that I could learn and see, I am satisfied that there is a good pass, and that when it is thoroughly explored, it will prove no real impediment. In all this distance, you find no impediment from snow whatever. Now, if the country east of the Wahsatch is equal to that part of the route west of the Wahsatch, I have no hesitancy in saying that, for distance and locality, it has greatly the preference over every other. I have personal knowledge, and actual observation, of a part, at least, of both the North and South routes."

THE END.

UNIV. OF MICHIGAN,
JUN 29 1912

CATALOGUE
OF
VALUABLE BOOKS,
PUBLISHED BY
LIPPINCOTT, GRAMBO & CO.,
(SUCCESSORS TO GRIGG, ELLIOT & CO.)

NO. 14 NORTH FOURTH STREET, PHILADELPHIA;

CONSISTING OF A LARGE ASSORTMENT OF

Bibles, Prayer-Books, Commentaries, Standard Poets,

MEDICAL, THEOLOGICAL AND MISCELLANEOUS WORKS, ETC.,

PARTICULARLY SUITABLE FOR

PUBLIC AND PRIVATE LIBRARIES.

FOR SALE BY BOOKSELLERS AND COUNTRY MERCHANTS GENERALLY THROUGHOUT THE UNITED STATES.

THE BEST & MOST COMPLETE FAMILY COMMENTARY.

The Comprehensive Commentary on the Holy Bible;

CONTAINING

THE TEXT ACCORDING TO THE AUTHORIZED VERSION,

SCOTT'S MARGINAL REFERENCES; MATTHEW HENRY'S COMMENTARY, CONDENSED, BUT RETAINING EVERY USEFUL THOUGHT; THE PRACTICAL OBSERVATIONS OF REV. THOMAS SCOTT, D. D.;

WITH EXTENSIVE

EXPLANATORY, CRITICAL AND PHILOLOGICAL NOTES,

Selected from Scott, Doddridge, Gill, Adam Clarke, Patrick, Poole, Lowth, Burder, Harmer, Calmet, Rosenmueller, Bloomfield, Stuart, Bush, Dwight, and many other writers on the Scriptures.

The whole designed to be a digest and combination of the advantages of the best Bible Commentaries, and embracing nearly all that is valuable in

HENRY, SCOTT, AND DODDRIDGE.

Conveniently arranged for family and private reading, and, at the same time, particularly adapted to the wants of Sabbath-School Teachers and Bible Classes; with numerous useful tables, and a neatly engraved Family Record.

Edited by Rev. William Jenks, D. D.,

PASTOR OF GREEN STREET CHURCH, BOSTON.

Embellished with five portraits, and other elegant engravings, from steel plates; with several maps and many wood-cuts, illustrative of Scripture Manners, Customs, Antiquities, &c. In 6 vols. super-royal 8vo.

Including Supplement, bound in cloth, sheep, calf, &c., varying in

Price from $10 to $15.

The whole forming the most valuable as well as the cheapest Commentary published in the world.

NOTICES AND RECOMMENDATIONS
OF THE
COMPREHENSIVE COMMENTARY.

The Publishers select the following from the testimonials they have received as to the value of the work:

We, the subscribers, having examined the *Comprehensive Commentary*, issued from the press of Messrs. L., G. & Co., and highly approving its character, would cheerfully and confidently recommend it as containing more matter and more advantages than any other with which we are acquainted; and considering the expense incurred, and the excellent manner of its mechanical execution, we believe it to be one of the *cheapest* works ever issued from the press. We hope the publishers will be sustained by a liberal patronage, in their expensive and useful undertaking. We should be pleased to learn that every family in the United States had procured a copy.

B. B. WISNER, D. D., Secretary of Am. Board of Com. for For. Missions.
WM. COGSWELL, D. D., " " Education Society.
JOHN CODMAN, D. D., Pastor of Congregational Church, Dorchester.
Rev. HUBBARD WINSLOW, " " Bowdoin street, Dorchester.
Rev. SEWALL HARDING, Pastor of T. C. Church, Waltham.
Rev. J. H. FAIRCHILD, Pastor of Congregational Church, South Boston.
GARDINER SPRING, D. D., Pastor of Presbyterian Church, New York city.
CYRUS MASON, D. D., " " " " "
THOS. M'AULEY, D. D., " " " " "
JOHN WOODBRIDGE, D. D., " " " " "
THOS. DEWITT, D. D., " Dutch Ref. " " "
E. W. BALDWIN, D. D., " " " " "
Rev. J. M. M'KREBS, " Presbyterian " " "
Rev. ERSKINE MASON, " " " " "
Rev. J. S. SPENCER, " " " Brooklyn.
EZRA STILES ELY, D. D., Stated Clerk of Gen. Assem. of Presbyterian Church.
JOHN M'DOWELL, D. D., Permanent " " " "
JOHN BRECKENRIDGE, Corresponding Secretary of Assembly's Board of Education.
SAMUEL B. WYLIE, D. D., Pastor of the Reformed Presbyterian Church.
N. LORD, D. D., President of Dartmouth College.
JOSHUA BATES, D. D., President of Middlebury College.
H. HUMPHREY, D. D., " Amherst College.
E. D. GRIFFIN, D. D., " Williamstown College.
J. WHEELER, D. D., " University of Vermont, at Burlington.
J. M. MATTHEWS, D. D., " New York City University.
GEORGE E. PIERCE, D. D., " Western Reserve College, Ohio.
Rev. Dr. BROWN, " Jefferson College, Penn.
LEONARD WOODS, D. D., Professor of Theology, Andover Seminary.
THOS. H. SKINNER, D. D., " Sac. Rhet. " "
Rev. RALPH EMERSON, " Eccl. Hist. " "
Rev. JOEL PARKER, Pastor of Presbyterian Church, New Orleans.
JOEL HAWES, D. D., " Congregational Church, Hartford, Conn.
N. S. S. BEAMAN, D. D., " Presbyterian Church, Troy, N. Y.
MARK TUCKER, D. D., " " " " "
Rev. E. N. KIRK, " " " Albany, N. Y.
Rev. E. B. EDWARDS, Editor of Quarterly Observer.
Rev. STEPHEN MASON, Pastor First Congregational Church, Nantucket.
Rev. ORIN FOWLER, " " " " Fall River.
GEORGE W. BETHUNE, D. D., Pastor of the First Reformed Dutch Church, Philada.
Rev. LYMAN BEECHER, D. D., Cincinnati, Ohio.
Rev C. D. MALLORY, Pastor Baptist Church, Augusta, Ga.
Rev. S. M. NOEL, " " " Frankfort, Ky.

From the Professors at Princeton Theological Seminary.

The Comprehensive Commentary contains the whole of Henry's Exposition in a condensed form, Scott's Practical Observations and Marginal References, and a large number of very valuable philological and critical notes, selected from various authors. The work appears to be executed with judgment, fidelity, and care; and will furnish a rich treasure of scriptural knowledge to the Biblical student, and to the teachers of Sabbath-Schools and Bible Classes.

A. ALEXANDER, D. D.
SAMUEL MILLER, D. D.
CHARLES HODGE, D. D.

The Companion to the Bible.

In one super-royal volume.

DESIGNED TO ACCOMPANY

THE FAMILY BIBLE,

OR HENRY'S, SCOTT'S, CLARKE'S, GILL'S, OR OTHER COMMENTARIES:

CONTAINING

1. A new, full, and complete Concordance;

Illustrated with monumental, traditional, and oriental engravings, founded on Butterworth's, with Cruden's definitions; forming, it is believed, on many accounts, a more valuable work than either Butterworth, Cruden, or any other similar book in the language.

The value of a Concordance is now generally understood; and those who have used one, consider it indispensable in connection with the Bible.

2. A Guide to the Reading and Study of the Bible;

being Carpenter's valuable Biblical Companion, lately published in London, containing a complete history of the Bible, and forming a most excellent introduction to its study. It embraces the evidences of Christianity, Jewish antiquities, manners, customs, arts, natural history, &c., of the Bible, with notes and engravings added.

3. Complete Biographies of Henry, by Williams; Scott, by his son; Doddridge, by Orton;

with sketches of the lives and characters, and notices of the works, of the writers on the Scriptures who are quoted in the Commentary, living and dead, American and foreign.

This part of the volume not only affords a large quantity of interesting and useful reading for pious families, but will also be a source of gratification to all those who are in the habit of consulting the Commentary; every one naturally feeling a desire to know some particulars of the lives and characters of those whose opinions he seeks. Appended to this part, will be a

BIBLIOTHECA BIBLICA,

or list of the best works on the Bible, of all kinds, arranged under their appropriate heads.

4. A complete Index of the Matter contained in the Bible Text.

5. A Symbolical Dictionary.

A very comprehensive and valuable Dictionary of Scripture Symbols, (occupying about *fifty-six* closely printed pages,) by Thomas Wemyss, (author of "Biblical Gleanings," &c.) Comprising Daubuz, Lancaster, Hutcheson, &c.

6. The Work contains several other Articles,

Indexes, Tables, &c. &c., and is,

7. Illustrated by a large Plan of Jerusalem,

identifying, as far as tradition, &c., go, the original sites, drawn on the spot by F. Catherwood, of London, architect. Also, two steel engravings of portraits of seven foreign and eight American theological writers, and numerous wood engravings.

The whole forms a desirable and necessary fund of instruction for the use not only of clergymen and Sabbath-school teachers, but also for families. When the great amount of matter it must contain is considered, it will be deemed exceedingly cheap.

"I have examined 'The Companion to the Bible,' and have been surprised to find so much information introduced into a volume of so moderate a size. It contains a library of sacred knowledge and criticism. It will be useful to ministers who own large libraries, and cannot fail to be an invaluable help to every reader of the Bible."
HENRY MORRIS,
Pastor of Congregational Church, Vermont.

The above work can be had in several styles of binding. Price varying from $1 75 to $5 00.

ILLUSTRATIONS OF THE HOLY SCRIPTURES,

In one super-royal volume.

DERIVED PRINCIPALLY FROM THE MANNERS, CUSTOMS, ANTIQUITIES, TRADITIONS, AND FORMS OF SPEECH, RITES, CLIMATE, WORKS OF ART, AND LITERATURE OF THE EASTERN NATIONS:

EMBODYING ALL THAT IS VALUABLE IN THE WORKS OF

ROBERTS, HARMER, BURDER, PAXTON, CHANDLER,

And the most celebrated oriental travellers. Embracing also the subject of the Fulfilment of Prophecy, as exhibited by Keith and others; with descriptions of the present state of countries and places mentioned in the Sacred Writings.

ILLUSTRATED BY NUMEROUS LANDSCAPE ENGRAVINGS,

FROM SKETCHES TAKEN ON THE SPOT.

Edited by Rev. George Bush,

Professor of Hebrew and Oriental Literature in the New York City University.

The importance of this work must be obvious, and, being altogether *illustrative*, without reference to doctrines, or other points in which Christians differ, it is hoped it will meet with favour from all who love the sacred volume, and that it will be sufficiently interesting and attractive to recommend itself, not only to professed Christians of *all* denominations, but also to the general reader. The arrangement of the texts illustrated with the notes, in the order of the chapters and verses of the authorized version of the Bible, will render it convenient for reference to particular passages; while the *copious Index* at the end will at once enable the reader to turn to every subject discussed in the volume.

This volume is not designed to take the place of Commentaries, but is a distinct department of biblical instruction, and may be used as a companion to the Comprehensive or any other Commentary, or the Holy Bible.

THE ENGRAVINGS

in this volume, it is believed, will form no small part of its attractions. No pains have been spared to procure such as should embellish the work, and, at the same time, illustrate the text. Objections that have been made to the pictures commonly introduced into the Bible, as being mere creations of fancy and the imagination, often unlike nature, and frequently conveying false impressions, cannot be urged against the pictorial illustrations of this volume. Here the fine arts are made subservient to utility, the landscape views being, without an exception, *matter-of-fact views of places mentioned in Scripture, as they appear at the present day;* thus in many instances exhibiting, in the most forcible manner, *to the eye*, the strict and *literal* fulfilment of the remarkable prophecies; "the present ruined and desolate condition of the cities of Babylon, Nineveh, Selah, &c., and the countries of Edom and Egypt, are astonishing examples, and so completely exemplify, in the most minute particulars, every thing which was foretold of them in the height of their prosperity, that no better description can now be given of them than a simple quotation from a chapter and verse of the Bible written nearly two or three thousand years ago." The publishers are enabled to select from several collections lately published in London, the proprietor of one of which says that "several distinguished travellers have afforded him the use of nearly *Three Hundred Original Sketches*" of Scripture places, made upon the spot. "The land of Palestine, it is well known, abounds in scenes of the most picturesque beauty. Syria comprehends the snowy heights of Lebanon, and the majestic ruins of Tadmor and Baalbec."

The above work can be had in various styles of binding.

Price from $1 50 to $5 00.

THE ILLUSTRATED CONCORDANCE,

In one volume, royal 8vo.

A new, full, and complete Concordance; illustrated with monumental, traditional, and oriental engravings, founded on Butterworth's, with Cruden's definitions; forming, it is believed, on many accounts, a more valuable work than either Butterworth, Cruden, or any other similar book in the language.

The value of a Concordance is now generally understood; and those who have used one, consider it indispensable in connection with the Bible. Some of the many advantages the Illustrated Concordance has over all the others, are, that it contains near two hundred appropriate engravings: it is printed on fine white paper, with beautiful large type.

Price One Dollar.

LIPPINCOTT'S EDITION OF
BAGSTER'S COMPREHENSIVE BIBLE.

In order to develope the peculiar nature of the Comprehensive Bible, it will only be necessary to embrace its more prominent features.

1st. The SACRED TEXT is that of the Authorized Version, and is printed from the edition corrected and improved by Dr. Blaney, which, from its accuracy, is considered the standard edition.

2d. The VARIOUS READINGS are faithfully printed from the edition of Dr. Blaney, inclusive of the translation of the proper names, without the addition or diminution of one.

3d. In the CHRONOLOGY, great care has been taken to fix the date of the particular transactions, which has seldom been done with any degree of exactness in any former edition of the Bible.

4th. The NOTES are exclusively philological and explanatory, and are not tinctured with sentiments of any sect or party. They are selected from the most eminent Biblical critics and commentators.

It is hoped that this edition of the Holy Bible will be found to contain the essence of Biblical research and criticism, that lies dispersed through an immense number of volumes.

Such is the nature and design of this edition of the Sacred Volume, which, from the various objects it embraces, the freedom of its pages from all sectarian peculiarities, and the beauty, plainness, and correctness of the typography, that it cannot fail of proving acceptable and useful to Christians of every denomination.

In addition to the usual references to parallel passages, which are quite full and numerous, the student has all the marginal readings, together with a rich selection of *Philological, Critical, Historical, Geographical*, and other valuable notes and remarks, which explain and illustrate the sacred text. Besides the general introduction, containing valuable essays on the genuineness, authenticity, and inspiration of the Holy Scriptures, and other topics of interest, there are introductory and concluding remarks to each book—a table of the contents of the Bible, by which the different portions are so arranged as to read in an historical order.

Arranged at the top of each page is the period in which the prominent events of sacred history took place. The calculations are made for the year of the world before and after Christ, Julian Period, the year of the Olympiad, the year of the building of Rome, and other notations of time. At the close is inserted a Chronological Index of the Bible, according to the computation of Archbishop Ussher. Also, a full and valuable index of the *subjects* contained in the Old and New Testaments, with a careful analysis and arrangement of texts under their appropriate subjects.

Mr. Greenfield, the editor of this work, and for some time previous to his death the superintendent of the editorial department of the British and Foreign Bible Society, was a most extraordinary man. In editing the Comprehensive Bible, his varied and extensive learning was called into successful exercise, and appears in happy combination with sincere piety and a sound judgment. The Editor of the Christian Observer, alluding to this work, in an obituary notice of its author, speaks of it as a work of "prodigious labour and research, at once exhibiting his varied talents and profound erudition."

LIPPINCOTT'S EDITION OF
THE OXFORD QUARTO BIBLE.

The Publishers have spared neither care nor expense in their edition of the Bible; it is printed on the finest white vellum paper, with large and beautiful type, and bound in the most substantial and splendid manner, in the following styles: Velvet, with richly gilt ornaments; Turkey super extra, with gilt clasps; and in numerous others, to suit the taste of the most fastidious.

OPINIONS OF THE PRESS.

"In our opinion, the Christian public generally will feel under great obligations to the publishers of this work for the beautiful taste, arrangement, and delicate neatness with which they have got it out. The intrinsic merit of the Bible recommends itself; it needs no tinsel ornament to adorn its sacred pages. In this edition every superfluous ornament has been avoided, and we have presented us a perfectly chaste specimen of the Bible, without note or comment. It appears to be just what is needed in every family—'the *unsophisticated* word of God.'

"The size is quarto, printed with beautiful type, on white, sized vellum paper, of the finest texture and most beautiful surface. The publishers seem to have been solicitous to make a perfectly unique book, and they have accomplished the object very successfully. We trust that a liberal community will afford them ample remuneration for all the expense and outlay they have necessarily incurred in its publication. It is a standard Bible.

"The publishers are Messrs. Lippincott, Grambo & Co., No. 14 North Fourth street, Philadelphia." — *Baptist Record.*

"A beautiful quarto edition of the Bible, by L., G. & Co. Nothing can exceed the type in clearness and beauty: the paper is of the finest texture, and the whole execution is exceedingly neat. No illustrations or ornamental type are used. Those who prefer a Bible executed in perfect simplicity, yet elegance of style, without adornment, will probably never find one more to their taste." — *M. Magazine.*

LIPPINCOTT'S EDITIONS OF

THE HOLY BIBLE.

SIX DIFFERENT SIZES,

Printed in the best manner, with beautiful type, on the finest sized paper, and bound in the most splendid and substantial styles. Warranted to be correct, and equal to the best English editions, at much less price. To be had with or without plates; the publishers having supplied themselves with over fifty steel engravings, by the first artists.

Baxter's Comprehensive Bible,

Royal quarto, containing the various readings and marginal notes; disquisitions on the genuineness, authenticity, and inspiration of the Holy Scriptures; introductory and concluding remarks to each book; philological and explanatory notes; table of contents, arranged in historical order; a chronological index, and various other matter; forming a suitable book for the study of clergymen, Sabbath-school teachers, and students.

In neat plain binding, from $4 00 to $5 00.—In Turkey morocco, extra, gilt edges, from $8 00 to $12 00.—In do., with splendid plates, $10 00 to $15 00.—In do., bevelled side, gilt clasps and illuminations, $15 00 to $25 00.

The Oxford Quarto Bible,

Without note or comment, universally admitted to be the most beautiful Bible extant.

In neat plain binding, from $4 00 to $5 00.—In Turkey morocco, extra, gilt edges, $8 00 to $12 00.—In do., with steel engravings, $10 00 to $15 00.—In do., clasps, &c., with plates and illuminations, $15 00 to $25 00.—In rich velvet, with gilt ornaments, $25 00 to $50 00.

Crown Octavo Bible,

Printed with large clear type, making a most convenient hand Bible for family use.

In neat plain binding, from 75 cents to $1 50.—In English Turkey morocco, gilt edges, $1 00 to $2 00.—In do., imitation, &c., $1 50 to $3 00.—In do., clasps, &c., $2 50 to $5 00.—In rich velvet, with gilt ornaments, $5 00 to $10 00.

The Sunday-School Teacher's Polyglot Bible, with Maps, &c.,

In neat plain binding, from 60 cents to $1 00.—In imitation gilt edge, $1 00 to $1 50.—In Turkey, super extra, $1 75 to $2 25.—In do. do., with clasps, $2 50 to $3 75.—In velvet, rich gilt ornaments, $3 50 to $8 00.

The Oxford 18mo., or Pew Bible,

In neat plain binding, from 50 cents to $1 00.—In imitation gilt edge, $1 00 to $1 50.—In Turkey, super extra, $1 75 to $2 25.—In do. do., with clasps, $2 50 to $3 75.—In velvet, rich gilt ornaments, $3 50 to $8 00.

Agate 32mo. Bible,

Printed with larger type than any other small or pocket edition extant.

In neat plain binding, from 50 cents to $1 00.—In tucks, or pocket-book style, 75 cents to $1 00.—In roan, imitation gilt edge, $1 00 to $1 50.—In Turkey, super extra, $1 00 to $2 00.—In do. do., gilt clasps, $2 50 to $3 50.—In velvet, with rich gilt ornaments, $3 00 to $7 00.

32mo. Diamond Pocket Bible;

The neatest, smallest, and cheapest edition of the Bible published.

In neat plain binding, from 30 to 50 cents.—In tucks, or pocket-book style, 60 cents to $1 00.—In roan, imitation gilt edge, 75 cents to $1 25.—In Turkey, super extra, $1 00 to $1 50.—In do. do., gilt clasps, $1 50 to $2 00.—In velvet, with richly gilt ornaments, $2 50 to $6 00.

CONSTANTLY ON HAND,

A large assortment of BIBLES, bound in the most splendid and costly styles, with gold and silver ornaments, suitable for presentation; ranging in price from $10 00 to $100 00.

A liberal discount made to Booksellers and Agents by the Publishers.

ENCYCLOPÆDIA OF RELIGIOUS KNOWLEDGE;

OR, DICTIONARY OF THE BIBLE, THEOLOGY, RELIGIOUS BIOGRAPHY, ALL RELIGIONS, ECCLESIASTICAL HISTORY, AND MISSIONS.

Designed as a complete Book of Reference on all Religious Subjects, and Companion to the Bible; forming a cheap and compact Library of Religious Knowledge. Edited by Rev. J. Newton Brown. Illustrated by wood-cuts, maps, and engravings on copper and steel. In one volume, royal 8vo. Price, $4 00.

Lippincott's Standard Editions of

THE BOOK OF COMMON PRAYER.

IN SIX DIFFERENT SIZES,

ILLUSTRATED WITH A NUMBER OF STEEL PLATES AND ILLUMINATIONS.

COMPREHENDING THE MOST VARIED AND SPLENDID ASSORTMENT IN THE UNITED STATES.

THE ILLUMINATED OCTAVO PRAYER-BOOK,

Printed in seventeen different colours of ink, and illustrated with a number of Steel Plates and Illuminations; making one of the most splendid books published. To be had in any variety of the most superb binding, ranging in prices.

In Turkey, super extra, from $5 00 to $8 00.—In do. do., with clasps, $6 00 to $10 00.—In do. do., bevelled and panelled edges, $8 00 to $15 00.—In velvet, richly ornamented, $12 00 to $20 00.

8vo.

In neat plain binding, from $1 50 to $2 00.—In imitation gilt edge, $2 00 to $3 00.—In Turkey, super extra, $2 50 to $4 50.—In do. do., with clasps, $3 00 to $5 00.—In velvet, richly gilt ornaments, $5 00 to $12 00.

16mo.

Printed throughout with large and elegant type.

In neat plain binding, from 75 cents to $1 50.—In Turkey morocco, extra, with plates, $1 75 to $3 00.—In do. do., with plates, clasps, &c., $2 50 to $5 00.—In velvet, with richly gilt ornaments, $4 00 to $9 00.

18mo.

In neat plain binding, from 25 to 75 cents.—In Turkey morocco, with plates, $1 25 to $2 00.—In velvet, with richly gilt ornaments, $3 00 to $8 00.

32mo.

A beautiful Pocket Edition, with large type.

In neat plain binding, from 50 cents to $1 00.—In roan, imitation gilt edge, 75 cents to $1 50.—In Turkey, super extra, $1 25 to $2 00.—In do. do., gilt clasps, $2 00 to $3 00.—In velvet, with richly gilt ornaments, $3 00 to $7 00.

32mo., Pearl type.

In plain binding, from 25 to 37 1-2 cents.—Roan, 37 1-2 to 50 cents.—Imitation Turkey, 50 cents to $1 00.—Turkey, super extra, with gilt edge, $1 00 to $1 50.—Pocket-book style, 60 to 75 cents.

PROPER LESSONS.

18mo.

A BEAUTIFUL EDITION, WITH LARGE TYPE.

In neat plain binding, from 50 cents to $1 00.—In roan, imitation gilt edge, 75 cents to $1 50.—In Turkey, super extra, $1 50 to $2 00.—In do. do., gilt clasps, $2 50 to $3 00.—In velvet, with richly gilt ornaments, $3 00 to $7 00.

THE BIBLE AND PRAYER-BOOK,

In one neat and portable volume.

32mo., in neat plain binding, from 75 cents to $1 00.—In imitation Turkey, $1 00 to $1 50.—In Turkey, super extra, $1 50 to $2 50.

18mo, in large type, plain, $1 75 to $2 50.—In imitation, $1 00 to $1 75.—In Turkey, super extra, $1 75 to $3 00. Also, with clasps, velvet, &c. &c.

The Errors of Modern Infidelity Illustrated and Refuted.

BY S. M. SCHMUCKER, A. M.

In one volume, 12mo.; cloth. Just published.

We cannot but regard this work, in whatever light we view it in reference to its design, as one of the most masterly productions of the age, and fitted to uproot one of the most fondly cherished and dangerous of all ancient or modern errors. God must bless such a work, armed with his own truth, and doing fierce and successful battle against black infidelity, which would bring His Majesty and Word down to the tribunal of human reason, for condemnation and annihilation.—*Alb. Spectator.*

The Clergy of America:

CONSISTING OF

ANECDOTES ILLUSTRATIVE OF THE CHARACTER OF MINISTERS OF RELIGION IN THE UNITED STATES.

BY JOSEPH BELCHER, D. D.,

Editor of "The Complete Works of Andrew Fuller," "Robert Hall," &c.

"This very interesting and instructive collection of pleasing and solemn remembrances of many pious men, illustrates the character of the day in which they lived, and defines the men more clearly than very elaborate essays."—*Baltimore American.*

"We regard the collection as highly interesting, and judiciously made."—*Presbyterian.*

JOSEPHUS'S (FLAVIUS) WORKS,

FAMILY EDITION.

BY THE LATE WILLIAM WHISTON, A. M.

FROM THE LAST LONDON EDITION, COMPLETE.

One volume, beautifully illustrated with Steel Plates, and the only readable edition published in this country.

As a matter of course, every family in our country has a copy of the Holy Bible; and as the presumption is that the greater portion often consult its pages, we take the liberty of saying to all those that do, that the perusal of the writings of Josephus will be found very interesting and instructive.

All those who wish to possess a beautiful and correct copy of this valuable work, would do well to purchase this edition. It is for sale at all the principal bookstores in the United States, and by country merchants generally in the Southern and Western States.

Also, the above work in two volumes.

BURDER'S VILLAGE SERMONS;

Or, 101 Plain and Short Discourses on the Principal Doctrines of the Gospel.

INTENDED FOR THE USE OF FAMILIES, SUNDAY-SCHOOLS, OR COMPANIES ASSEMBLED FOR RELIGIOUS INSTRUCTION IN COUNTRY VILLAGES.

BY GEORGE BURDER.

To which is added to each Sermon, a Short Prayer, with some General Prayers for Families, Schools, &c., at the end of the work.

COMPLETE IN ONE VOLUME, OCTAVO.

These sermons, which are characterized by a beautiful simplicity, the entire absence of controversy, and a true evangelical spirit, have gone through many and large editions, and been translated into several of the continental languages. "They have also been the honoured means not only of converting many individuals, but also of introducing the Gospel into districts, and even into parish churches, where before it was comparatively unknown."

"This work fully deserves the immortality it has attained."

This is a fine library edition of this invaluable work; and when we say that it should be found in the possession of every family, we only reiterate the sentiments and sincere wishes of all who take a deep interest in the eternal welfare of mankind.

FAMILY PRAYERS AND HYMNS,

ADAPTED TO FAMILY WORSHIP,

AND

TABLES FOR THE REGULAR READING OF THE SCRIPTURES.

By Rev. S. C. WINCHESTER, A. M.,

Late Pastor of the Sixth Presbyterian Church, Philadelphia; and the Presbyterian Church at Natchez, Miss.

One volume, 12mo.

SPLENDID LIBRARY EDITIONS.

ILLUSTRATED STANDARD POETS.

ELEGANTLY PRINTED, ON FINE PAPER, AND UNIFORM IN SIZE AND STYLE.

The following Editions of Standard British Poets are illustrated with numerous Steel Engravings, and may be had in all varieties of binding.

BYRON'S WORKS.

COMPLETE IN ONE VOLUME, OCTAVO.

INCLUDING ALL HIS SUPPRESSED AND ATTRIBUTED POEMS; WITH SIX BEAUTIFUL ENGRAVINGS.

This edition has been carefully compared with the recent London edition of Mr. Murray, and made complete by the addition of more than fifty pages of poems heretofore unpublished in England. Among these there are a number that have never appeared in any American edition; and the publishers believe they are warranted in saying that this is *the most complete edition of Lord Byron's Poetical Works* ever published in the United States.

The Poetical Works of Mrs. Hemans.

Complete in one volume, octavo; with seven beautiful Engravings.

This is a new and complete edition, with a splendid engraved likeness of Mrs. Hemans, on steel, and contains all the Poems in the last London and American editions. With a Critical Preface by Mr. Thatcher, of Boston.

"As no work in the English language can be commended with more confidence, it will argue bad taste in a female in this country to be without a complete edition of the writings of one who was an honour to her sex and to humanity, and whose productions, from first to last, contain no syllable calculated to call a blush to the cheek of modesty and virtue. There is, moreover, in Mrs. Hemans's poetry, a moral purity and a religious feeling which commend it, in an especial manner, to the discriminating reader. No parent or guardian will be under the necessity of imposing restrictions with regard to the free perusal of every production emanating from this gifted woman. There breathes throughout the whole a most eminent exemption from impropriety of thought or diction; and there is at times a pensiveness of tone, a winning sadness in her more serious compositions, which tells of a soul which has been lifted from the contemplation of terrestrial things, to divine communings with beings of a purer world."

MILTON, YOUNG, GRAY, BEATTIE, AND COLLINS'S POETICAL WORKS.

COMPLETE IN ONE VOLUME, OCTAVO.

WITH SIX BEAUTIFUL ENGRAVINGS.

Cowper and Thomson's Prose and Poetical Works.

COMPLETE IN ONE VOLUME, OCTAVO.

Including two hundred and fifty Letters, and sundry Poems of Cowper, never before published in this country; and of Thomson a new and interesting Memoir, and upwards of twenty new Poems, for the first time printed from his own Manuscripts, taken from a late Edition of the Aldine Poets, now publishing in London.

WITH SEVEN BEAUTIFUL ENGRAVINGS.

The distinguished Professor Silliman, speaking of this edition, observes: "I am as much gratified by the elegance and fine taste of your edition, as by the noble tribute of genius and moral excellence which these delightful authors have left for all future generations; and Cowper, especially, is not less conspicuous as a true Christian, moralist and teacher, than as a poet of great power and exquisite taste."

THE POETICAL WORKS OF ROGERS, CAMPBELL, MONTGOMERY, LAMB, AND KIRKE WHITE.

COMPLETE IN ONE VOLUME, OCTAVO.

WITH SIX BEAUTIFUL ENGRAVINGS.

The beauty, correctness, and convenience of this favourite edition of these standard authors are so well known, that it is scarcely necessary to add a word in its favour. It is only necessary to say, that the publishers have now issued an illustrated edition, which greatly enhances its former value. The engravings are excellent and well selected. It is the best library edition extant.

CRABBE, HEBER, AND POLLOK'S POETICAL WORKS.

COMPLETE IN ONE VOLUME, OCTAVO.

WITH SIX BEAUTIFUL ENGRAVINGS.

A writer in the Boston Traveller holds the following language with reference to these valuable editions:—

"Mr. Editor:—I wish, without any idea of puffing, to say a word or two upon the 'Library of English Poets' that is now published at Philadelphia, by Lippincott, Grambo & Co. It is certainly, taking into consideration the elegant manner in which it is printed, and the reasonable price at which it is afforded to purchasers, the best edition of the modern British Poets that has ever been published in this country. Each volume is an octavo of about 500 pages, double columns, stereotyped, and accompanied with fine engravings and biographical sketches; and most of them are reprinted from Galignani's French edition. As to its value, we need only mention that it contains the entire works of Montgomery, Gray, Beattie, Collins, Byron, Cowper, Thomson, Milton, Young, Rogers, Campbell, Lamb, Hemans, Heber, Kirke White, Crabbe, the Miscellaneous Works of Goldsmith, and other masters of the lyre. The publishers are doing a great service by their publication, and their volumes are almost in as great demand as the fashionable novels of the day; and they deserve to be so: for they are certainly printed in a style superior to that in which we have before had the works of the English Poets."

No library can be considered complete without a copy of the above beautiful and cheap editions of the English Poets; and persons ordering all or any of them, will please say Lippincott, Grambo & Co.'s illustrated editions.

A COMPLETE

Dictionary of Poetical Quotations:

COMPRISING THE MOST EXCELLENT AND APPROPRIATE PASSAGES IN THE OLD BRITISH POETS; WITH CHOICE AND COPIOUS SELECTIONS FROM THE BEST MODERN BRITISH AND AMERICAN POETS.

EDITED BY SARAH JOSEPHA HALE.

As nightingales do upon glow-worms feed,
So poets live upon the living light
Of Nature and of Beauty.

Bailey's Festus.

Beautifully illustrated with Engravings. In one super-royal octavo volume, in various bindings.

The publishers extract, from the many highly complimentary notices of the above valuable and beautiful work, the following:

"We have at last a volume of Poetical Quotations worthy of the name. It contains nearly six hundred octavo pages, carefully and tastefully selected from all the home and foreign authors of celebrity. It is invaluable to a writer, while to the ordinary reader it presents every subject at a glance."—*Godey's Lady's Book.*

"The plan or idea of Mrs. Hale's work is felicitous. It is one for which her fine taste, her orderly habits of mind, and her long occupation with literature, has given her peculiar facilities; and thoroughly has she accomplished her task in the work before us."—*Sartain's Magazine.*

"It is a choice collection of poetical extracts from every English and American author worth perusing, from the days of Chaucer to the present time."—*Washington Union.*

"There is nothing negative about this work; it is *positively* good."—*Evening Bulletin.*

THE DIAMOND EDITION OF BYRON.

THE POETICAL WORKS OF LORD BYRON,

WITH A SKETCH OF HIS LIFE.

COMPLETE IN ONE NEAT DUODECIMO VOLUME, WITH STEEL PLATES.

The type of this edition is so perfect, and it is printed with so much care, on fine white paper, that it can be read with as much ease as most of the larger editions. This work is to be had in plain and superb binding, making a beautiful volume for a gift.

"*The Poetical Works of Lord Byron*, complete in one volume; published by L., G. & Co., Philadelphia. We hazard nothing in saying that, take it altogether, this is the most elegant work ever issued from the American press.

"'In a single volume, not larger than an ordinary duodecimo, the publishers have embraced the whole of Lord Byron's Poems, usually printed in ten or twelve volumes; and, what is more remarkable, have done it with a type so clear and distinct, that, notwithstanding its necessarily small size, it may be read with the utmost facility, even by failing eyes. The book is stereotyped; and never have we seen a finer specimen of that art. Everything about it is perfect—the paper, the printing, the binding, all correspond with each other; and it is embellished with two fine engravings, well worthy the companionship in which they are placed.

"'This will make a beautiful Christmas present.'

"We extract the above from Godey's Lady's Book. The notice itself, we are given to understand, is written by Mrs. Hale.

"We have to add our commendation in favour of this beautiful volume, a copy of which has been sent us by the publishers. The admirers of the noble bard will feel obliged to the enterprise which has prompted the publishers to dare a competition with the numerous editions of his works already in circulation; and we shall be surprised if this convenient travelling edition does not in a great degree supersede the use of the large octavo works, which have little advantage in size and openness of type, and are much inferior in the qualities of portability and lightness."—*Intelligencer.*

THE DIAMOND EDITION OF MOORE.

(CORRESPONDING WITH BYRON.)

THE POETICAL WORKS OF THOMAS MOORE,

COLLECTED BY HIMSELF.

COMPLETE IN ONE VOLUME.

This work is published uniform with Byron, from the last London edition, and is the most complete printed in the country.

THE DIAMOND EDITION OF SHAKSPEARE,

(COMPLETE IN ONE VOLUME,)

INCLUDING A SKETCH OF HIS LIFE.

UNIFORM WITH BYRON AND MOORE.

THE ABOVE WORKS CAN BE HAD IN SEVERAL VARIETIES OF BINDING.

GOLDSMITH'S ANIMATED NATURE.

IN TWO VOLUMES, OCTAVO.

BEAUTIFULLY ILLUSTRATED WITH 385 PLATES.

CONTAINING A HISTORY OF THE EARTH, ANIMALS, BIRDS, AND FISHES; FORMING THE MOST COMPLETE NATURAL HISTORY EVER PUBLISHED.

This is a work that should be in the library of every family, having been written by one of the most talented authors in the English language.

"Goldsmith can never be made obsolete while delicate genius, exquisite feeling, fine invention, the most harmonious metre, and the happiest diction, are at all valued."

BIGLAND'S NATURAL HISTORY

Of Animals, Birds, Fishes, Reptiles, and Insects. Illustrated with numerous and beautiful Engravings. By JOHN BIGLAND, author of a "View of the World," "Letters on Universal History," &c. Complete in 1 vol., 12mo.

THE POWER AND PROGRESS OF THE UNITED STATES.

THE UNITED STATES; Its Power and Progress.

BY GUILLAUME TELL POUSSIN,

LATE MINISTER OF THE REPUBLIC OF FRANCE TO THE UNITED STATES.

FIRST AMERICAN, FROM THE THIRD PARIS EDITION.

TRANSLATED FROM THE FRENCH BY EDMOND L. DU BARRY, M. D.,

SURGEON U. S. NAVY.

In one large octavo volume.

SCHOOLCRAFT'S GREAT NATIONAL WORK ON THE INDIAN TRIBES OF THE UNITED STATES.

WITH BEAUTIFUL AND ACCURATE COLOURED ILLUSTRATIONS.

HISTORICAL AND STATISTICAL INFORMATION

RESPECTING THE

HISTORY, CONDITION AND PROSPECTS

OF THE

Indian Tribes of the United States.

COLLECTED AND PREPARED UNDER THE DIRECTION OF THE BUREAU OF INDIAN AFFAIRS, PER ACT OF MARCH 3, 1847,

BY HENRY R. SCHOOLCRAFT, LL.D.

ILLUSTRATED BY S. EASTMAN, CAPT. U. S. A.

PUBLISHED BY AUTHORITY OF CONGRESS.

THE AMERICAN GARDENER'S CALENDAR,

ADAPTED TO THE CLIMATE AND SEASONS OF THE UNITED STATES.

Containing a complete account of all the work necessary to be done in the Kitchen Garden, Fruit Garden, Orchard, Vineyard, Nursery, Pleasure-Ground, Flower Garden, Green-house, Hot-house, and Forcing Frames, for every month in the year; with ample Practical Directions for performing the same.

Also, general as well as minute instructions for laying out or erecting each and every of the above departments, according to modern taste and the most approved plans; the Ornamental Planting of Pleasure Grounds, in the ancient and modern style; the cultivation of Thorn Quicks, and other plants suitable for Live Hedges, with the best methods of making them, &c. To which are annexed catalogues of Kitchen Garden Plants and Herbs; Aromatic, Pot, and Sweet Herbs; Medicinal Plants, and the most important Grapes, &c., used in rural economy; with the soil best adapted to their cultivation. Together with a copious Index to the body of the work.

BY BERNARD M'MAHON.

Tenth Edition, greatly improved. In one volume, octavo.

THE USEFUL AND THE BEAUTIFUL;

OR, DOMESTIC AND MORAL DUTIES NECESSARY TO SOCIAL HAPPINESS.

BEAUTIFULLY ILLUSTRATED.

16mo. square cloth. Price 50 and 75 cents.

THE FARMER'S AND PLANTER'S ENCYCLOPÆDIA.

The Farmer's and Planter's Encyclopædia of Rural Affairs.

BY CUTHBERT W. JOHNSON.

ADAPTED TO THE UNITED STATES BY GOUVERNEUR EMERSON.

Illustrated by seventeen beautiful Engravings of Cattle, Horses, Sheep, the varieties of Wheat, Barley, Oats, Grasses, the Weeds of Agriculture, &c.; besides numerous Engravings on wood of the most important implements of Agriculture, &c.

This standard work contains the latest and best information upon all subjects connected with farming, and appertaining to the country; treating of the great crops of grain, hay, cotton, hemp, tobacco, rice, sugar, &c. &c.; of horses and mules; of cattle, with minute particulars relating to cheese and butter-making; of fowls, including a description of capon-making, with drawings of the instruments employed; of bees, and the Russian and other systems of managing bees and constructing hives. Long articles on the uses and preparation of bones, lime, guano, and all sorts of animal, mineral, and vegetable substances employed as manures. Descriptions of the most approved ploughs, harrows, threshers, and every other agricultural machine and implement; of fruit and shade trees, forest trees, and shrubs; of weeds, and all kinds of flies, and destructive worms and insects, and the best means of getting rid of them; together with a thousand other matters relating to rural life, about which information is so constantly desired by all residents of the country.

IN ONE LARGE OCTAVO VOLUME.

MASON'S FARRIER—FARMERS' EDITION.

Price, 62 cents.

THE PRACTICAL FARRIER, FOR FARMERS:

COMPRISING A GENERAL DESCRIPTION OF THE NOBLE AND USEFUL ANIMAL,

THE HORSE;

WITH MODES OF MANAGEMENT IN ALL CASES, AND TREATMENT IN DISEASE.

TO WHICH IS ADDED,

A PRIZE ESSAY ON MULES; AND AN APPENDIX,

Containing Recipes for Diseases of Horses, Oxen, Cows, Calves, Sheep, Dogs, Swine, &c. &c.

BY RICHARD MASON, M. D.,

Formerly of Surry County, Virginia.

In one volume, 12mo.; bound in cloth, gilt.

MASON'S FARRIER AND STUD-BOOK—NEW EDITION.

THE GENTLEMAN'S NEW POCKET FARRIER:

COMPRISING A GENERAL DESCRIPTION OF THE NOBLE AND USEFUL ANIMAL,

THE HORSE;

WITH MODES OF MANAGEMENT IN ALL CASES, AND TREATMENT IN DISEASE.

BY RICHARD MASON, M. D.,

Formerly of Surry County, Virginia.

To which is added, A PRIZE ESSAY ON MULES; and AN APPENDIX, containing Recipes for Diseases of Horses, Oxen, Cows, Calves, Sheep, Dogs, Swine, &c. &c.; with Annals of the Turf, American Stud-Book, Rules for Training, Racing, &c.

WITH A SUPPLEMENT,

Comprising an Essay on Domestic Animals, especially the Horse; with Remarks on Treatment and Breeding; together with Trotting and Racing Tables, showing the best time on record at one, two, three and four mile heats; Pedigrees of Winning Horses, since 1839, and of the most celebrated Stallions and Mares; with useful Calving and Lambing Tables. By J. S. SKINNER, Editor now of the Farmer's Library, New York, &c. &c.

HINDS'S FARRIERY AND STUD-BOOK—NEW EDITION.

FARRIERY,

TAUGHT ON A NEW AND EASY PLAN:

BEING

A Treatise on the Diseases and Accidents of the Horse;

With Instructions to the Shoeing Smith, Farrier, and Groom; preceded by a Popular Description of the Animal Functions in Health, and how these are to be restored when disordered.

BY JOHN HINDS, VETERINARY SURGEON.

With considerable Additions and Improvements, particularly adapted to this country,

BY THOMAS M. SMITH,

Veterinary Surgeon, and Member of the London Veterinary Medical Society.

WITH A SUPPLEMENT, BY J. S. SKINNER.

The publishers have received numerous flattering notices of the great practical value of these works. The distinguished editor of the American Farmer, speaking of them, observes:—"We cannot too highly recommend these books, and therefore advise every owner of a horse to obtain them."

"There are receipts in those books that show how *Founder* may be cured, and the traveller pursue his journey the next day, by giving a *tablespoonful of alum*. This was got from Dr. P. Thornton, of Montpelier, Rappahannock county, Virginia, as founded on his own observation in several cases."

"The constant demand for Mason's and Hinds's Farrier has induced the publishers, Messrs. Lippincott, Grambo & Co., to put forth new editions, with a 'Supplement' of 100 pages, by J. S. Skinner, Esq. We should have sought to render an acceptable service to our agricultural readers, by giving a chapter from the Supplement, 'On the Relations between Man and the Domestic Animals, especially the Horse, and the Obligations they impose;' or the one on 'The Form of Animals;' but that either one of them would overrun the space here allotted to such subjects."

"Lists of Medicines, and other articles which ought to be at hand about every training and livery stable, and every Farmer's and Breeder's establishment, will be found in these valuable works."

TO CARPENTERS AND MECHANICS.

Just Published.

A NEW AND IMPROVED EDITION OF

THE CARPENTER'S NEW GUIDE,

A COMPLETE BOOK OF LINES FOR

CARPENTRY AND JOINERY;

Treating fully on Practical Geometry, Soffits, Groins, Niches, Roofs, and Domes; and containing a great variety of original Designs.

ALSO, A FULL EXEMPLIFICATION OF THE

Theory and Practice of Stair Building,

Cornices, Mouldings, and Dressings of every description. Including also some observations and calculations on the Strength of Timber.

BY PETER NICHOLSON,

Author of "The Carpenter's and Joiner's Assistant," "The Student's Instructor to the Five Orders," &c. The whole being carefully and thoroughly revised,

BY N. K. DAVIS,

And containing numerous New, Improved, and Original Designs, for Roofs, Domes, &c.,

BY SAMUEL SLOAN, ARCHITECT,

Author of "The Model Architect."

SIXTEENTH EDITION. PRICE, FOUR DOLLARS.

A DICTIONARY OF SELECT AND POPULAR QUOTATIONS,

WHICH ARE IN DAILY USE.

TAKEN FROM THE LATIN, FRENCH, GREEK, SPANISH AND ITALIAN LANGUAGES.

Together with a copious Collection of Law Maxims and Law Terms, translated into English, with Illustrations, Historical and Idiomatic.

NEW AMERICAN EDITION, CORRECTED, WITH ADDITIONS.

One volume, 12mo.

This volume comprises a copious collection of legal and other terms which are in common use, with English translations and historical illustrations; and we should judge its author had surely been to a great "Feast of Languages," and stole all the scraps. A work of this character should have an extensive sale, as it entirely obviates a serious difficulty in which most readers are involved by the frequent occurrence of Latin, Greek, and French passages, which we suppose are introduced by authors for a mere show of learning—a difficulty very perplexing to readers in general. This "Dictionary of Quotations," concerning which too much cannot be said in its favour, effectually removes the difficulty, and gives the reader an advantage over the author; for we believe a majority are themselves ignorant of the meaning of the terms they employ. Very few truly learned authors will insult their readers by introducing Latin or French quotations in their writings, when "plain English" will do as well; but we will not enlarge on this point.

If the book is useful to those unacquainted with other languages, it is no less valuable to the classically educated as a book of reference, and answers all the purposes of a Lexicon—indeed, on many accounts, it is better. It saves the trouble of tumbling over the larger volumes, to which every one, and especially those engaged in the legal profession, are very often subjected. It should have a place in every library in the country.

RUSCHENBERGER'S NATURAL HISTORY,

COMPLETE, WITH NEW GLOSSARY.

The Elements of Natural History,

EMBRACING ZOOLOGY, BOTANY AND GEOLOGY:

FOR SCHOOLS, COLLEGES AND FAMILIES.

BY W. S. W. RUSCHENBERGER, M. D.

IN TWO VOLUMES.

WITH NEARLY ONE THOUSAND ILLUSTRATIONS, AND A COPIOUS GLOSSARY.

Vol. I. contains *Vertebrate Animals.* Vol. II. contains *Intervertebrate Animals, Botany, and Geology.*

GREAT TRUTHS BY GREAT AUTHORS.

GREAT TRUTHS BY GREAT AUTHORS;

A DICTIONARY

OF AIDS TO REFLECTION, QUOTATIONS OF MAXIMS, METAPHORS, COUNSELS, CAUTIONS, APHORISMS. ETC.,

FROM WRITERS OF ALL AGES AND BOTH HEMISPHERES,

ONE VOLUME, DEMI-OCTAVO.

"I have somewhere seen it observed, that we should make the same use of a book, that a bee does of a flower; she steals sweets from it, but does not injure it."—Cotton.

STYLES OF BINDING.

Ultramarine cloth, bevelled board, price $1 50; Ultramarine cloth, bevelled and panelled, gilt sides and edges, $2 00; Half calf, or Turkey antique, fancy edges, $2 50; Full calf, or Turkey antique, brown or gilt edges, $3 50.

THE YOUNG DOMINICAN;
OR, THE MYSTERIES OF THE INQUISITION,

AND OTHER SECRET SOCIETIES OF SPAIN.

BY M. V. DE FEREAL.

WITH HISTORICAL NOTES, BY M. MANUEL DE CUENDIAS,

TRANSLATED FROM THE FRENCH.

ILLUSTRATED WITH TWENTY SPLENDID ENGRAVINGS BY FRENCH ARTISTS.

One volume, octavo.

SAY'S POLITICAL ECONOMY.

A TREATISE ON POLITICAL ECONOMY;
Or, The Production, Distribution and Consumption of Wealth.

BY JEAN BAPTISTE SAY.

FIFTH AMERICAN EDITION, WITH ADDITIONAL NOTES,

BY C. C. BIDDLE, Esq.

In one volume, octavo.

It would be beneficial to our country if all those who are aspiring to office, were required by their constituents to be familiar with the pages of Say.

The distinguished biographer of the author, in noticing this work, observes: "Happily for science, he commenced that study, which forms the basis of his admirable Treatise on *Political Economy*; a work which not only improved under his hand with every successive edition, but has been translated into most of the European languages."

The Editor of the North American Review, speaking of Say, observes, that "he is the most popular, and perhaps the most able writer on Political Economy, since the time of Smith."

LAURENCE STERNE'S WORKS,

WITH A LIFE OF THE AUTHOR:

WRITTEN BY HIMSELF.

WITH SEVEN BEAUTIFUL ILLUSTRATIONS, ENGRAVED BY GILBERT AND GIHON, FROM DESIGNS BY DARLEY.

One volume, octavo; cloth, gilt.

To commend or to criticise Sterne's Works, in this age of the world, would be all "wasteful and extravagant excess." Uncle Toby—Corporal Trim—the Widow—Le Fevre—Poor Maria—the Captive—even the Dead Ass,—this is all we have to say of Sterne; and in the memory of these characters, histories, and sketches, a thousand follies and worse than follies are forgotten. The volume is a very handsome one.

THE MEXICAN WAR AND ITS HEROES;

BEING

A COMPLETE HISTORY OF THE MEXICAN WAR,

EMBRACING ALL THE OPERATIONS UNDER GENERALS TAYLOR AND SCOTT.

WITH A BIOGRAPHY OF THE OFFICERS.

ALSO,

AN ACCOUNT OF THE CONQUEST OF CALIFORNIA AND NEW MEXICO,

Under Gen. Kearny, Cols. Doniphan and Fremont. Together with Numerous Anecdotes of the War, and Personal Adventures of the Officers. Illustrated with Accurate Portraits, and other Beautiful Engravings.

In one volume, 12mo.

NEW AND COMPLETE COOK-BOOK.

THE PRACTICAL COOK-BOOK,

CONTAINING UPWARDS OF

ONE THOUSAND RECEIPTS,

Consisting of Directions for Selecting, Preparing, and Cooking all kinds of Meats, Fish, Poultry, and Game; Soups, Broths, Vegetables, and Salads. Also, for making all kinds of Plain and Fancy Breads, Pastes, Puddings, Cakes, Creams, Ices, Jellies, Preserves, Marmalades, &c. &c. &c. Together with various Miscellaneous Recipes, and numerous Preparations for Invalids.

BY MRS. BLISS.

In one volume, 12mo.

The City Merchant; or, The Mysterious Failure.

BY J. B. JO[illegible]

AUTHOR OF "WILD WESTERN SCENES," "THE WEST[illegible] [illegible]CHANT," &c.

ILLUSTRATED WITH TEN ENGRAVINGS.

In one volume, 12mo.

CALIFORNIA AND OREGON;

OR, SIGHTS IN THE GOLD REGION, AND SCENES BY THE WAY.

BY THEODORE T. JOHNSON.

WITH NOTES, BY HON. SAMUEL R. THURSTON,

Delegate to Congress from that Territory.

With numerous Plates and Maps.

AUNT PHILLIS'S CABIN;

OR, SOUTHERN LIFE AS IT IS.

BY MRS. MARY H. EASTMAN.

PRICE, 50 AND 75 CENTS.

This volume presents a picture of Southern Life, taken at different points of view from the one occupied by the authoress of "*Uncle Tom's Cabin.*" The writer, being a native of the South, is familiar with the many varied aspects assumed by domestic servitude in that sunny region, and therefore feels competent to give pictures of "Southern Life, as it is."

Pledged to no clique or party, and free from the pressure of any and all extraneous influences, she has written her book with a view to its truthfulness; and the public at the North, as well as at the South, will find in "Aunt Phillis's Cabin" not the distorted picture of an interested painter, but the faithful transcript of a Daguerreotypist.

WHAT IS CHURCH HISTORY?

A VINDICATION OF THE IDEA OF HISTORICAL DEVELOPMENTS.

BY PHILIP SCHAF.

TRANSLATED FROM THE GERMAN.

In one volume, 12mo.

DODD'S LECTURES.

DISCOURSES TO YOUNG MEN.

ILLUSTRATED BY NUMEROUS HIGHLY INTERESTING ANECDOTES.

BY WILLIAM DODD, LL. D.,

CHAPLAIN IN ORDINARY TO HIS MAJESTY GEORGE THE THIRD.

FIRST AMERICAN EDITION, WITH ENGRAVINGS.

One volume, 18mo.

THE IRIS:

AN ORIGINAL SOUVENIR.

With Contributions from the First Writers in the Country.

EDITED BY PROF. JOHN S. HART.

With Splendid Illuminations and Steel Engravings. Bound in Turkey Morocco and rich Papier Mache Binding.

IN ONE VOLUME, OCTAVO.

Its contents are entirely original. Among the contributors are names well known in the republic of letters; such as Mr. Boker, Mr. Stoddard, Prof. Moffat, Edith May, Mrs. Sigourney, Caroline May, Mrs. Kinney, Mrs. Butler, Mrs. Pease, Mrs. Swift, Mr. Van Bibber, Rev. Charles T. Brooks, Mrs. Dorr, Erastus W. Ellsworth, Miss E. W. Barnes, Mrs. Williams, Mary Young, Dr. Gardette, Alice Carey, Phebe Carey, Augusta Browne, Hamilton Browne, Caroline Eustis, Margaret Junkin, Maria J. B. Browne, Miss Starr, Mrs. Brotherson, Kate Campbell, &c.

Gems from the Sacred Mine;

OR, HOLY THOUGHTS UPON SACRED SUBJECTS.

BY CLERGYMEN OF THE EPISCOPAL CHURCH.

EDITED BY THOMAS WYATT, A. M.

In one volume, 12mo.

WITH SEVEN BEAUTIFUL STEEL ENGRAVINGS.

The contents of this work are chiefly by clergymen of the Episcopal Church. Among the contributors will be found the names of the Right Rev. Bishop Potter, Bishop Hopkins, Bishop Smith, Bishop Johns, and Bishop Doane; and the Rev. Drs. H. V. D. Johns, Coleman, and Butler; Rev. G. T. Bedell, M'Cabe, Ogilsby, &c. The illustrations are rich and exquisitely wrought engravings upon the following subjects: — "Samuel before Eli," "Peter and John healing the Lame Man," "The Resurrection of Christ," "Joseph sold by his Brethren," "The Tables of the Law," "Christ's Agony in the Garden," and "The Flight into Egypt." These subjects, with many others in prose and verse, are ably treated throughout the work.

ANCIENT CHRISTIANITY EXEMPLIFIED,

In the Private, Domestic, Social, and Civil Life of the Primitive Christians, and in the Original Institutions, Offices, Ordinances, and Rites of the Church.

BY REV. LYMAN COLEMAN, D. D.

In one volume 8vo. Price $2 50.

LONZ POWERS; Or, The Regulators.

A ROMANCE OF KENTUCKY.

FOUNDED ON FACTS.

BY JAMES WEIR, ESQ.

IN TWO VOLUMES.

The scenes, characters, and incidents in these volumes have been copied from nature, and from real life. They are represented as taking place at that period in the history of Kentucky, when the Indian, driven, after many a hard-fought field, from his favourite hunting-ground, was succeeded by a rude and unlettered population, interspersed with organized bands of desperadoes, scarcely less savage than the red men they had displaced. The author possesses a vigorous and graphic pen, and has produced a very interesting romance, which gives us a striking portrait of the times he describes.

A PRACTICAL TREATISE ON BUSINESS;

OR, HOW TO GET, SAVE, SPEND, GIVE, LEND, AND BEQUEATH MONEY;

WITH AN INQUIRY INTO THE CHANCES OF SUCCESS AND CAUSES OF FAILURE IN BUSINESS.

BY EDWIN T. FREEDLY.

Also, Prize Essays, Statistics, Miscellanies, and numerous private letters from successful and distinguished business men.

12mo., cloth. Price One Dollar.

The object of this treatise is fourfold. First, the elevation of the business character, and to define clearly the limits within which it is not only proper but obligatory to get money. Secondly, to lay down the principles which must be observed to insure success, and what must be avoided to escape failure. Thirdly, to give the mode of management in certain prominent pursuits adopted by the most successful, from which men in all kinds of business may derive profitable hints. Fourthly, to afford a work of solid interest to those who read without expectation of pecuniary benefit.

A MANUAL OF POLITENESS,

COMPRISING THE

PRINCIPLES OF ETIQUETTE AND RULES OF BEHAVIOUR

IN GENTEEL SOCIETY, FOR PERSONS OF BOTH SEXES.

18mo., with Plates.

Book of Politeness.

THE GENTLEMAN AND LADY'S

BOOK OF POLITENESS AND PROPRIETY OF DEPORTMENT.

DEDICATED TO THE YOUTH OF BOTH SEXES.

BY MADAME CELNART.

Translated from the Sixth Paris Edition, Enlarged and Improved.

Fifth American Edition.

One volume, 18mo.

THE ANTEDILUVIANS; Or, The World Destroyed.

A NARRATIVE POEM, IN TEN BOOKS.

BY JAMES M'HENRY, M.D.

One volume, 18mo.

Bennett's (Rev. John) Letters to a Young Lady,

ON A VARIETY OF SUBJECTS CALCULATED TO IMPROVE THE HEART, TO FORM THE MANNERS, AND ENLIGHTEN THE UNDERSTANDING.

"That our daughters may be as polished corners of the temple."

The publishers sincerely hope (for the happiness of mankind) that a copy of this valuable little work will be found the companion of every young lady, as much of the happiness of every family depends on the proper cultivation of the female mind.

THE DAUGHTER'S OWN BOOK:

OR, PRACTICAL HINTS FROM A FATHER TO HIS DAUGHTER.

One volume, 18mo.

This is one of the most practical and truly valuable treatises on the culture and discipline of the female mind, which has hitherto been published in this country; and the publishers are very confident, from the great demand for this invaluable little work, that ere long it will be found in the library of every young lady.

THE AMERICAN CHESTERFIELD:

Or, "Youth's Guide to the Way to Wealth, Honour, and Distinction," &c. 18mo.

CONTAINING ALSO A COMPLETE TREATISE ON THE ART OF CARVING.

"We most cordially recommend the American Chesterfield to general attention; but to young persons particularly, as one of the best works of the kind that has ever been published in this country. It cannot be too highly appreciated, nor its perusal be unproductive of satisfaction and usefulness."

SENECA'S MORALS.

BY WAY OF ABSTRACT TO WHICH IS ADDED, A DISCOURSE UNDER THE TITLE OF AN AFTER-THOUGHT.

BY SIR ROGER L'ESTRANGE, KNT.

A new, fine edition; one volume, 18mo.

A copy of this valuable little work should be found in every family library.

NEW SONG-BOOK.

Grigg's Southern and Western Songster;

BEING A CHOICE COLLECTION OF THE MOST FASHIONABLE SONGS, MANY OF WHICH ARE ORIGINAL.

In one volume, 18mo.

Great care was taken, in the selection, to admit no song that contained, in the slightest degree, any indelicate or improper allusions; and with great propriety it may claim the title of "The Parlour Song-Book, or Songster." The immortal Shakspeare observes—

"The man that hath not music in himself,
Nor is not moved with concord of sweet sounds,
Is fit for treasons, stratagems, and spoils."

ROBOTHAM'S POCKET FRENCH DICTIONARY,

CAREFULLY REVISED,

AND THE PRONUNCIATION OF ALL THE DIFFICULT WORDS ADDED.

THE LIFE AND OPINIONS OF TRISTRAM SHANDY, GENTLEMAN.

COMPRISING THE HUMOROUS ADVENTURES OF

UNCLE TOBY AND CORPORAL TRIM.

BY L. STERNE.

Beautifully Illustrated by Darley. Stitched.

A SENTIMENTAL JOURNEY.

BY L. STERNE.

Illustrated as above by Darley. Stitched.

The beauties of this author are so well known, and his errors in style and expression so few and far between, that one reads with renewed delight his delicate turns, &c.

THE LIFE OF GENERAL JACKSON,

WITH A LIKENESS OF THE OLD HERO.

One volume, 18mo.

LIFE OF PAUL JONES.

In one volume, 12mo.

WITH ONE HUNDRED ILLUSTRATIONS.

BY JAMES HAMILTON.

The work is compiled from his original journals and correspondence, and includes an account of his services in the American Revolution, and in the war between the Russians and Turks in the Black Sea. There is scarcely any Naval Hero, of any age, who combined in his character so much of the adventurous, skilful and daring, as Paul Jones. The incidents of his life are almost as startling and absorbing as those of romance. His achievements during the American Revolution—the fight between the Bon Homme Richard and Serapis, the most desperate naval action on record—and the alarm into which, with so small a force, he threw the coasts of England and Scotland—are matters comparatively well known to Americans; but the incidents of his subsequent career have been veiled in obscurity, which is dissipated by this biography. A book like this, narrating the actions of such a man, ought to meet with an extensive sale, and become as popular as Robinson Crusoe in fiction, or Weems's Life of Marion and Washington, and similar books, in fact. It contains 400 pages, has a handsome portrait and medallion likeness of Jones, and is illustrated with numerous original wood engravings of naval scenes and distinguished men with whom he was familiar.

THE GREEK EXILE;

Or, A Narrative of the Captivity and Escape of Christophorus Plato Castanis,

DURING THE MASSACRE ON THE ISLAND OF SCIO BY THE TURKS.

TOGETHER WITH VARIOUS ADVENTURES IN GREECE AND AMERICA.

WRITTEN BY HIMSELF,

Author of an Essay on the Ancient and Modern Greek Languages; Interpretation of the Attributes of the Principal Fabulous Deities; The Jewish Maiden of Scio's Citadel; and the Greek Boy in the Sunday-School.

One volume, 12mo.

THE YOUNG CHORISTER;

A Collection of New and Beautiful Tunes, adapted to the use of Sabbath-Schools, from some of the most distinguished composers; together with many of the author's compositions.

EDITED BY MINARD W. WILSON.

CAMP LIFE OF A VOLUNTEER.

A Campaign in Mexico; Or, A Glimpse at Life in Camp.

BY "ONE WHO HAS SEEN THE ELEPHANT."

Life of General Zachary Taylor,

COMPRISING A NARRATIVE OF EVENTS CONNECTED WITH HIS PROFESSIONAL CAREER, AND AUTHENTIC INCIDENTS OF HIS EARLY YEARS.

BY J. REESE FRY AND R. T. CONRAD.

With an original and accurate Portrait, and eleven elegant Illustrations, by Darley.

In one handsome 12mo. volume.

"It is by far the fullest and most interesting biography of General Taylor that we have ever seen." —*Richmond (Whig) Chronicle.*

"On the whole, we are satisfied that this volume is the most correct and comprehensive one yet published." —*Hunt's Merchants' Magazine.*

"The superiority of this edition over the ephemeral publications of the day consists in fuller and more authentic accounts of his family, his early life, and Indian wars. The narrative of his proceedings in Mexico is drawn partly from reliable private letters, but chiefly from his own official correspondence."

"It forms a cheap, substantial, and attractive volume, and one which should be read at the fireside of every family who desire a faithful and true life of the Old General."

GENERAL TAYLOR AND HIS STAFF:

Comprising Memoirs of Generals Taylor, Worth, Wool, and Butler; Cols. May, Cross, Clay, Hardin, Yell, Hays, and other distinguished Officers attached to General Taylor's Army. Interspersed with

NUMEROUS ANECDOTES OF THE MEXICAN WAR,

and Personal Adventures of the Officers. Compiled from Public Documents and Private Correspondence. With

ACCURATE PORTRAITS, AND OTHER BEAUTIFUL ILLUSTRATIONS.

In one volume, 12mo.

GENERAL SCOTT AND HIS STAFF:

Comprising Memoirs of Generals Scott, Twiggs, Smith, Quitman, Shields, Pillow, Lane, Cadwalader, Patterson, and Pierce; Cols. Childs, Riley, Harney, and Butler; and other distinguished officers attached to General Scott's Army.

TOGETHER WITH

Notices of General Kearny, Col. Doniphan, Col. Fremont, and other officers distinguished in the Conquest of California and New Mexico; and Personal Adventures of the Officers. Compiled from Public Documents and Private Correspondence. With

ACCURATE PORTRAITS, AND OTHER BEAUTIFUL ILLUSTRATIONS.

In one volume, 12mo.

THE FAMILY DENTIST,

INCLUDING THE SURGICAL, MEDICAL AND MECHANICAL TREATMENT OF THE TEETH.

Illustrated with thirty-one Engravings.

By CHARLES A. DU BOUCHET, M. D., Dental Surgeon.

In one volume, 18mo.

MECHANICS FOR THE MILLWRIGHT, ENGINEER AND MACHINIST, CIVIL ENGINEER, AND ARCHITECT:

CONTAINING

THE PRINCIPLES OF MECHANICS APPLIED TO MACHINERY

Of American models, Steam-Engines, Water-Works, Navigation, Bridge-building, &c. &c. By

FREDERICK OVERMAN,

Author of "The Manufacture of Iron," and other scientific treatises.

Illustrated by 150 Engravings. In one large 12mo. volume.

WILLIAMS'S TRAVELLER'S AND TOURIST'S GUIDE

Through the United States, Canada, &c.

This book will be found replete with information, not only to the traveller, but likewise to the man of business. In its preparation, an entirely new plan has been adopted, which, we are convinced, needs only a trial to be fully appreciated.

Among its many valuable features, are tables showing at a glance the *distance, fare*, and *time* occupied in travelling from the principal cities to the most important places in the Union; so that the question frequently asked, without obtaining a satisfactory reply, is here answered in full. Other tables show the distances from New York, &c., to domestic and foreign ports, by sea; and also, by way of comparison, from New York and Liverpool to the principal ports beyond and around Cape Horn, &c., as well as *via* the Isthmus of Panama. Accompanied by a large and accurate Map of the United States, including a separate Map of California, Oregon, New Mexico and Utah. Also, a Map of the Island of Cuba, and Plan of the City and Harbor of Havana; and a Map of Niagara River and Falls.

THE LEGISLATIVE GUIDE:

Containing directions for conducting business in the House of Representatives; the Senate of the United States; the Joint Rules of both Houses; a Synopsis of Jefferson's Manual, and copious Indices; together with a concise system of Rules of Order, based on the regulations of the U. S. Congress. Designed to economise time, secure uniformity and despatch in conducting business in all secular meetings, and also in all religious, political, and Legislative Assemblies.

BY JOSEPH BARTLETT BURLEIGH, LL. D.

In one volume, 12mo.

This is considered by our Judges and Congressmen as decidedly the best work of the kind extant. Every young man in the country should have a copy of this book.

THE INITIALS; A Story of Modern Life.

THREE VOLUMES OF THE LONDON EDITION COMPLETE IN ONE VOLUME 12MO.

A new novel, equal to "Jane Eyre."

WILD WESTERN SCENES:

A NARRATIVE OF ADVENTURES IN THE WESTERN WILDERNESS.

Wherein the Exploits of Daniel Boone, the Great American Pioneer, are particularly described. Also, Minute Accounts of Bear, Deer, and Buffalo Hunts—Desperate Conflicts with the Savages—Fishing and Fowling Adventures—Encounters with Serpents, &c.

By LUKE SHORTFIELD, Author of "The Western Merchant."

BEAUTIFULLY ILLUSTRATED. One volume, 12mo.

POEMS OF THE PLEASURES:

Consisting of the PLEASURES OF IMAGINATION, by Akenside; the PLEASURES OF MEMORY, by Samuel Rogers; the PLEASURES OF HOPE, by Campbell; and the PLEASURES OF FRIENDSHIP, by M'Henry. With a Memoir of each Author, prepared expressly for this work. 18mo.

BALDWIN'S PRONOUNCING GAZETTEER.

A PRONOUNCING GAZETTEER:

CONTAINING

TOPOGRAPHICAL, STATISTICAL, AND OTHER INFORMATION, OF ALL THE MORE IMPORTANT PLACES IN THE KNOWN WORLD, FROM THE MOST RECENT AND AUTHENTIC SOURCES.

BY THOMAS BALDWIN.

Assisted by several other Gentlemen.

To which is added an APPENDIX, containing more than TEN THOUSAND ADDITIONAL NAMES, chiefly of the small Towns and Villages, &c., of the United States and of Mexico.

NINTH EDITION, WITH A SUPPLEMENT,

Giving the Pronunciation of near two thousand names, besides those pronounced in the Original Work: Forming in itself a Complete Vocabulary of Geographical Pronunciation.

ONE VOLUME 12MO.—PRICE, $1.50.

Arthur's Library for the Household.

Complete in Twelve handsome 18mo. Volumes, bound in Scarlet Cloth.

1. WOMAN'S TRIALS; OR, TALES AND SKETCHES FROM THE LIFE AROUND US.
2. MARRIED LIFE; ITS SHADOWS AND SUNSHINE.
3. THE TWO WIVES; OR LOST AND WON.
4. THE WAYS OF PROVIDENCE; OR, "HE DOETH ALL THINGS WELL."
5. HOME SCENES AND HOME INFLUENCES.
6. STORIES FOR YOUNG HOUSEKEEPERS.
7. LESSONS IN LIFE, FOR ALL WHO WILL READ THEM.
8. SEED-TIME AND HARVEST; OR, WHATSOEVER A MAN SOWETH THAT SHALL HE ALSO REAP.
9. STORIES FOR PARENTS.
10. OFF-HAND SKETCHES, A LITTLE DASHED WITH HUMOR.
11. WORDS FOR THE WISE.
12. THE TRIED AND THE TEMPTED.

The above Series are sold together or separate, as each work is complete in itself. No Family should be without a copy of this interesting and instructive Series. Price Thirty-seven and a Half Cents per Volume.

FIELD'S SCRAP BOOK.—New Edition.

Literary and Miscellaneous Scrap Book.

Consisting of Tales and Anecdotes — Biographical, Historical, Patriotic, Moral, Religious, and Sentimental Pieces, in Prose and Poetry.

COMPILED BY WILLIAM FIELDS.

SECOND EDITION, REVISED AND IMPROVED.

In one handsome 8vo. Volume. Price, $2.00.

POLITICS FOR AMERICAN CHRISTIANS;

A WORD UPON OUR EXAMPLE AS A NATION, OUR LABOUR, &c.

TOGETHER WITH

THE POLITICS OF THE NEW TESTAMENT.

BY THE AUTHOR OF "NEW THEMES FOR THE PROTESTANT CLERGY."

One vol. 8vo., half cloth. Price 50 cents. For sale by all the Trade.

THE HUMAN BODY AND ITS CONNEXION WITH MAN.

ILLUSTRATED BY THE PRINCIPAL ORGANS.

BY JAMES JOHN GARTH WILKINSON,

Member of the Royal College of Surgeons of England.

IN ONE VOLUME, 12MO — PRICE $1 25.

BOARDMAN'S BIBLE IN THE FAMILY.

The Bible in the Family:

OR,

HINTS ON DOMESTIC HAPPINESS.

BY H. A. BOARDMAN,

PASTOR OF THE TENTH PRESBYTERIAN CHURCH, PHILADELPHIA.

One Volume 12mo.—Price, One Dollar.

WHEELER'S HISTORY OF NORTH CAROLINA.

Historical Sketches

OF

NORTH CAROLINA,

From 1584 to 1851.

Compiled from Original Records, Official Documents, and Traditional Statements; with Biographical Sketches of her Distinguished Statesmen, Jurists, Lawyers, Soldiers, Divines, &c.

BY JOHN H. WHEELER,

Late Treasurer of the State.

IN ONE VOLUME OCTAVO.—PRICE, $2.00.

THE NORTH CAROLINA READER:

CONTAINING

A HISTORY AND DESCRIPTION OF NORTH CAROLINA, SELECTIONS IN PROSE AND VERSE, (MANY OF THEM BY EMINENT CITIZENS OF THE STATE), HISTORICAL AND CHRONOLOGICAL TABLES,

And a Variety of Miscellaneous Information and Statistics.

BY C. H. WILEY.

"My own green land for ever!
Land of the beautiful and brave—
The freeman's home—the martyr's grave."

Illustrated with Engravings, and designed for Families and Schools.

ONE VOLUME 12MO. PRICE $1.00.

THIRTY YEARS WITH THE INDIAN TRIBES.

PERSONAL MEMOIRS

OF A

Residence of Thirty Years with the Indian Tribes

ON THE AMERICAN FRONTIERS:

With brief Notices of passing Events, Facts, and Opinions,

A. D. 1812 TO A. D. 1842.

BY HENRY R. SCHOOLCRAFT.

ONE LARGE OCTAVO VOLUME. PRICE THREE DOLLARS.

THE SCALP HUNTERS:

OR,

ROMANTIC ADVENTURES IN NORTHERN MEXICO.

BY CAPTAIN MAYNE REID,

AUTHOR OF THE "RIFLE RANGERS."

Complete in One Volume. Price Fifty Cents.

THE CONFESSIONS OF A HOUSEKEEPER.

BY MRS. JOHN SMITH.

WITH THIRTEEN HUMOROUS ILLUSTRATIONS.

One Volume 12mo. Price 50 Cents.

Splendid Illustrated Books, suitable for Gifts for the Holidays

THE IRIS: AN ORIGINAL SOUVENIR FOR ANY YARE.

EDITED BY PROF. JOHN S. HART.

WITH TWELVE SPLENDID ILLUMINATIONS, ALL FROM ORIGINAL DESIGNS.

THE DEW-DROP: A TRIBUTE OF AFFECTION.

WITH NINE STEEL ENGRAVINGS.

GEMS FROM THE SACRED MINE.

WITH TEN STEEL PLATES AND ILLUMINATIONS.

The Poet's Offering.

WITH FOURTEEN STEEL PLATES AND ILLUMINATIONS.

THE STANDARD EDITIONS OF THE POETS.

WITH ILLUSTRATIONS.

LORD AND LADY HARCOURT:

OR, COUNTRY HOSPITALITIES.

BY CATHARINE SINCLAIR,

Author of "Jane Bouverie," "The Business of Life," "Modern Accomplishments," &c.

One Volume 12mo. Price 50 cents, paper; cloth, fine, 75 cents.

A Book for every Family.

THE DICTIONARY OF DOMESTIC MEDICINE AND HOUSEHOLD SURGERY

BY SPENCER THOMPSON, M.D., F.R.C.S.,

Of Edinburgh.

ILLUSTRATED WITH NUMEROUS CUTS.

EDITED AND ADAPTED TO THE WANTS OF THIS COUNTRY, BY A WELL-KNOWN PRACTITIONER OF PHILADELPHIA.

In one volume, demi-octavo.

The Regicide's Daughter:

A TALE OF TWO WORLDS.

BY W. H. CARPENTER,

AUTHOR OF "CLAIBORNE THE REBEL," "JOHN THE BOLD," &C., &C.

One Volume 18mo. Price Thirty-seven and a Half Cents.

WILLIAMS'S NEW MAP OF THE UNITED STATES, ON ROLLERS.

SIZE TWO AND A HALF BY THREE FEET.

A new Map of the United States, upon which are delineated its vast works of Internal Communication, Routes across the Continent, &c., showing also Canada and the Island of Cuba,

BY W. WILLIAMS.

This Map is handsomely colored and mounted on rollers, and will be found a beautiful and useful ornament to the Counting-House and Parlor, as well as the School-Room. Price Two Dollars.

VALUABLE STANDARD MEDICAL BOOKS.

DISPENSATORY OF THE UNITED STATES.

BY DRS. WOOD AND BACHE.

New Edition, much enlarged and carefully revised. One volume, royal octavo.

A TREATISE ON THE PRACTICE OF MEDICINE.

BY GEORGE B. WOOD, M. D.,

One of the Authors of the "Dispensatory of the U. S.," &c. New edition, improved. 2 vols. 8vo.

AN ILLUSTRATED SYSTEM OF HUMAN ANATOMY; SPECIAL, MICROSCOPIC, AND PHYSIOLOGICAL.

BY SAMUEL GEORGE MORTON, M. D.

With 391 beautiful Illustrations. One volume, royal octavo.

SMITH'S OPERATIVE SURGERY.

A SYSTEM OF OPERATIVE SURGERY, BASED UPON THE PRACTICE OF SURGEONS IN THE UNITED STATES; AND COMPRISING A Bibliographical Index and Historical Record of many of their Operations, FOR A PERIOD OF 200 YEARS.

BY HENRY H. SMITH, M.D.

Illustrated with nearly 1000 Engravings on Steel.

MATERIA MEDICA AND THERAPEUTICS,

With ample Illustrations of Practice in all the Departments of Medical Science, and copious Notices of Toxicology.

BY THOMAS D. MITCHELL, A.M., M.D.,

Prof. of the Theory and Practice of Medicine in the Philadelphia College of Medicine, &c. 1 vol. 8vo.

THE THEORY AND PRACTICE OF SURGERY.

By GEORGE M'CLELLAN, M. D. 1 vol. 8vo.

EBERLE'S PRACTICE OF MEDICINE.

New Edition. Improved by GEORGE M'CLELLAN, M. D. Two volumes in 1 vol. 8vo.

EBERLE'S THERAPEUTICS.

TWO VOLUMES IN ONE.

A TREATISE ON THE DISEASES AND PHYSICAL EDUCATION OF CHILDREN,

By JOHN EBERLE, M. D., &c. Fourth Edition. With Notes and very large Additions,

By THOMAS D. MITCHELL, A. M., M. D., &c. 1 vol. 8vo.

EBERLE'S NOTES FOR STUDENTS—NEW EDITION,

*** These works are used as text-books in most of the Medical Schools in the United States.

A PRACTICAL TREATISE ON POISONS:

Their Symptoms, Antidotes, and Treatment. By O. H. Costill, M. D. 18mo.

IDENTITIES OF LIGHT AND HEAT, OF CALORIC AND ELECTRICITY,

BY C. CAMPBELL COOPER.

UNITED STATES' PHARMACOPŒIA,

Edition of 1851. Published by authority of the National Medical Convention. 1 vol. 8vo

SCHOOLCRAFTS GREAT NATIONAL WORK ON THE

Indian Tribes of the United States.

PART SECOND—QUARTO.

WITH EIGHTY BEAUTIFUL ILLUSTRATIONS ON STEEL,

Engraved in the first style of the art, from Drawings by Captain Eastman, U. S. A.

PRICE, FIFTEEN DOLLARS.

COCKBURN'S LIFE OF LORD JEFFREY.

LIFE OF LORD JEFFREY,

WITH A SELECTION FROM HIS CORRESPONDENCE,

BY LORD COCKBURN,

One of the Judges of the Court of Sessions in Scotland. Two volumes, demi-octavo.

"Those who know Lord Jeffrey only through the pages of the Edinburgh Review, get but a one-sided, and not the most pleasant view of his character."

"We advise our readers to obtain the book, and enjoy it to the full themselves. They will unite with us in saying that the self-drawn character portrayed in the letters of Lord Jeffrey, is one of the most delightful pictures that has ever been presented to them."—*Evening Bulletin.*

"Jeffrey was for a long period editor of the Review, and was admitted by all the other contributors to be the leading spirit in it. In addition to his political articles, he soon showed his wonderful powers of criticism in literature. He was equally at home whether censuring or applauding; in his onslaughts on the mediocrity of Southey, or the misused talents of Byron, or in his noble essays on Shakspeare, or Scott, or Burns."—*New York Express.*

PRICE, TWO DOLLARS AND A HALF.

ROMANCE OF NATURAL HISTORY;

OR, WILD SCENES AND WILD HUNTERS.

WITH NUMEROUS ILLUSTRATIONS, IN ONE VOLUME OCTAVO, CLOTH.

BY C. W. WEBBER.

"We have rarely read a volume so full of life and enthusiasm, so capable of transporting the reader into an actor among the scenes and persons described. The volume can hardly be opened at any page without arresting the attention, and the reader is borne along with the movement of a style whose elastic spring and life knows no weariness."—*Boston Courier and Transcript.*

PRICE, TWO DOLLARS.

THE LIFE OF WILLIAM PENN,

WITH SELECTIONS FROM HIS CORRESPONDENCE AND AUTOBIOGRAPHY,

BY SAMUEL M. JANNEY.

Second Edition, Revised.

"Our author has acquitted himself in a manner worthy of his subject. His style is easy, flowing, and yet sententious. Altogether, we consider it a highly valuable addition to the literature of our age, and a work that should find its way into the library of every Friend."—*Friends' Intelligencer, Philadelphia.*

"We regard this life of the great founder of Pennsylvania as a valuable addition to the literature of the country."—*Philadelphia Evening Bulletin.*

"We have no hesitation in pronouncing Mr. Janney's life of Penn the best, because the most satisfactory, that has yet been written. The author's style is clear and uninvolved, and well suited to the purposes of biographical narrative."—*Louisville Journal.*

PRICE, TWO DOLLARS.

LIPPINCOTT'S CABINET HISTORIES OF THE STATES,

CONSISTING OF A SERIES OF

Cabinet Histories of all the States of the Union,

TO EMBRACE A VOLUME FOR EACH STATE.

We have so far completed all our arrangements, as to be able to issue the whole series in the shortest possible time consistent with its careful literary production. SEVERAL VOLUMES ARE NOW READY FOR SALE. The talented authors who have engaged to write these Histories, are no strangers in the literary world.

NOTICES OF THE PRESS.

"These most tastefully printed and bound volumes form the first instalment of a series of State Histories, which, without superseding the bulkier and more expensive works of the same character, may enter household channels from which the others would be excluded by their cost and magnitude."

"In conciseness, clearness, skill of arrangement, and graphic interest, they are a most excellent earnest of those to come. They are eminently adapted both to interest and instruct, and should have a place in the family library of every American."—*N. Y. Courier and Enquirer.*

"The importance of a series of State History like those now in preparation, can scarcely be estimated. Being condensed as carefully as accuracy and interest of narrative will permit, the size and price of the volumes will bring them within the reach of every family in the country, thus making them home-reading books for old and young. Each individual will, in consequence, become familiar, not only with the history of his own State, but with that of the other States; thus mutual interests will be re-awakened, and old bonds cemented in a firmer re-union."—*Home Gazette.*

NEW THEMES FOR THE PROTESTANT CLERGY;

CREEDS WITHOUT CHARITY, THEOLOGY WITHOUT HUMANITY, AND PROTESTANTISM WITHOUT CHRISTIANITY:

With Notes by the Editor on the Literature of Charity, Population, Pauperism, Political Economy, and Protestantism.

"The great question which the book discusses is, whether the Church of this age is what the primitive Church was, and whether Christians—both pastors and people—are doing their duty. Our anthor believes not, and, to our mind, he has made out a strong case. He thinks there is abundant room for reform at the present time, and that it is needed almost as much as in the days of Luther. And why? Because, in his own words, 'While one portion of nominal Christians have busied themselves with forms and ceremonies and observances; with pictures, images, and processions; others have given to doctrines the supremacy, and have busied themselves in laying down the lines by which to enforce human belief—lines of interpretation by which to control human opinion—lines of discipline and restraint, by which to bring human minds to uniformity of faith and action. They have formed creeds and catechisms; they have spread themselves over the whole field of the sacred writings, and scratched up all the surface; they have gathered all the straws, and turned over all the pebbles, and detected the colour and determined the outline of every stone and tree and shrub; they have dwelt with rapture upon all that was beautiful and sublime; but they have trampled over mines of golden wisdom, of surpassing richness and depth, almost without a thought, and almost without an effort to fathom these priceless treasures, much less to take possession of them.'"

PRICE, ONE DOLLAR.

SIMPSON'S MILITARY JOURNAL.

JOURNAL OF A MILITARY RECONNOISSANCE FROM SANTA FE, NEW MEXICO, TO THE NAVAJO COUNTRY,

BY JAMES H. SIMPSON, A. M.,

FIRST LIEUTENANT CORPS OF TOPOGRAPHICAL ENGINEERS.

WITH SEVENTY-FIVE COLOURED ILLUSTRATIONS.

One volume, octavo. Price, Three Dollars.

TALES OF THE SOUTHERN BORDER.

BY C. W. WEBBER.

ONE VOLUME OCTAVO, HANDSOMELY ILLUSTRATED.

The Hunter Naturalist, a Romance of Sporting;

OR, WILD SCENES AND WILD HUNTERS,

BY C. W. WEBBER,

Author of "Shot in the Eye," "Old Hicks the Guide," "Gold Mines of the Gila," &c.

ONE VOLUME, ROYAL OCTAVO.

ILLUSTRATED WITH FORTY BEAUTIFUL ENGRAVINGS, FROM ORIGINAL DRAWINGS,

MANY OF WHICH ARE COLOURED.

Price, Five Dollars.

NIGHTS IN A BLOCK-HOUSE;

OR, SKETCHES OF BORDER LIFE,

Embracing Adventures among the Indians, Feats of the Wild Hunters, and Exploits of Boone, Brady, Kenton, Whetzel, Fleehart, and other Border Heroes of the West

BY HENRY C. WATSON,

Author of "Camp-Fires of the Revolution."

WITH NUMEROUS ILLUSTRATIONS.

One volume, 8vo. Price, $2 00.

HAMILTON, THE YOUNG ARTIST.

BY AUGUSTA BROWNE.

WITH

AN ESSAY ON SCULPTURE AND PAINTING,

BY HAMILTON A. C. BROWNE.

1 vol. 18mo. Price, 37 1-2 cents.

THE FISCAL HISTORY OF TEXAS:

EMBRACING AN ACCOUNT OF ITS REVENUES, DEBTS, AND CURRENCY, FROM THE COMMENCEMENT OF THE REVOLUTION IN 1834, TO 1851-2, WITH REMARKS ON AMERICAN DEBTS.

BY WM. M. GOUGE,

Author of "A Short History of Paper Money and Banking in the United States."

In one vol. 8vo., cloth. Price $1 50.

INGERSOLL'S HISTORY OF THE SECOND WAR:

A HISTORY OF THE SECOND WAR BETWEEN THE U. STATES AND GT. BRITAIN.

BY CHARLES J. INGERSOLL.

Second series. 2 volumes, 8vo. Price $4 00.

These two volumes, which embrace the hostile transactions between the United States and Great Britain during the years 1814 and '15, complete Mr. Ingersoll's able work on the Second or "Late War," as it has usually been called. A great deal of new and valuable matter has been collected by the author from original sources, and is now first introduced to the public.

FROST'S JUVENILE SERIES.

TWELVE VOLUMES, 16mo., WITH FIVE HUNDRED ENGRAVINGS.

WALTER O'NEILL, OR THE PLEASURE OF DOING GOOD. 25 Engrav'gs.
JUNKER SCHOTT, and other Stories. 6 Engravings.
THE LADY OF THE LURLEI, and other Stories. 12 Engravings.
ELLEN'S BIRTHDAY, and other Stories. 20 Engravings.
HERMAN, and other Stories. 9 Engravings.
KING TREGEWALL'S DAUGHTER, and other Stories. 16 Engravings.
THE DROWNED BOY, and other Stories. 6 Engravings.
THE PICTORIAL RHYME-BOOK. 122 Engravings.
THE PICTORIAL NURSERY BOOK. 117 Engravings.
THE GOOD CHILD'S REWARD. 115 Engravings.
ALPHABET OF QUADRUPEDS. 26 Engravings.
ALPHABET OF BIRDS. 26 Engravings.

PRICE, TWENTY-FIVE CENTS EACH.

The above popular and attractive series of New Juveniles for the Young, are sold together or separately.

THE MILLINER AND THE MILLIONAIRE.

BY MRS. REBECCA HICKS,

(Of Virginia,) Author of "The Lady Killer," &c. One volume, 12mo.

Price, 37½ cents.

STANSBURY'S
EXPEDITION TO THE GREAT SALT LAKE.

AN EXPLORATION
OF THE VALLEY OF THE GREAT SALT LAKE
OF UTAH,

CONTAINING ITS GEOGRAPHY, NATURAL HISTORY, MINERALOGICAL RESOURCES, ANALYSIS OF ITS WATERS, AND AN AUTHENTIC ACCOUNT OF

THE MORMON SETTLEMENT.

ALSO,

A RECONNOISSANCE OF A NEW ROUTE THROUGH THE ROCKY MOUNTAINS.

WITH SEVENTY BEAUTIFUL ILLUSTRATIONS,

FROM DRAWINGS TAKEN ON THE SPOT,

AND TWO LARGE AND ACCURATE MAPS OF THAT REGION.

BY HOWARD STANSBURY,

CAPTAIN TOPOGRAPHICAL ENGINEERS.

One volume, royal octavo. Price Five Dollars.

THE ABBOTSFORD EDITION

OF

The Waverley Novels,

PRINTED UPON FINE WHITE PAPER, WITH NEW AND BEAUTIFUL TYPE,

FROM THE LAST ENGLISH EDITION,

EMBRACING

THE AUTHOR'S LATEST CORRECTIONS, NOTES, ETC.,

COMPLETE IN TWELVE VOLUMES, DEMI-OCTAVO, AND NEATLY BOUND IN CLOTH,

With Illustrations,

FOR ONLY TWELVE DOLLARS,

CONTAINING

WAVERLEY, or 'Tis Sixty Years Since............THE FORTUNES OF NIGEL.
GUY MANNERING............PEVERIL OF THE PEAK.
THE ANTIQUARY............QUENTIN DURWARD.
THE BLACK DWARF............ST. RONAN'S WELL.
OLD MORTALITY............REDGAUNTLET.
ROB ROY............THE BETROTHED.
THE HEART OF MID-LOTHIAN............THE TALISMAN.
THE BRIDE OF LAMMERMOOR............WOODSTOCK.
A LEGEND OF MONTROSE............THE HIGHLAND WIDOW, &c.
IVANHOE............THE FAIR MAID OF PERTH.
THE MONASTERY............ANNE OF GEIERSTEIN.
THE ABBOT............COUNT ROBERT OF PARIS.
KENILWORTH............CASTLE DANGEROUS.
THE PIRATE............THE SURGEON'S DAUGHTER, &c.

ANY OF THE ABOVE NOVELS SOLD, IN PAPER COVERS, AT FIFTY CENTS EACH.

ALSO,

AN ILLUSTRATED EDITION

OF

THE WAVERLEY NOVELS,

In Twelve Volumes, Royal Octavo, on Superfine Paper, with

SEVERAL HUNDRED CHARACTERISTIC AND BEAUTIFUL ENGRAVINGS.

ELEGANTLY BOUND IN CLOTH, GILT.

Price, Only Twenty-Four Dollars.

A NEW AND COMPLETE

Gazetteer of the United States,

EDITED BY T. BALDWIN AND J. THOMAS, M.D.

WITH

A NEW AND SUPERB MAP OF THE UNITED STATES,

ENGRAVED ON STEEL.

Above Twelve Hundred Pages, Octavo.

The Publishers take pleasure in announcing the completion of this, the most elaborate, comprehensive, and perfect Gazetteer of the United States, that has ever issued from the press. In its preparation, no considerations of expense or labor have been allowed to interfere with a work designed to be as perfect as possible in every department, and in all of its details. Nor have the successive issues of other Gazetteers, hurried through the press to claim the market, tempted the publishers to offer their book before all the ample census of 1850, and other material in the hands of the editors, were fully digested and accurately arranged.

When this Gazetteer was first announced, 800 pages, or, at the most, 900, were designed as the limit of the book. But so vast was the amount of matter accumulated through the personal labors of the editors and their assistants, as well as through the active efforts of several thousand correspondents in all parts of the United States, the work has swelled to near 1300 pages. The amount of new matter which it contains, all of a recent character, is very large, and in many instances embraces statistics and populations to 1853. This gives it an intrinsic value over every other work of the kind in existence.

We therefore offer our Gazetteer confidently, as the only complete and thoroughly reliable Gazetteer of the United States yet published. Price, four dollars.

In Press,

A UNIVERSAL GAZETTEER, OR GEOGRAPHICAL DICTIONARY,

Of the most complete and comprehensive character. It will be compiled from the best English, French, and German authorities, and will be published the moment that the returns of the present census of Europe can be obtained.

REPORT OF A GEOLOGICAL SURVEY

OF

WISCONSIN, IOWA, AND MINNESOTA,

AND INCIDENTALLY OF

A PORTION OF NEBRASKA TERRITORY,

MADE UNDER INSTRUCTIONS FROM THE U. S. TREASURY DEPARTMENT,

BY DAVID DALE OWEN,

United States' Geologist.

WITH OVER 150 ILLUSTRATIONS ON STEEL AND WOOD.

Two volumes, quarto. Price Ten Dollars.

MERCHANTS' MEMORANDUM BOOK,

CONTAINING LISTS OF ALL GOODS PURCHASED BY COUNTRY MERCHANTS, &c

One volume, 18mo., Leather cover. Price, 50 cents.

ARTHUR'S
New Juvenile Library.
BEAUTIFULLY ILLUSTRATED.

1. WHO IS GREATEST? and other Stories.
2. WHO ARE HAPPIEST? and other Stories.
3. THE POOR WOOD-CUTTER, and other Stories.
4. MAGGY'S BABY, and other Stories.
5. MR. HAVEN'T-GOT-TIME AND MR. DON'T-BE-IN-A-HURRY.
6. THE PEACEMAKERS.
7. UNCLE BEN'S NEW-YEAR'S GIFT, and other Stories.
8. THE WOUNDED BOY, and other Stories.
9. THE LOST CHILDREN, and other Stories.
10. OUR HARRY, and other Poems and Stories.
11. THE LAST PENNY, and other Stories.
12. PIERRE, THE ORGAN BOY, and other Stories.

EACH VOLUME IS ILLUSTRATED WITH

ENGRAVINGS FROM ORIGINAL DESIGNS BY CROOME,

And are sold together or separately.

"YIEGER'S CABINET."

SPIRITUAL VAMPIRISM:

The History of Etherial Softdown and her Friends of the New Light.

BY C. W. WEBBER.

One Volume, demi-octavo. Price, One Dollar.

LIBRARY EDITION OF SHAKSPEARE.

(LARGE TYPE.)

THE DRAMATIC WORKS OF WILLIAM SHAKSPEARE,

WITH A LIFE OF THE POET,

AND NOTES ORIGINAL AND SELECTED, TOGETHER WITH A COPIOUS GLOSSARY.

4 VOLUMES OCTAVO.

STYLES OF BINDING:

Cloth, extra	$6 00
Library style	7 00
Half-Turkey morocco	9 00
Half-calf and Turkey, antique style	12 00
Full calf and Turkey, antique style	15 00

The Footpath and Highway;

OR,

WANDERINGS OF AN AMERICAN IN GREAT BRITAIN,

IN 1851 AND '52.

BY BENJAMIN MORAN,

This volume embodies the observations of the anthor, made during eight months' wanderings, as a correspondent for American Journals; and as he travelled much on foot, differs essentially from those on the same countries, by other writers. The habits, manners, customs, and condition of the people have been carefully noted, and his views of them are given in clear, bold language. His remarks take a wide range, and as he visited every county in England but three, there will be much in the work of a novel and instructive character.

One vol. 12mo. Price $1 25.

DAY DREAMS.

BY MISS MARTHA ALLEN.

ONE VOLUME 12mo.

Price, paper, 50 cents. Cloth, 75 cents.

SIMON KENTON: OR, THE SCOUT'S REVENGE.

AN HISTORICAL ROMANCE.

BY JAMES WEIR.

Illustrated, cloth, 75 cents. Paper, 50 cents.

MARIE DE BERNIERE, THE MAROON,

AND OTHER TALES.

BY W. GILMORE SIMMS.

1 vol. 12mo., cloth. Price $1 25.

HISTORY OF THE NATIONAL FLAG OF THE UNITED STATES.

WITH COLOURED ILLUSTRATIONS.

BY SCHUYLER HAMILTON,

CAPTAIN BY BREVET, U. S. A.

One vol., crown 8vo. Price $1 00.

THE DOUBTING COMMUNICANT ENCOURAGED.

BY THE REV. SEPTIMUS TUSTIN, D. D.

SECOND EDITION.

One Volume, 32mo. Price, 38 cents.

A REVIEW
OF
"NEW THEMES FOR THE PROTESTANT CLERGY."

ONE VOLUME 12mo.

Price, paper, 25 cents. Cloth, 50 cents.

THE BIBLE IN THE COUNTING-HOUSE.

BY H. A. BOARDMAN, D.D.,

AUTHOR OF "THE BIBLE IN THE FAMILY."

One vol. 12mo., cloth. Price One Dollar.

AUTOBIOGRAPHY OF A NEW CHURCHMAN.

BY JOHN A. LITTLE.

ONE VOLUME 12mo. PRICE 75 CENTS.

MILTON'S WORKS—NEW AND COMPLETE EDITION.

Milton's Poetical Works,

WITH A LIFE, DISSERTATION, INDEX, AND NOTES,

BY PROF. C. D. CLEVELAND.

ONE VOLUME ROYAL 12mo., CLOTH. PRICE $1 25.

UNIFORM AND DRESS
OF THE
ARMY OF THE UNITED STATES.

WITH COLOURED ILLUSTRATIONS.

QUARTO, CLOTH. PRICE FIVE DOLLARS.

UNIFORM AND DRESS
OF THE
NAVY OF THE UNITED STATES.

WITH COLOURED ILLUSTRATIONS.

QUARTO, CLOTH. PRICE FIVE DOLLARS.

Types of Mankind,

OR

ETHNOLOGICAL RESEARCHES,

BASED UPON THE

ANCIENT MONUMENTS, PAINTINGS, SCULPTURES, AND CRANIA OF RACES,

AND UPON THEIR

NATURAL, GEOGRAPHICAL, PHILOLOGICAL AND BIBLICAL HISTORY,

ILLUSTRATED BY SELECTIONS FROM THE INEDITED PAPERS OF

SAMUEL GEORGE MORTON, M. D.,

(LATE PRESIDENT OF THE ACADEMY OF NATURAL SCIENCES AT PHILADELPHIA)

AND BY ADDITIONAL CONTRIBUTIONS FROM

PROF. L. AGASSIZ, LL.D.; W. USHER, M. D.; AND PROF. H. S. PATTERSON, M. D.

BY

J. C. NOTT, M. D., and GEO. R. GLIDDON,

MOBILE, ALABAMA. FORMERLY U. S. CONSUL AT CAIRO.

WITH FOUR HUNDRED ILLUSTRATIONS.

One volume, quarto. Price, Five Dollars.

Iron Tables, Price 25 Cents—A Useful New Work.

WEIGHT TABLES

OF DIFFERENT LENGTHS OF

ROUND, SQUARE, AND FLAT BAR IRON, STEEL, ETC.

BY A PRACTICAL MECHANIC.

This is one of the most useful works published for Dealers and Workers in Iron. So correct are the calculations, that any person can safely sell and buy with the book, without even weighing the Iron and Steel.

THE RACE FOR RICHES,

And some of the Pits into which the Runners fall.

SIX LECTURES,

APPLYING THE WORD OF GOD TO THE TRAFFIC OF MEN.

BY WILLIAM ARNOT,

MINISTER OF FREE ST. PETER'S, GLASGOW.

With a Preface and Notes,

BY STEPHEN COLWELL, AUTHOR OF "NEW THEMES," ETC.

One volume, 12mo. Price, 62 cents.

LIBRARY EDITION OF

ROLLIN'S ANCIENT HISTORY,

A NEW STEREOTYPED EDITION.

Four volumes, octavo, large type.

STYLES OF BINDING.

Cloth gilt	$6 00
Library style	7 00
Half Turkey morocco, plain	8 00
Half calf, or Turkey antique	10 00
Half calf, or Turkey antique, brown edge	11 00
Full calf, or Turkey antique, gilt edge	16 00

THE LIFE OF LORD BYRON,

WITH HIS LETTERS AND JOURNALS.

BY THOMAS MOORE,

One volume, Octavo, of over Thirteen Hundred Pages.

Price, cloth, $2 00. Library style, $2 25.

Lines for the Gentle and Loving.

By Thomas MacKellar.

Man's chief duty to his brethren is, to endeavor to make them good and happy. — Abler pens have amused the fancy and instructed the mind; be it my privilege to touch the heart.—T. M.

One volume, 12mo. Price, Fifty Cents.

NOTES ON UNCLE TOM'S CABIN.

BEING A LOGICAL ANSWER TO ITS ALLEGATIONS AND INFERENCES AGAINST SLAVERY AS AN INSTITUTION,

With a Supplementary Note on "The Key,"

AND AN INDEX OF AUTHORITIES.

BY REV. E. J. STEARNS, A. M.,

LATE PROFESSOR IN ST. JOHN'S COLLEGE, ANNAPOLIS, MARYLAND.

Price, paper covers, 50 cents; cloth, 75 cents.

THE AMERICAN HANDBOOK OF ORNAMENTAL TREES.

BY THOMAS MEHAN, GARDENER.

One volume, 18mo. Price, Seventy-five cents.

The Wars of America,

CONTAINING A COMPLETE HISTORY OF THE

Early Indian Wars from the Landing of the Pilgrims;

THE WAR OF THE REVOLUTION;

THE SECOND WAR WITH GREAT BRITAIN;

AND THE MEXICAN WAR.

WITH 300 CUTS, AND NUMEROUS COLORED ILLUSTRATIONS.

One volume, large octavo. Price, $3 00.

LIFE AND ITS AIMS.

IN TWO PARTS.

Part I., Ideal Life—Part II., Actual Life.

One Volume, 12mo. Price, One Dollar.

THE UNIVERSAL LETTER WRITER.

Price, 25 cents,

AN HISTORICAL TEXT-BOOK AND ATLAS OF BIBLICAL GEOGRAPHY.

BY LYMAN COLEMAN, D. D.

ILLUSTRATED WITH SEVEN NEW ENGRAVED MAPS, COLORED.

One volume, imperial octavo. Price, $2 00.

ELEMENTS OF THE LAWS,

Or Outlines of the System of Civil and Criminal Law in Force in the United States,

AND THE SEVERAL STATES OF THE UNION.

Designed for popular use, and to enable any one to acquire a popular knowledge of his legal rights and privileges, in all the most important political and business relations of the citizens of the country, with the principles on which they are founded, and the means of asserting and maintaining them.

BY THE HON. THOMAS J. SMITH,

One of the Judges of the Supreme Court of the State of Indiana.

In one handsome demi-octavo volume. Price, One Dollar.

THE LIFE OF GEORGE FOX,

WITH DISSERTATIONS ON HIS VIEWS CONCERNING THE DOCTRINES, TESTIMONIES, AND DISCIPLINE OF THE CHRISTIAN CHURCH.

BY SAMUEL M. JANNEY.

One volume, 8vo. Price, $1 75.

KOLLIKER'S ANATOMY OF THE HUMAN BODY.

A Manual of Microscopical Anatomy of the Human Body.

BY ALBERT KOLLIKER,

Professor of Anatomy and Physiology in Wirtemberg.

TRANSLATED FROM THE GERMAN,

BY J. DA COSTA, M. D.,

Member of the Academy of Natural Sciences, Philadelphia.

WITH 315 WOOD-CUTS

One volume, 8vo.

THE

American Aboriginal Portfolio.

By Mrs. Mary H. Eastman.

WITH TWENTY-SEVEN SUPERB LINE ENGRAVINGS ON STEEL,

BY THE FIRST ARTISTS OF THE COUNTRY.

One volume folio, richly bound in ultramarine cloth, extra gilt. Price, $6 00.

LIBRARY FOR TRAVELLERS AND THE FIRESIDE.

The British Cabinet in 1853.

Being Sketches of the Lives of the Earl of Aberdeen, Lord John Russell, Lord Palmerston, Sir James Graham, Mr. Gladstone, Earl of Clarendon, Duke of Argyle, &c.

"This remarkable coalition Ministry is now in power, and its existence is regarded by many as marking a great epoch in the political history of Great Britain, in which the old barriers of class and party rivalry are seen to have at length given way, superseded entirely by the new and purer principles of an age of progress."

PRICE, SIXTY-THREE CENTS.

ELLET ON THE OHIO AND MISSISSIPPI RIVERS.

With Twelve Illustrations. One volume, octavo. Price, $3 00.

CASSIN'S BIRDS OF NORTH AMERICA.

Illustrations of the Birds of California, Texas, Oregon, BRITISH AND RUSSIAN AMERICA.

Intended to contain Descriptions and Figures of all North American Birds, not given by former American Authors, and

A General Synopsis of North American Ornithology.

By John Cassin,

Member of the Academy of Natural Sciences of Philadelphia; of the American Philosophical Society; of the Horticultural Society of Pennsylvania; of the New York Lyceum of Natural History, &c. &c.

The publication will be completed in thirty parts, to be furnished at as early periods as their proper execution can be effected, and which will probably be at intervals of from one to two months. Every part will contain five colored plates, and the work, when completed, will form two volumes, octavo. Price, One Dollar each part.

PERSONAL NARRATIVE OF SCENES AND ADVENTURES

IN THE

Semi-Alpine Region of the Ozark Mountains

OF MISSOURI AND ARKANSAS,

WHICH WERE FIRST TRAVERSED BY DE SOTO IN 1541.

BY HENRY ROWE SCHOOLCRAFT.

One Volume, demi-octavo. Price, $1 50.

Life and Adventures of a Country Merchant.

BY THE AUTHOR OF "WILD WESTERN SCENES," ETC.

ILLUSTRATED.

One volume, 12mo. Cloth, gilt. Price, One Dollar.

THE WINTER LODGE, OR VOW FULFILLED.

AN HISTORICAL NOVEL

THE SEQUEL TO SIMON KENTON.

BY JAMES WEIR.

One volume, 12mo. Price, paper, 50 cents; cloth, 75 cents.

ÆSOP'S FABLES.

A NEW STEREOTYPED EDITION, BEAUTIFULLY ILLUSTRATED.

18mo., cloth, gilt. Price, Fifty Cents.

CENTRAL ROUTE TO THE PACIFIC,

From the Valley of the Mississippi to California.

JOURNAL OF THE EXPEDITION OF E. F. BEALE,

SUPERINTENDENT OF INDIAN AFFAIRS IN CALIFORNIA,

AND

GWINN HARRIS HEAP,

From Missouri to California, in 1853.

BY GWINN HARRIS HEAP.

One volume, octavo, with fourteen Maps and Illustrations. Price, $1 50.

LARDNER'S

KEIGHTLEY'S UNIVERSAL HISTORY,

COMPRISING

A Concise History of the World from the Earliest Period.

BY THOMAS KEIGHTLEY,

Author of Mythology, Histories of Greece and Rome, England, &c.

REVISED AND BROUGHT DOWN TO THE PRESENT PERIOD,

With Questions and Illustrations.

One volume, 12mo. Cloth, embossed. Price, One Dollar.

The Beauties of History;

OR,

EXAMPLES OF THE OPPOSITE EFFECTS OF VIRTUE AND VICE.

FOR THE USE OF SCHOOLS AND FAMILIES.

One volume, 12mo., with Plates. Price, 62½ cents.

"There are here collected, within a narrow compass, the most striking examples of individual virtue and vice which are spread forth on the pages of history, or are recorded in personal biography. The noblest precepts are recommended for the guidance of youth, and in the most impressive manner is he taught to conquer the degrading impulses which lower the standard of the human character."

WINCHESTER'S CAMPAIGN IN 1812-13.

BY ELIAS DARNELL.

Half roan. Price, Twenty-five cents.

Weems's Life of Marion.

THE LIFE OF GEN. FRANCIS MARION,

A celebrated Partisan Officer in the Revolutionary War against the British and Tories in South Carolina and Georgia.

By Brig. Gen. P. Horry, of Marion's Brigade, and M. L. Weems.

12mo.; cloth, gilt; with five Engravings. Price, 75 cents.

WEEMS'S LIFE OF WASHINGTON.

THE LIFE OF GEORGE WASHINGTON,

WITH CURIOUS ANECDOTES, EQUALLY HONORABLE AND EXEMPLARY TO HIS YOUNG COUNTRYMEN.

BY M. L. WEEMS,

FORMERLY RECTOR OF MOUNT VERNON PARISH.

One volume, 12mo.; cloth, gilt; with six Engravings. Price, 75 cents.

RAMSEY'S HISTORY OF TENNESSEE.

THE ANNALS OF TENNESSEE,

FROM ITS SETTLEMENT,

TO THE

END OF THE EIGHTEENTH CENTURY.

By J. G. M. Ramsey, A. M., M. D.

One volume, 8vo. Price, cloth, $3 00; Library style, $3 50.

TRAVELS IN EGYPT AND PALESTINE.

BY J. THOMAS, M. D.

One Volume, 12mo. Price, 63 cents.

LIPPINCOTT, GRAMBO & CO.

Have made arrangements with the extensive Publishers, W. & R. CHAMBERS, of Edinburgh, to publish and supply the Trade in this country with their Publications, and hereafter will issue their Books simultaneously with publication in Great Britain. The following works will be the first issued:

CHAMBERS'S INFORMATION FOR THE PEOPLE.

AN ENTIRELY NEW AND IMPROVED EDITION.

Two volumes royal octavo, cloth.

CHAMBERS'S CYCLOPEDIA OF ENGLISH LITERATURE.

TWO VOLUMES ROYAL OCTAVO, CLOTH.

A Critical and Biographical History of English Writers in all departments of Literature, illustrated by specimens of their writings.

Chambers's Miscellany of Useful and Entertaining Tracts.

TWENTY VOLUMES, CAP OCTAVO.

This work was written with the view of supplying a useful and entertaining species of reading among the great mass of the community, and will be found adapted for SCHOOL and DISTRICT LIBRARIES.

Chambers's Repository of Instructive and Amusing Tracts.

FIVE VOLUMES ISSUED.

This work resembles in some respects the preceding Miscellany of Tracts, aiming at a higher, though not less popular tone, and will satisfy, it is hoped, the new requirements of the day in regard to literary elegance. Each volume is illustrated with wood engravings, and has a neatly engraved title-page.

CHAMBERS'S PAPERS FOR THE PEOPLE.

Twelve volumes, crown 12mo., fancy boards.

This series embraces History, Archæology, Biography, Science, the Industrial and Fine Arts, the leading topics in Social Economy, together with Criticism, Fiction, Personal Narrative, and other branches of Elegant Literature — each number containing a distinct subject.

CHAMBERS'S POCKET MISCELLANY,

In monthly volumes, 18mo.

TWENTY-ONE VOLUMES ISSUED.

This work consists partly of amusing papers reprinted from the early quarto volumes of "Chambers's Edinburgh Journal" — now irrecoverably out of print, and unknown to the young generation of readers — and partly of articles of a similar kind, for which space has not been found in the current numbers of that periodical, and is an excellent literary companion for the railway and the fireside.

CHAMBERS'S LIBRARY FOR YOUNG PEOPLE.

In twenty volumes, 12mo.; neatly done up in cloth.

This Series embraces Moral and Religious Tales, History, Poetry, and Subjects of General Information.

ALFRED IN INDIA; OR, SCENES IN HINDOOSTAN.
CLEVER BOYS, and other Stories.
DUTY AND AFFECTION; A TALE.
ENGLAND, HISTORY OF. By Frederica Rowan.
FIRESIDE AMUSEMENTS.
FRANCE, HISTORY OF. By Leitch Ritchie.
GRANDMAMMA'S POCKETS. By Mrs. S. C. Hall.
LITTLE ROBINSON, and other Tales.
MORAL COURAGE, and other Tales.
OLD ENGLAND, A TALE OF. By Thomas Miller.
ORLANDINO, A TALE. By Miss Edgeworth.
POEMS FOR YOUNG PEOPLE.
SCOTLAND, HISTORY OF. By Frederica Rowan.
SELF-DENIAL, JACOPO, and other Tales.
STEADFAST GABRIEL, A TALE. By Mary Howitt.
SWANN'S EGG, THE. By Mrs. S. C. Hall.
TRUE HEROISM, and other Stories.
TRUTH AND TRUST.
UNCLE SAM'S MONEY-BOX. By Mrs. S. C. Hall.
WHISPERER, THE. By Mrs. S. C. Hall.

Chambers's Instructive and Entertaining Library.

History of the French Revolutions from 1789 to 1849.

BY T. W. REDHEAD.

THREE VOLUMES.

Lamartine's Travels in the East,

INCLUDING A JOURNEY IN THE HOLY LAND.

WITH A MEMOIR OF THE AUTHOR.

IN TWO VOLUMES.

STORIES OF THE IRISH PEASANTRY.

BY MRS. S. C. HALL.

Biography, Exemplary and Instructive.

This work contains the Lives of the Principal Persons who have advanced Science and Art, the most remarkable Discoverers and Inventors, or those who have otherwise distinguished themselves.

THE PICTORIAL TREASURY,

A LARGE QUARTO,

WITH

SEVEN HUNDRED FINE ENGRAVINGS.

With an Illuminated Cover, Printed in Six Oil Colors.

PRICE, ONE DOLLAR.

THE CHILDREN'S PLEASURE BOOK,

A QUARTO,

WITH NEARLY

FIVE HUNDRED FINE ENGRAVINGS,

WITH A

Splendid Illuminated Cover, printed in Six Oil Colors.

PRICE, FIFTY CENTS.

THE CHILD'S PICTORIAL ALBUM,

A QUARTO,

WITH UPWARDS OF

FIVE HUNDRED FINE ENGRAVINGS,

With an Illuminated Cover, printed in Six Oil Colors.

PRICE, FIFTY CENTS.

DAY DREAMS.

With Additions by Martha Allen.

One volume, 12mo., cloth. Second Edition.

PRICE, SIXTY-THREE CENTS.

"'Tis to create, and in creating live
A being more intense, that we endow
With form or fancy, gaining as we give
The life we image, even as I do now."

Sketches of a romantic character, displaying a warm imagination and an ornate style.—Philada. Ledger.

Their perusal, we doubt not, will diffuse a general satisfaction; for they are beautiful, though brief.—M'Makin's Courier.

www.ingramcontent.com/pod-product-compliance
Lightning Source LLC
LaVergne TN
LVHW010742120826
845150LV00009B/1397

* 9 7 8 1 4 2 5 5 1 7 1 0 6 *

away. We were delayed some time after sunrise in consequence of most of the mules having gone astray; they were not recovered until near seven o'clock, when we resumed our journey. Our course was generally east, down a succession of valleys, whose surface was level and moist, with hills rising abruptly on either side. We saw a great abundance of game, but killed nothing but a grouse. These mountains teem with antelope, deer, and mountain sheep.

The valleys down which we travelled, and which opened into each other with the regularity of streets, grew gradually broader as we descended. We finally entered one watered by Carnero Creek, which joins the Garita in San Luis valley, and at noon encamped a short distance above a gate or gap through which the stream passes. Half a mile below this gap there is another, and a quarter of a mile farther a third; the passage through them is level, whilst the trail around them is steep and stony. In the afternoon, we went through the first gap, made a circuit around the second, as it was much obstructed with trees and bushes, and, leaving the third on our left, rode over some low hills, and five miles from camp crossed the Garita. We were once more in San Luis valley, and all before us was a perfect level, as far as the sight could reach. We encamped on the Rio Grande del Norte, as the sun was setting behind the pass in the Sierra de San Juan, at the head of the Del Norte. This pass was in sight of us, and is the one in which Colonel Frémont met with so terrible a disaster in the winter of 1848–49, so near was he to the object of his search, the Coochatope.

From the plains this pass appears to be more practicable than either the Carnero or the Coochatope; but it can be traversed only by mules, and by them only from the middle of August until the first snows fall, early in December. In winter it is impassable, and in spring, and until August, the River Del Norte, which flows through part of it, and is swollen with melting snows, is the principal obstruction. This pass is known to the Mexicans as the Puerto del Rio Del Norte (the Pass of the River Del Norte), but Americans call it *Williams's Pass*, in honor of "Old Bill Williams," who discovered it, and was Colonel Frémont's guide. Through it is the shortest road to Grand River, it being one day shorter than by the Carnero, and nearly two days shorter than by the Coochatope. The hills, for, as they appeared to us the band on foot. She said that they had subsisted on meat left them by their tribe, and ended by telling us that she had just buried her companion, who had died the previous night, and that she was now on her way to the summer rendezvous of her people, ladened with her own and her companion's packs. We informed her that she would probably overtake a band of Utahs that night or the next day, and placed her on their trail. She seemed glad to receive this news, and still more so when we turned our mules' heads to leave her, though we had shown her all possible kindness—so hard is it in them to believe in the sincerity of white people.

The trail led over low hills and down a succession of beautiful slopes, running mostly in a southerly direction, until we entered a narrow winding valley two and a half miles in length by one hundred to two hundred yards in breadth. It was shut in on each side by perpendicular walls of rock rising from fifty to seventy-five feet above the level of the valley, whose surface was flat and carpeted with tender grass. A stream of clear water meandered through its centre, and the grade was so slight that the stream, overflowing its banks in many places, moistened the whole surface.

As we descended this beautiful and singular valley, we occasionally passed others of a similar character opening into it. It ends in Sahwatch valley, which we entered about an hour before sunset.

We had here the choice of two routes: the first was down Sahwatch valley to its outlet near the head of the valley of San Luis, which would have taken us over the same ground that we had traversed in coming from Fort Massachusetts; the second crossed Sahwatch valley here, passed over a shorter and as good a route, and entered San Luis valley near where the Garita leaves the mountains. We selected the last route.

Coochatope Pass enters Sahwatch Valley a mile below Carnero Pass. Crossing Sahwatch valley, here half a mile broad, and the creek about ten yards in breadth and three feet in depth, we travelled up a narrow valley for a short distance into the hills, and encamped at dark. Day's travel, 47 miles; distance from Grand River, 138 miles.

July 3. During the early part of the night the mosquitos swarmed around us, but it soon became cold, which drove them

PREFACE TO THE AMERICAN EDITION.

THE following work was issued by the author in London, under the unassuming title of "Thoughts on Parts of the Book of Leviticus." The original work consists of an essay on each of the Offerings, together with notes on the first six chapters of Leviticus, in which the law of true offering is laid down. The present edition consists only of the essays, into which have been inserted such portions of the notes as seemed desirable for the more full presentation of the author's views. Some few foot notes have also been added by the editor from the writings of the author and from other sources. There has been no change of the author's language except in a few instances where a mere verbal correction has been made.

The author throughout recognizes, with Archbishop Magee, that the Sacrifices of the Mosaic economy "terminate in that grand and comprehensive Offering which was the primary object and the final consummation of the sacrificial institution." His aim is simply to place side by side the type and the antitype, in order that those for whom the great Sacrifice was offered may behold and rejoice in its perfectness.

Those who peruse the work with care will probably be led to admire the wisdom of God, as shown in the types which he has been pleased to use for the instruction of his children. It has been well said, "By them does God bring within the range of our capacity definite views of the details of Christ's work, which, perhaps, but for these pictures, we should never fully, or at least so fully, apprehend."

In his views of the significance of the Offerings the author is in essential accord with the most judicious expounders of the Mosaic ritual. Those who have attempted to unfold the meaning of the special offerings while overlooking their distinct reference to the one perfect sacrifice of Christ, have been always involved in hopeless embarrassments. What Kurtz, in his "Sacrificial Worship of the Old Testament," says of the Sin and Trespass-offerings, may well be applied to the offerings in general: "There is scarcely a single question connected with the whole range of biblical theology on which there has been so much pure conjecture, and about the settlement of which theological science was so late in arriving at a correct conclusion, although the foundations for it evidently existed in the biblical text, and were not very difficult to find." We should not have had so much vain conjecture had interpreters fully understood and faithfully applied the principle of Augustine: "The New Testament is hidden in the Old; the Old Testament is unfolded in the New."

The work is now reproduced in the hope that it may be used by the Holy Spirit to promote the peace and joy of believers in Christ. It is his blessed office-work to cause believers to "know the things that are freely given to us of God." In doing this he fulfills the word of the Lord: "He shall glorify me; for he shall receive of mine, and shall show it unto you." Christ is too often regarded by believers as merely their Sin-offering or their Trespass-offering. These are important and precious aspects of his work. But they do not represent fully his Perfect Sacrifice. Those who have been led by the Holy Spirit to know him also in the Burnt-offering, the Meat-offering, and the Peace-offering, will find in the view thus opened to them fresh occasion for gratitude and love. When the Lord Jesus Christ is known in all the aspects of his Perfect Sacrifice, the believer will begin to comprehend more fully the blessedness of those who are "complete in him."

CONTENTS.

THE PERFECT SACRIFICE.

CHAPTER I.

INTRODUCTORY.

THE first anxiety of every soul awakened to consider its relation to God concerns its own salvation. Its cry is, "What must I do to be saved?" That cry God has answered. He has said, and the words remain written forever, "BELIEVE ON THE LORD JESUS CHRIST, AND THOU SHALT BE SAVED." Our faith may be feeble; our appreciation of sin weak; our knowledge of Christ poor. We may be little able to say, that we are humbled as we should be humbled; or that we reverence God as we should reverence him; or that we value Christ as we should value him: nevertheless, whosoever with the feeblest faith casts himself on God thus preaching peace through Jesus Christ, "HATH everlasting life, and shall not come into condemnation, but IS PASSED from death unto life." John v. 24. His own worthless name is set aside ; it is, as it were, blotted out ; and he stands accepted in the name of Another. He is "justified freely"—"has peace with God"—"has received reconciliation."

But whilst the Scripture thus plainly points to the door by which we enter the everlasting fold, another of its objects is to instruct those who are within. We enter the fold not as sheep that have never wandered, but as sheep that have gone astray—ignorant, therefore, and weak—still exposed to temptation—still prone to wander; and as such, needing instruction, guidance, consolation. This the Scripture is intended to supply; and such peculiarly is the object of the book of Leviticus. It explains to those who *have* believed, the fullness and completeness of their redemption. Israel, to whom were given in types the shadows of those mercies which are made to *us* verities in Christ—Israel received the book of Leviticus, not whilst they were in

Egypt, not *before* they received the typical sign of salvation in the blood of the Passover lamb, but *after* they had quitted Egypt—*after* they had been saved from its judgment—*after* they had been recognized as the redeemed of the Lord. The midnight cry which suddenly arose from every Egyptian dwelling, was heard in none of the families of Israel. Strengthened by the food on which they had secretly fed in their houses marked with the blood of the lamb, they entered the wilderness, not as strangers to God and to his mercies, but as a people whom God had chosen for himself, to learn his ways, and to maintain his testimonies.

One of the chief and most peculiar mercies granted to them in the wilderness, was the Tabernacle—the place of "appointed meeting" between themselves and God. There, as soon as it was reared up, God instituted those sacrifices which formed the basis of Israel's rest in *him*, and of his ability, without derogation from his holiness, to rest in *them*. SACRIFICE, therefore, is the great thought of Leviticus throughout. The altar with its holy fire seeking that whereon it might feed—the claim of the altar duly met by accepted offering—God satisfied and honored—the worshiper protected, instructed, and blessed—these are the subjects of which the book of Leviticus treats. Believers learn in it the riches which are theirs in Christ Jesus : they learn also to see in the light of God's holiness, as well as of his grace, the nature of those short-comings and sins which need that those riches should be substituted for their poverty in the presence of God. They learn, too, how they are consecrated as his priestly servants to serve him in the midst of holy, and also in the midst of unholy things.

The commencing chapters of Leviticus present to us *five* different aspects of the sacrificial service of Christ, varied according to the variety of those needs in us, which the grace of the One Sacrifice is designed to meet. The want of that *full and unreserved devotedness* which is due on our part to God, and claimed by him, but which is by us never rendered, is met by that abounding grace which has appointed Another, perfect in devotedness and self-renunciation, to be a *Burnt-offering* in our room. The manifold deficiencies in our personal *characters*—the presence in them of so much that should be absent, and the absence of so much that should be present, is met by the presentation of him for us, the perfectness of whose character is here typified by the excellency of the *Meat-offering.* The condition of our *nature,* which is enmity against God, because sin, essential sin dwells in it, is met by the efficacy of the *Peace-sacrifice,* whereby, notwithstanding the enmity of our nature, peace with the Holy One becomes our portion. *Sin,* even when committed in such intensity of blindness, as that we understand not the heinousness of that which we are doing, and perhaps mistake it for good—such sin is met by the *Sin-offering:* or if it be *committed knowingly,* not under the blindness of ignorance, but in the willfulness of a heart that consciously refuses to be restrained, it is met by the grace of the *Trespass-offering.* Such are the aspects under which the perfectness of the One Sacrifice is presented to us in the first chapters of Leviticus. The aspects are various, but the sacrifice is one; just as the colors of the rainbow may for instruction-sake be presented to us separately, but the rainbow which they unitedly constitute is one. After we have learned in distinctness, we combine in unity. Nor is there any division of the perfectness of the One Sacrifice in its application to them that believe. From the first moment we believe, the perfectness of Christ's sacrifice is in all its totality ours. We may not, perhaps, either appreciate or understand all that is typified by these various offerings, yet the united value of them all is reckoned to us by God. As we "grow in grace, and in the knowledge of our Lord and Saviour," we understand more, and appreciate better; but by such growth in understanding we do not *make* the blessing ours—we only apprehend that which *is* ours.

CHAPTER II.

THE BURNT OFFERINGS.

LEVITICUS I.

It must be self-evident to all who reflect on the perfections of God, that he as the Governor of the universe must maintain those perfections unsullied, and must require that they should be duly recognized, and duly responded to by his creatures. The claims of God are never arbitrary. He only requires that which is needful to the happiness, as well as to the holiness of his creatures. The happiness of heaven is this, that God being known and his character appreciated, he is necessarily, and if I may so say, naturally loved and honored. It requires no effort in sinless beings to love and honor One who is essentially worthy of all honor, and all love. In heaven, as soon as God is known, he is loved—spontaneously loved; and we can easily conceive how the absence of such love must, in the judgment of heaven, be deemed the evidence of deepest sin. The power of that first and greatest commandment, "Thou shalt love the Lord thy God with all thy heart, and with all thy soul, and with all thy might," is well understood in heaven; and a heart that for one moment fails therein, is instantly understood to be under the plague of sin.

But the thoughts of earth are very diverse from those of heaven. Here we are so accustomed to fall short of God's glory, and failure in glorifying him is so much regarded as the necessary law of our condition, that even believers find it difficult to look on failure in devotedness as sin—sin that needs atonement as much as their most dire transgressions. Even after we have owned the blood of the Paschal Lamb as delivering from the judgment due to our natural condition, and after we have recognized the necessity of the Holy One bearing the curse earned by our trangressions, we nevertheless fail to estimate the want of perfect devotedness as being positive sin; and hence the appreciation of our own condition, as well as of the grace that meets it, becomes proportionately enfeebled.

In order to correct this error—an error fatal to all right apprehension of God, and our relation both to his holiness and to his grace—the first lesson given to us in the Tabernacle respects the whole Burnt-offering. We might perhaps have expected on entering that place of appointed meeting with God, to hear first respecting our palpable trangressions or sins. Our minds intuitively turn to the Trespass-offering, or to the Sin-offering; for conscience without much difficulty recognizes that trangression violates our relation to a holy God. Yet neither of these offerings is presented to our regard when God first speaks from the Tabernacle of Congregation. His first commandment respected the Holocaust, or whole Burnt-offering.

The Hebrew word which is rendered in the Greek version "Holocaust" (whole Burnt-offering), and in our version "Burnt-offering," means properly "that which ascends." It was called "the Ascending-offering," either because it was wholly lifted up or caused to ascend upon the altar, or because it was wholly burned on the altar and thence ascended in sweet smelling fragrance as a sweet savor of rest before Jehovah. In other offerings part was sometimes given to the priest, sometimes to the offerer; but the Burnt-offering was *all* (the skin only excepted) rendered to God, and *all* burnt upon his altar. In the Burnt-offering, therefore, there was a distinct recognition of the righteous claim of God on the unreserved devotedness of his creatures; but it was also the confession that that claim was responded to by none. When an offerer presented a victim to be accepted in his room, the very act of substitution implied, that the offerer acknowledged himself to be destitute of the qualifications which were found in his offering: otherwise, substitution would not be needed, for the offerer would stand in his own integrity. There was the confession, too, that the absence of these qualifications involved guilt—guilt deserving death; for otherwise the offering would not have been substantially slain—"killed before Jehovah;" and lastly, there was the acknowledgment that because no unreserved devotedness had been found in him, he needed an offering to be wholly given in his stead as "a sweet savor of rest before Jehovah."

The Burnt-offering therefore may be regarded as the type of Christ in respect of that full, unreserved devotedness of service, which caused him as the Servant of Jehovah, in all things to renounce himself, and to render every energy, and every feeling, and finally his life itself, as a whole Burnt-offering unto God. Perfect in understanding, perfect in every mental, as well as moral power, he nevertheless glorified not himself by these powers, but unreservedly devoted them to God. If he meditated, it was for God; if he spake, or if he acted, it was for him. He knew him whom he served, and he fully loved him. He appreciated the character of God—understood his counsels—knew what was needful to the maintenance of his glory, and met perfectly all its claims. Christ only could say, "I have set the Lord always before me." "My meat and my drink is to do my Father's will." "I came not to do mine own will, but the will of him that sent me, and to finish his work." And when, at the close of his course of sorrow, he might have asked the Father to deliver him from the Cross and from the wrath thereon endured—when, to use his own words, he could have prayed to the Father, and he would presently have given him more than twelve legions of angels, he refused so to pray—he asked for no such deliverance, but meekly said, "Father, glorify thy name." Here was the unreserved devotedness unto God which the Burnt-offering typified. "He was obedient unto death, even the death of the Cross." The Cross had many other significations, many other relations; but one thing marked on it was the unshrinking obedience of him who there suffered—One indeed who had ever said, "Father, not my will, but thine, be done."

The first act in offering the Holocaust was its solemn presentation before Jehovah. Before it was placed upon the altar, and before it was slain, it was brought in its living perfectness to the door of the Tabernacle of Congregation, and was there presented before Jehovah. There the offerer, standing as in the presence of Jehovah, identified himself with the offering by firmly leaning his hand upon its head. It was equivalent to saying, "Let this offering be regarded, as if it were myself; I lean on it as my support before thee." The offering thus presented for his acceptance, was accepted for him to make "atonement for him," or literally, "to place a covering over him."*

The offering was thus presented *"for the acceptance"* of the offerer—I say for his acceptance, for such is the right translation of the words, לרצנו as they are rightly rendered by the Septuagint (δεκτον) and by the Vulgate (*acceptabilis*). Indeed, our own translators have so rendered

* "In this way," says Kurtz, "we understand the covering of Sin in the Sacrificial worship, as a covering by which the accusating and damnatory power of sin—its power to excite the anger and wrath of God—is broken; by which, in fact, it is rendered both harmless and impotent. * * * It is so complete, effectual and overpowering a covering that all real and active force in that which is covered up is thereby rendered impossible, or slain." Katmis says, "To expiate, literally to cover up, does not mean to cause a sin not to have been committed, for that is impossible; nor to represent it as having no existence, for that would be opposed to the correctness of the law; nor to pay or compensate it by any performance; but to cover it before God, i. e., to deprive it of its power to come between us and God."

them in Lev. xxiii. 11, "He shall wave the sheaf before Jehovah *to be accepted for you.*" And again, in Exod. xxviii. 38, "And it (that is, the golden plate) shall always be upon Aaron's forehead that they may *be accepted* before the Lord." When this alteration is made, the concluding words of the following verse are brought into their proper correspondency: "He shall offer it *for his acceptance* before Jehovah . . . . and *it shall be accepted for him.*"

The mis-translation of these words has led many to imagine that the Burnt-offering was distinctively a voluntary offering: whereas, it is contrasted with voluntary offerings, as in the following passage, "a Burnt-offering or sacrifice in performing a vow or in a *free-will-offering.*" Num. xv. 2. Not only was the Burnt-offering *demanded* by the ordinance of God from Israel unitedly, as in the daily Burnt-offering, and in the annual ceremonies of the Day of Atonement, but it was continually required of individual Israelites. See Lev. xii. and xiv. Indeed, an Israelite, who walked in the fear of God, would feel himself under perpetual obligation to bring a

Burnt-offering, whenever he became conscious of failing in right devotedness towards God—and that might be more often than the day. When seeking through the Burnt-offering *atonement*, because of *not* having loved the Lord his God with *all* his strength, he would no more think that he was bringing "a free-will-offering," than he would think so, when bringing a sin-offering or a trespass-offering. If the latter were required when he *had* done things that were *forbidden*, the Burnt-offering was equally required when he had *not* done that which was commanded. The same Law that said, "Thou shalt *not* covet," said also, "Thou *shalt* love."

This presentation of the living victim in its *perfectness* (for it was to be a male—the type of strength and energy; and it was to be without blemish) is to be distinguished from its death, and from its being burned upon the altar. It was presented indeed in order that it might be slain and burned; and without its being so slain and burned, there could have been no atonement, no acceptance for the offerer. Nevertheless, the act of presentation is to be considered by itself. It typifies the believer's recognition of the living excellency which individually characterized the Lord Jesus here—that excellency in virtue of which he was known as the "righteous Servant,"—"the faithful and the true Witness"—"the Lover of righteousness," and "the Hater of iniquity." The Lord Jesus had a personal, individual history of his own; and we can easily understand how, in the case of those, who, like John and Peter, knew, loved, and followed him, the thought of what Jesus personally had been, formed as real and distinct a subject of meditation as any of the results which flowed from his having been given unto death for them. They knew indeed the value of that death; they estimated the value of its results, but they knew also the value of THE PERSON who had died. They remembered, and they understood those words once and again uttered from heaven, "This is my beloved Son, in whom I am well pleased." Indeed, their apprehension of the living service of their Master, formed one of the chief elements in their knowledge of him, and of God. Understanding the excellency of him in whom they trusted, they appreciated the blessedness of those who, like themselves, had leaned their sinful hand upon the holy head of the Burnt-offering.

After having been thus presented, the victim was slain. If there should be in our minds a disposition to speak lightly of failure in devotedness, and to extenuate its evil, as if it were something easily to be excused in persons circumstanced as we, we find in the death of the Burnt-offering the answer which God has given to thoughts so dishonoring to himself, and so destructive of all right apprehensions of sin. The fact of the Burnt-offering being slain—*slain for atonement*, is an abiding witness, that want of devotedness to God is a sin that can only be "covered" by death—expiatory death. There are, indeed, other aspects in which we may consider sin. We may see it in the hidden depravity and uncleanness of our nature; we may trace it in the facility with which we fall ignorantly into transgression; or we may discover it in many a form of deliberate and willful disobedience; but there is no more convincing evidence of its power, to those who are acquainted with the character of God, than that want of devotedness to him, whereby ourselves, and not God, become the chief object of our heart's devotion and love. When the disciples learned at last to know God in and through Christ, when they began to appreciate the perfect devotedness that had marked the service of their Lord, they found in their own want of likeness to him, evidences of guilt too deep to be met availingly by any thing else than atoning death. They needed not to look to their palpable transgressions for proof that they required that another should die in their room; they found it in the fact that they had *chiefly* loved themselves.

But before the offering was placed upon the altar, another ceremony was appointed: it was to be flayed and divided into its parts. The head, representing powers of intelligence, observation, and directive control; the fat, which indicates healthfulness and vigor in the parts to which it pertains; the inwards, which typify the inward activities of thought and feeling; the legs, which denote the path practicallv pursued—these various parts were all carefully distinguished from each other before they were given to the altar. In this, again, we see the importance attached in Scripture to a knowledge of what Christ was whilst living and acting here ; for it was here that he showed how all his powers, inward and outward, were wholly and always dedicated to God. Even if no results had ever flowed to us therefrom, the living dedication of Christ would not have lost its excellency. It was excellent in itself apart rom all its results, and, as we learn from this type, is to be considered not carelessly, but with minute and accurate discrimination by all who would appreciate the full value of the Burnt-offering. It must be observed, however, that that living value is, at this stage of the offering, regarded as something past: the victim *had been* slain—its energies arrested by death—its life taken from the earth. In such knowledge, therefore, apart from the altar, and from the priestly ministration thereon, there would have been only sorrow—sorrow like that of the disciples who went to the sepulchre with their spices, or who journeyed to Emmaus and were sad.

They mourned over him who was gone, but they understood not the purposes of God—they had, as yet, no view of the altar—no knowledge of the manner in which the holy fire of that altar had fed on and been satisfied with the excellency of him for whom they sorrowed. But the moment their eyes were opened to understand the work which God's hand had wrought—the moment they stood, as it were, by the side of the Burnt-offering altar and understood the ministrations there, their sorrow was turned into joy. There they could consider all the sinfulness of their deficiencies, and think of God in all the fullness of his attributes, and yet rejoice in the knowledge, that all had been met by an offering that had ascended, as a sweet savor of rest, before Jehovah forever.

We can, indeed, scarcely estimate the change that took place in the apprehensions of the disciples, when first they began to think of God as accepting them in the perfectness of the offering of Christ, or to use typical language, when they became acquainted with the fire which had fed on the perfectness of the Burnt-offering. That fire represented the searching holiness of God. Israel had beheld that holy fire in Egypt when it burned terribly against the Egyptians. Peter became conscious of its presence, when, astounded by the manifestation of Almighty power in Jesus, he said, "Depart from me; for I am a sinful man, O Lord." The lesson of the Burnt-offering altar he had not yet learned. There, indeed, the fire was seen unchanged as to its holiness: its relation to every thing merely human was taught in the wood given to it to be consumed: but the wood was not the only thing that was given—the Burnt-offering, also, was laid upon the altar; and the fire, as it fed thereon, although still the type of holiness, became the type of holiness *placated.* The coal from the altar could, after this, touch the lips of the unclean, and it could be said, "Lo, this hath touched thy lips, and thy iniquity is taken away, and thy sin purged."

The Burnt-offering was a sweet savor of rest unto Jehovah. The word "rest,"* omitted in

* "Savor of rest or sweetness," that which delights or satisfies.—AM. ED.

our version, is important, as showing how much it is the object of the whole passage to keep prominently before us the great doctrine of SATISFACTION in connection with this offering. Two things were needful in order that God might rest in his people. In the first place his violated law required a satisfaction that could be rendered only by death—atoning death; but his claim for positive perfectness must be satisfied, too. God could not rest in those to whom no righteousness attached, any more than he could rest in those whose guilt was unforgiven. Imputation of righteousness, therefore, was needed, and was granted in virtue of the same great act that gave them immunity from wrath. He who bore in their stead the stroke of judgment, did at the same moment present for them his own personal excellency to God. The offerer, as he beheld the altar breathing forth towards heaven its cloud of fragrance, saw in that fragrance something that was attributed to himself. He learned in it the blessed truth of IMPUTATION.*

* It has been said by some of late that there never can be any progress in real truth, unless we get rid

How far believers need such "imputation," it must be left to their own consciences to decide. The history of Christianity is no bright picture. The path even of real Christians has been sorrowfully marked by the want of single-eyed devotedness to God. Eager to reign as kings before the hour for the supremacy of Truth has come, and impatient of "the endurance of the kingdom of Jesus," even real Christians early despised the Apostle's chiefest honor, and shrunk from being regarded as "the filth of the earth, and the offscouring of all things," for Christ's sake. Even the brightest instances of individual faith, when narrowly examined, show how little any among the sons of men can say—"I have set the

---

of the absurd doctrine of imputation. No doubt it is a doctrine peculiarly adverse to the schemes of those who wish to make men happy apart from Christ. Men say, where is it taught in Scripture? We might rather ask, where is it *not* taught? Every page that alludes to the altar sending up the sweet-smelling savor of its offerings teaches it. Would the Scripture, which cannot lie, teach me that that ascends for me which does not ascend for me; and if it ascends for me, its excellency is attributed to me; and that is imputation.

Lord always before me." We are they of whom the Lord Jesus prophetically said, that "offences should abound" amongst us, and that because of them, the love, even of the greater part of us—his people—should wax cold. Yet the sin even of believers cannot frustrate the purposes of the grace of God. The Burnt-offering altar remains what it ever was; its offering retains its efficacy, and in virtue thereof, the church unitedly, and each believer individually, stands before God, not only protected from the consequences of their failure, but accepted according to the excellency of him who has lived and who has died for them. They will enter into the presence of God, not as those who are to be oppressed by the recollection and sense of their failure; but as those who are to be welcomed and rejoiced over, because encompassed by the results of the sacrifice and service of Another. Our title to this blessing is not affected by the degree of our faith, nor by the depth of our spiritual experience, nor by the character of our service. It is given on the ground of what Christ is, and becomes the inheritance of the believer solely because of him.

The thief on the cross, and the jailer at Philippi, when they believed, could have had little knowledge of their condition—little estimate of sin—little experimental acquaintance with truth—little appreciation of Christ and the fullness of his salvation. Yet Paul himself, when able to say, "I have fought the good fight, I have finished my course, I have kept the faith," was not more certainly under the efficacy of this most precious offering than were they, from the first moment they believed. The babe that falls asleep in Jesus has, as regards this, the same title as an apostle; because that title is, in either case, derived exclusively from Another.

But whilst we have firmly to maintain the prerogative of grace, in giving according to its own bountifulness out of its own riches; and have jealously to guard those blessings which are the common heritage of believers, we must not on that account despise such present blessings, as are by God's own appointment made dependent on *growth* in the knowledge of Christ our Saviour. A knowledge not necessary for acceptance may be necessary for our comfort, and for the right direction of our service here. When first our eye is turned believingly towards Christ our Passover, we are quickened by the Spirit, and he begins to dwell within us. To quicken is the work of the Spirit towards us when we are in the world; to teach us respecting Christ, and to cause us to appreciate the things freely given to us of God, is his work towards us when we are in the church. If then the Scriptures describe our relation to God after we have believed, by the type of one standing at the altar under the full acceptance of the ascending offering, should we not seek to recognize this as our position, even though it be true that we are safe without such recognition? If the priests bearing the holy fire, and laying thereon the wood, be a type of believers occupied in the service of the sanctuary, there learning to estimate God's holiness which is as the fire, in contrast with all that is merely natural which is as the wood, who would not desire to have an experimental acquaintance with such things? Yet the soul of a believer may, as regards its experience, linger in the Land of Egypt, and never know the lessons of the Tabernacle. It may think of Christ as One who delivers from coming wrath —it may recognize the fire of divine holiness as burning destructively against Egypt and its works—it may even appreciate its own immunity from that wrath through the blood marked on the door-posts and doors, and yet be a stranger to the Tabernacle; for to know the blood so sprinkled (blessed as such knowledge is) is not the same thing as beholding it presented at the altar, and there accepted with the offering of sweet-smelling savor. The one speaks of deliverance from destruction; the other of heavenly acceptance and joy in God. How different the place of an Israelite standing in the dark midnight scene of Egypt's judgment, and an Israelite standing as an accepted worshiper by the side of the altar in the Tabernacle of God! How different the aspect of that holy fire which on the night of Israel's release shone terribly against their foes, and the aspect of the same holy fire when seen in the Tabernacle on the Burnt-offering altar! There it could be approached—there the priests could handle it—could consider its nature and acquaint themselves with its character. There they could learn what it eschewed, and on what it delighted to feed. If in Egypt they found deliverance, in the Tabernacle they found him who had delivered. In thinking of Egypt, we learn what we leave; in entering the Tabernacle we learn whereunto we have come. New interests, new comforts, new prospects, new employments open on us when first we begin to appreciate our place at the altar. The abiding interests of eternal life are there.

I have already said that the appreciation of these things is not necessary to our acceptance; nevertheless, none that desire to advance in the knowledge of Christ will despise that typical unfolding of the riches of redemption which the book of Leviticus supplies. We *ought* to estimate Christ as there typified; we *ought* to apprehend his various relations to God and to ourselves as they are there shadowed. We should *desire* to be able to say of each particular type, that it had been verified, more or less, in the apprehensions of our souls. In this way, Leviticus becomes a most useful test, whereby to prove our spiritual experience. Our experience falls short of that which it might be, just in proportion as it fails to realize the manifold relations of the one great Sacrifice here typically indicated. Such falling short in our experience does not take from us the gift of salvation, for that is of grace through faith; yet, although not less secure, we are less happy—less able also to serve God. He might be very sure of having attained maturity in the knowledge of Christ, who could say that the experience of his heart accorded with the types of this holy book; but who amongst us will pretend to this? Are not our attempts even to sketch what these types are, mere feebleness? Nor should we have courage to attempt it, if God made us offenders for a word, or if he despised the day of small things.

In considering then the Burnt-offering, our minds are not directed, as in the case of some of the other offerings, to the effects resulting from positive trangression. They who can only discern sin when its consequences are made manifest in dark iniquity, will little appreciate the Burnt-offering. It will be estimated only by that heart that has well considered the duty and the joy of loving and serving God because of what he is, and the sin and misery of not serving him. He who is truly prepared to say, "I have never loved him as I should have loved him, and therein is my sin:" "I have never sought his favor as I should have sought it, although I know that in his favor is life"—he only who is prepared to make this confession will really appreciate the Burnt-offering. Want of devoted love is the sin that the Burnt-offering covers; the favor of the living God is the blessing that its acceptance brings. Through it we can look up and see, as it were, Heaven opened, and hear the voice which said, "This is my beloved Son, in whom I am well pleased," and appropriate the blessing of those words even to our own sinful selves, because we can say, "accepted in the beloved."

To use aright the grace of the Burnt-offering requires, whilst we remain in the flesh, continued watchfulness: else we may sit down under the shadow of its mercies and slumber. When protection in the earth was by the especial gift of God granted to Cain, the opportunities which that protection gave were instantly used by him against God. It may be said, what else could be expected from the unregenerate heart of Cain?—but it must be remembered that unregenerate energies are still found in the flesh even of the regenerate. "In our flesh no good thing dwelleth;" but sin—essential sin, is there. "The flesh lusteth against the Spirit." And although the protection vouchsafed to Cain was a temporary mercy only; and although no Burnt-offering spread the power of its acceptance over his guilty head, and therefore in him unregeneracy might be expected to work and to bring forth its proper fruits, yet what shall we say of another—him who is first mentioned in Scripture as standing by the side of a Burnt-offering altar? Noah offered whole burnt-offerings, and the Lord smelled a sweet savor of rest and made a covenant of blessing, and under it Noah rested: but to what did he devote his energies? to planting a vineyard for himself and cherishing its fruits, till he drank the wine thereof and became drunken and dishonored. Can there be any other result, when the church, forgetting its high and separate calling, finds its chief present use of the grace of redemption, in trying to sanctify to itself mere earthly joys? What then can be expected, but that it will drink of the wine of the earth, till it becomes naked and dishonored, and the voice of the mocker cries, Aha, Aha!

It was otherwise with the Apostle Paul. Who knew, as he, the value of the Burnt-offering and the joy of its acceptance? Yet to him, "to live was Christ;" and he labored on till he could say, "I have fought the good fight, I have kept the faith, I have finished my course with joy." And why this difference? It was because the Apostle better understood, that the only true place of blessing was "the *new* creation." His soul followed, as it were, the offering to the place into which its sweet-savor ascended—even above the heavens. Heaven, and not earth, he recognized as the sphere in which the results of its preciousness are alone to be made fully manifest. There he knew its excellency was being treasured for him—his hope was in the new creation. He sought therefore after no vineyard in the earth; his treasure was above, and his heart there also.

But there is yet another relation of the altar of Burnt-offering; it is the place at which we may ourselves serve. The grace of the Lord Jesus, which has given us acceptance, has not shut us out from that which he considered, whilst here, his peculiar joy—the service of God. Therefore, he has consecrated an altar for us, and left it as the place for *our* service, and for *our* gifts. The object indeed for which the Lord Jesus served, was essentially different from any that can be proposed to us; for he served in order that he might redeem. In life, and in death, he acted and suffered only as the Redeemer; but none of us can redeem our brother, nor give unto God "a ransom for him." Moreover his service was in itself perfect, and was accepted in its own intrinsic excellency; whereas ours, being imperfect, can only be accepted through him. Nevertheless, we through him draw nigh to serve the same God. He gave us an example, that we should follow his steps. If he found in devotedness to God the spring of his joys, in a world which was to him, otherwise, as the valley of the shadow of death, a path of similar character is, through his grace, opened to us. We too may render the powers of our being unto God. We too may spend upon others, and not upon ourselves. We too may receive the approbation and praise of God—his approbation here—his praise in the day of the glory of Jesus. It was but a small thing for the Philippians to part with a little of their worldly goods in order to relieve the need of an apostle of God, yet how is this their gift spoken of in the Scripture? It is spoken of as "an odor of a sweet smell, a sacrifice acceptable, well-pleasing to God." The value of Christ was reckoned to it: it ascended in the value of the offering that had been burned on the Burnt-offering altar. Who then would not desire to serve such a God—to serve on such terms as these? This is the true way of learning to deny ourselves. It is comparatively a light thing to lose our lives in this world, if we gain these employments, and these compensating joys in the Tabernacle of God. Self-denial, as self-denial, must necessarily be painful; but when accompanied by the happy consciousness of accepted service, the pain is counterbalanced; or rather commuted into joy. The self-devised austerity of ascetism has no element in common with this. It knows nothing of the altar of Burnt-offering, nothing of the happy liberty of the service of Christ.

When the soul even feebly apprehends these things, it cannot but desire to dwell in this Tabernacle, and to serve at this altar. "Blessed are they that dwell in thy courts: they shall be still praising thee." "I had rather be a door-keeper in the house of my God, than to dwell in the tents of wickedness." Nevertheless, we must be prepared to learn in the Tabernacle many an humbling lesson respecting our own incapacities, and our want of thorough devotedness to God. Humiliation will be one result of every right attempt to serve him fully. Yet this will only enhance our sense of the excellency of the service of him who served, and who died at that altar for us. We shall the more gladly lay our hands on the head of that holy victim, and bless God for that wondrous provision of his grace that has made its excellency ours. We shall meditate with the more joy on that coming hour, when the great manifested proof of our having been accepted in the value of the Great Offering will be given, by our receiving in attestation of its preciousness, change—such change as shall leave in us nothing that is weak, nothing that is unworthy, but shall give us new powers of being, to know as we are known, and to love, and to serve perfectly. Then only shall we fully understand the results of the Burnt-offering having been accepted for us.

CHAPTER III.

THE MEAT-OFFERING.

LEVITICUS II.

INSTANCES of devotedness have, through God's grace, been not altogether wanting in his church. Some have been enabled to make great personal sacrifices for the truth, and have even triumphed because of it over torture and death. Courage and constancy have thrown a lustre around the name of many a martyr; and in closely examining their personal histories, we expect perhaps to find all as bright as the halo that surrounds their memories. But who that has made such examination has not felt a measure of keen disappointment at the result? Minute inspection discloses numberless deficiencies in the character of those whose path seems most marked with brightness. Worldliness, impetuosity, and sometimes bitterness and pride, have tinged deeply the words and the ways of those who have been ready to submit unhesitatingly to torment or to death. Many whose devotedness has been extended through a lengthened series of years—who have received much discipline, and been subjected to countless sorrows, have nevertheless betrayed again and again thoughts little brought into harmony with those of Christ. Self-will and independency of spirit have ofttimes swayed their course. Ignorance, perhaps, of Scripture has led them to despise truth and justify evil: or else, their proud minds, refusing to bow to the simplicity of revealed truth, have, to use the words of the apostle, "replied against God." Every thought has not been brought into captivity to the mind of Christ.

There has however been One, whose unreserved devotedness, perfect as it was in life and in death, has been equalled by the perfectness of his character even in its minutest traits. Indeed, no *perfectness* of devotedness can exist where perfectness of character is wanting. Acts of devotedness there may be; but even those acts will, if the character of the agent be imperfect, exhibit some flaw, patent to the eye of God, even if hidden from the observation of men. *Acts* of devotedness may owe their origin to constraint of circumstances; as, for example, when there is no alternative between confession of the truth or apostacy: or they may spring from impulses that are irregular and fitful. Such devotedness may be sincere: it may have in it principles of faithfulness which God may recognize, and, through his grace in Christ, honor; but how different such *deeds* of devotedness from that *unreserved devotedness of heart* which is only found where the character is perfect! There can be nothing irregular, nothing wrongly balanced, nothing fitful in the thoughts and actions of one whose character is perfect. Perfectness of character can only be where every inward feeling, as well as every outward form of action, is in habitual conformity with God. The understanding, the desire, and the deliberate purpose of the heart, must all be ordered aright. The counsel that is formed within, the word that is expressed, or the deed that is done, must be perfect in the mode of its development, as well as of its conception. The will of God must be made the only test. No appeal must be made to any thing short of his perfectness; and, when all things have been measured by this standard and no deficiency found—when inward and outward conformity to the mind of God has been strictly and unvaryingly maintained—then, and then only, can perfectness of character be claimed. Such was the perfectness of the character of the Lord Jesus.*

But although there is this close connection between devotedness and perfectness of character, so that one in reality involves the other, yet they may be contemplated separately. The disciples when they called to remembrance the personal history of the Lord Jesus, might at one moment think of the manner in which he had dedicated himself and all his powers always to God, and this would have shown them the devoted One; at another moment they might consider the principles and habits he had developed: they

* "In accordance with this close connection between "devotedness" and "character," the Meat-offering may virtually be considered as an appendage to the Burnt-offering. See Numbers xv. 3, 4. The words Burnt-offering" and "his or its Meat-offering" are of continual occurrence. There was also a Burnt-offering perpetual, and a Meat-offering perpetual.

might ask what he had sanctioned, and what condemned, whom he had approved, and whom eschewed; and this would have taught them his character. Reflection on the manner in which the great devoted One had dedicated himself to God, would necessarily be accompanied by meditation on the aspect in which he had morally presented himself among men. They would see him holy, harmless, meek, lowly, and gentle; they would remember how the unction of the Spirit of holiness had ever characterized his ways; they would think how all that leavening power of evil that had infused its bitterness into the sentiments and habits of men, was in him never found—such would be their thoughts respecting him—thoughts that would teach them of his character, or, in other words, would lead them to the knowledge of the MEAT-OFFERING.*

* It has been sometimes asked how we know that the Meat-offering typifies *character*. The answer is this: no one doubts that the frankincense, salt, oil, etc., indicate certain moral features of good—that leaven, honey, etc., indicate certain moral features of evil—and that these features to be discerned must be

The earth into which Christ came to develop his character—a character new as the Person of him to whom it pertained—the earth had been from the beginning marked throughout all its history by self-will and arrogant insubjection to God. From the moment when the first murderer and his children builded and adorned with the arts of civilization those cities in which violence and rebellion found their first gathering place, on to the time when "ravening and roaring lions" encompassed the Cross of the Son of God, there had never been a period in which wilfulness and insubjection had not been the chief characteristics of man. Cedars of Lebanon high and lifted up; oaks of Bashan sturdy and unbending; fir trees vigorous in the wild strength of nature; beasts dreadful and terrible, and strong exceedingly—such are the emblems under which God has taught us to estimate the developed character of man. "Pride compasseth them about as a chain;

displayed in a living agent. Seeing, then, that this chapter typically describes the presence of all moral qualities of good, and the absence of all moral qualities of evil—what is this but perfectness of character?

violence covereth them as a garment. Their eyes stand out with fatness; they have more than heart could wish. They are corrupt, and speak wickedly concerning oppression; they speak loftily. They set their mouth against the heavens; and their tongue walketh through the earth." Such was the character of those among whom the Lord Jesus came; such are they among whom his truth still travails. Among such he was sent to display features of character in all respects opposite to theirs. Where self-will and arrogancy reigned—where God was hated, and his laws despised—there he came to manifest implicit obedience, implicit subjection to the will of another. "Lo, I come to do thy will, O God," were the characteristic words with which he entered the sphere of his suffering service here; and throughout its course he was ever able to say, "Not my will, but thine be done." Cheerful subservience to another's will, and that through a bitterness of suffering which none but himself ever knew; meek submission to insult and reproach; gentle kindness and love shown towards his fiercest enemies—such were the characteristics of him, who, because of these qualities, is here typified by one of the strongest types of meek subduedness that it is possible for nature to supply—an offering of FINE FLOUR. How different the thoughts suggested by such a type, from those which connect themselves with the fir trees of Lebanon, or the oaks of Bashan! Yet which of these emblems is suited best to him, who, though he could say, "I clothe the heavens with blackness, and make sackcloth their covering," yet "gave his back to the smiters, and his cheeks to them that plucked off the hair, and hid not his face from shame and spitting;" whose ear was "opened morning by morning to hear as the instructed;" who "did not strive, nor cry, neither did any hear his voice in the street;" who "glorified not himself;" who said, "Come unto me, all ye that labor and are heavy laden, ... for I am meek and lowly in heart." What type could better represent him, as to these qualities, than that of fine flour?

Observe, there is in this no type of subduedness conferred. No millstone was seen grinding the corn into its smoothness; no sifting to free it from its husks or roughness. The flour was brought already perfected in fineness, and as such became the type of what Christ was even when first born as a babe into the world. The many afflictions and sorrows that are needed to bring our hearts into the possession, even of a measure of meekness—a measure poor at the best—may help us to understand how wonderful must have been the character of him who needed no discipline, nor any sorrow, to soften or subdue his spirit: for he came into the world perfect in meekness and lowliness, and every power of submission. Affliction found in him these things; it did not bring them. It added to him no new qualities; it only developed those which were already there. The meekness which he manifested on the cross or in the judgment-hall, was not more perfect than that which marked him as he grew up beneath the care of Joseph and Mary—subject to them, and sharing their low estate. The excellencies of his character were intrinsic and essential—unchangeable as the holiness of his own eternal being.

We must remember, too, in the case of all these

types of moral excellency, that the Lord Jesus not only answered to them perfectly, but that he answered to them *always*. If fine flour be the type of perfect subduedness and meekness, the Lord Jesus was not only perfectly subdued and meek, but he was this *always*. How contrasted in this with all his servants! Their graces are, at the best, imperfect; but yet more, they manifest them uncertainly. Moses was the meekest of men, and yet in meekness Moses failed; speaking unadvisedly with his lips, he was not allowed to lead Israel into their land. John, the beloved disciple, who so well appreciated the value of *love* —John was he who wished to call down fire from heaven to consume those whom Jesus came to save. Paul, who knew well the need of bridling the tongue, allowed himself to say to one whom he was bound to honor, "God shall smite thee, thou whited wall:" but Jesus under all circumstances was the same. The equability of his character never varied. It was like himself, unchangeable—the same on earth as it had been in heaven.

There was nothing perhaps that more distinctively marked the character of the Lord Jesus, than the manner in which his various excellencies were developed. Whatever qualities he displayed, the mode, time, degree—in a word, all the circumstances of their development—were as perfect as the qualities themselves. In us, subduedness of character—if through his grace it measurably exist—is often accompanied by a weakness or a want of steadfastness that leads to compromise or abandonment of truth. We may acquiesce where we ought to resist, and be silent where we ought to reprove. Barnabas, no doubt, was one in whom the graciousness and gentleness of Christ were peculiarly seen, otherwise his name would not have been what it was, "son of consolation;" yet Barnabas, when occasion required that the conduct of Mark should be discountenanced and the dissimulation of Peter withstood, in both instances failed. Indeed, in the latter case, himself dissembled also, and compromised the truth of the gospel. And even when there is no such marked failure as this, the characters of those who are most mature in grace are seldom duly balanced. Some particular feature is allowed to predominate; some favorite tendency encouraged. We approve in others just what we approve in ourselves. Exclusiveness follows. We become partial judges, and make *our* predilections, rather than the will of God, the standard by which we sanction or condemn. But it was otherwise with the Lord Jesus. In him nothing unduly predominated; no feature of character became excessive. Though emphatically the meek and lowly One who could weep over Jerusalem and pray for his murderers, yet he could also, when the service of God required, turn on them in anger and say, "Woe unto you, Scribes and Pharisees, hypocrites! Ye serpents, ye generation of vipers, how can ye escape the damnation of hell?" All the actions of Christ were subordinated to the will of God—all were according to the Spirit. It was the recognition of this that was typically indicated by the offerer, when he poured oil, the emblem of heavenly unction, on the fine flour of the Meat-offering.* Oil was ever present in the character

* "The oil which imparted its bright and lasting luminous properties to the burning wicks of the

of Christ. That communion in holiness which subsisted between the Father, the Son, and the Spirit, before the world was, was not destroyed by the Son becoming flesh. The mode and circumstances of its development might be different, but the perfectness remained the same. The exhibitions of the meekness of Christ and of all his other qualities, were never in the power of mere human thought and feeling. Every word which he spake, every feeling he expressed, was in the power of that which he essentially was as heavenly and divine. "The Word became flesh, and dwelt among us, full of grace and truth." "Grace is poured into thy lips: therefore God hath blessed thee forever." Hence we may well understand why oil was poured upon the flour.

Frankincense was also added. "He shall pour oil upon it, and put frankincense thereon." Frankincense was a gum of snowy whiteness,

seven-armed candlestick in the holy place, with the oil which was mixed with the meat-offerings, according to the laws of symbolism must be regarded as anointing oil, and consequently as the symbol of the spirit of God.—*Kurtz, Sacrif. Worship of O. T.*

whence in Hebrew its name. It was the emblem therefore of purity — a purity which, when searched into by the fire of the altar, was found perfect in grateful fragrance. Such purity was, I need scarcely say, one of the distinctive features in the character of Christ. He was by birth the Holy One—"that holy thing that shall be born of thee shall be called the Son of God." He was God manifest in the flesh—flesh physically weak, physically like ours; yet morally so unlike, that every feeling there was, as to purity, in strict congeniality with the purity of that Holy One who had made that flesh his own. His character therefore was, as his person, pure and holy. No spot of darkness could be detected there. It was as the snow-white frankincense. It was the character of One who had never grieved, never hindered the Spirit of God, nor fallen short of his heavenly excellency. The ill-savor of fallen humanity was not there. Frankincense therefore, the type of fragrance as well as purity—fragrance suited to the altar of God—was appointed to crown the Meat-offering.

But whilst there was thus to be the presence

of oil and frankincense, leaven and honey were excluded. "No Meat-offering, which ye shall bring unto Jehovah, shall be made with leaven: for ye shall burn no leaven, nor any honey, in any offering of Jehovah made by fire." There are some things which even nature itself is wont to recognize as evil, and of such things leaven is the type. Leaven is sour and corrupted dough. No one, unless his senses are vitiated or depraved, can taste it without knowing it to be bitter; all who use it know that it infuses its own qualities into every thing in which it is allowed to work. But there are other things as unfit as leaven for the altar of God, in which, nevertheless, nature recognizes only sweetness. Of such things honey is the type—the type of mere earthly sweetness. It is the sweetest of natural things, but is a sweetness that has not in it the characteristics of heaven. Although formed, not under our tainting hand, but the result of an industry that finds its most suited sphere in distance from the haunts of man, where flowers bloom in unknown solitudes—although apparently, therefore, the purest and sweetest of the productions of the earth—it nevertheless soon shows that its sweetness is not the sweetness of the new creation, for it ferments, corrupts, and quickly turns to sourness. Leaven itself is not more repugnant to the taste, than the acrid corruption of honey. That which is capable of such a change has not the incorruptibility of the Paradise of God. It can find no place in the new creation, for all is unchangeable and incorruptible there.*

* "In frankincense the full fragrance is not brought out until the perfume is submitted to the action of fire. In honey it is just the reverse; the heat ferments and spoils it. The bearing of this on the offering of Jesus is too obvious to require comment. The fire of God's holiness tried him, but all was pure fragrance. Much of the precious odor of his offering was the very result of his fiery trial. How different is it in believers! There is in many a sweetness of nature—very sweet for a while it may seem to our taste—which yet will not stand the test of fire; the first trial is enough to sour it. Who is there that has been cast into sifting circumstances where God's holiness and our ease or interests have come into collision, without feeling how much there is in us which could not be a sweet savor upon the altar? And have we never found, in setting even before saints some plain but neglected command of our Master, that much

The moment we admit that in the flesh no good thing dwelleth ("flesh" being the name for *all* that we bring into this world with us as children of Adam), it follows that all such mere natural sweetness of disposition as is found in us, is not more acceptable to God, than are other features of character which are cast in a grosser mould of evil.

The Apostle Paul was well aware how the earthy, corruptible, honey-like sweetness of nature might insidiously infuse itself even into the very highest developments of Christian grace, such for example, as love. "I pray," said he, writing to the Philippians, "that your love may abound yet more and more *in knowledge and in all judgment*" (sensitive perception, discrimination), "that ye may approve things that are excellent," etc. Such would be the result of love being exercised on divine instead of natural principles—of having in it "salt" instead of "honey." But if, in

---

of the sweetness in them which we have taken to be frankincense has at once shown itself to be fermenting honey? It was not so with the blessed Jesus.—*Gukes on Offerings.*

loving others, we exercise no discrimination, and approve or sanction things that are not excellent, but evil—if we show no regard to truth or to character, but smile on those who are hindering Christ's truth, as much or more than on those who are sustaining it—if private predilections determine our preferences, instead of regard to the great principles of God—then either leaven or honey will be present; honey, if this wrongly-principled love be the result of a natural amiability of character that shrinks from giving pain, and makes quietness and repose the great desiderata in Christian life; leaven, if this exercise of undiscriminating love result from a disregard or contempt of truth, or from a desire to secure influence at any cost, by gratifying the natural feelings of others and pleasing them apart from God.

In the character of the Lord Jesus neither honey nor leaven were found. None of those principles which, operating age after age, had made human society what it was when he came into the world—principles which might properly be called "old leaven," neither any thing in which that leaven was working fresh developments of evil—no such elements of character were found in the Lord Jesus. Neither was there in his character any thing like honey. No sweetness that was the mere sweetness of earth was there. That which gave a savor to his actions was "salt," not "honey." Salt being in itself incorruptible, is repellant of, and preserves from, corruption Its incorruptibility and power of preserving from corruption make it also the emblem of perpetuity or unchangeableness, whence the expression, "covenant of salt." See Num. xviii. 19. As representing such things, it became the fit emblem of principles divine and heavenly—savoring of God, not of men, and giving to character those qualities which were demanded by the altar of God. "Every oblation of thy Meat-offering shalt thou season with salt; neither shalt thou suffer the salt of the covenant of thy God to be lacking from thy Meat-offering: with all thine offerings thou shalt offer salt." It formed therefore an essential element in the character of the Lord Jesus. The Lord Jesus loved the family at Bethany. God was exercising that family and teaching it. When the first blow fell on them they sent to the Lord Jesus, and entreated him to come. But he went not. Mere natural kindness would no doubt have caused him to go; but the Lord Jesus never loved any, nor helped any, apart from God. He knew that it was for God's glory and for their blessing that their request should not instantly be granted: he remained therefore where he was, and Lazarus died. If he had not primarily remembered God and God's glory, and had thought merely of gratifying them, then, whatever his kindness, there would have been "honey" in the character of Jesus: he would have lacked the "salt." But this was impossible. Again, mere natural kindness might have prompted him to spare his servant that terrible rebuke when he said to Peter, "Get thee behind me, Satan." In Peter, the "honey" had been found. It was mere natural feeling that caused him to say, in the apparent fervor of deep affection, "Be it far from thee, Lord; this shall not be unto thee." But Jesus was as the fire on the altar, quick to detect that which lacked the savor of God. Salt was in his words when he turned and said to Peter, "Get thee behind me, Satan; thou art an offence unto me; for thou savorest not the things that be of God, but those that be of men." These, however, were not the only occasions on which salt was seen in the character of our Lord and Saviour. If there was in his love towards God an incorruptible principle, that gave to it a perpetuity such as mere human love never knows, it is not otherwise in his love towards his people. That, too, is faithful and *perpetual*—love stronger than death, love from which nothing can separate. If the love of the Lord Jesus had had in it the mere sweetness of earth, would it not have failed when all his disciples forsook him, and Peter denied him, at the very hour when he most needed kindness—when men were raging around him, and when the terrors of the Cross were before him? Yet it failed not. It was the very moment at which it chiefly manifested its perpetuity, and showed that it was divine.

The perfectness of the character of the Lord Jesus was never more manifested than whilst he was dying on the Cross. If he had there silently died—if no word had been uttered by his lips, we should still have seen in him the devotedness of One who was rendering himself unreservedly as a whole Burnt-offering unto God. We should have known, too, that his character continued to be what it ever had been, perfect. But the perfectness of his character was livingly displayed on the Cross. His care for his mother; his forgiveness of the repentant sinner; his resolve to fulfill all that was written, when he said, "*I thirst;*" his prayer for his murderers; his use of the twenty-second Psalm, which is a psalm not of supplication merely but of thanksgiving and strong expression of joyful confidence as to the future—all these things showed that there was not one relation towards God or towards man which he was not sustaining perfectly, in all calm self-possession of spirit, just as if the unutterable anguish and weight of divine wrath had not been bearing upon him. It is then in respect of this excellency of character, perfect alike towards God and towards man, maintained unvaryingly through all circumstances, and offered in death for our sakes—it is in respect of this that Christ is typified by the Meat-offering.

If we had merely to consider the character of the Lord Jesus, and to contrast it with our own, the only result would be, anguish and despair. There would be the sense of necessary and everlasting severance, such as must subsist between purity and corruption. But it is not for this that we are brought to the altar where the Meat-offering is presented. We are brought there, not merely to discern its excellency and to judge our own condition in the light thereof, but to see it accepted on the altar for us, and burned for us, as an offering whose excellency is considered ours. It becomes our wealth—our endowment before God. Poor as the church is in all that constitutes heavenliness of character, it will nevertheless enter heaven in joyful consciousness that the results of all perfectness of character pertain inalienably to it, because of what Christ has been. All that pertained to the offering was attributed to him who brought it. As we behold the sweet savor ascending, we see, as in the case of the Burnt-offering before, the type of IMPUTATION. We are able to say that all the value of Christ's character is reckoned to be ours.

And here, we must again remember, that whilst it was needful for the Israelites to provide the Meat-offering, and to offer it in the appointed manner—otherwise its value would not be imputed to him—yet it is not so with us. God has provided for us the offering; God has caused it to be offered; and the moment we believe, all the value of Christ's sacrifice, under whatsoever type that value may be indicated, rests upon us. As we acquaint ourselves therewith we may strengthen our faith, but we do not strengthen the certainty of our blessing.

Nevertheless, nothing is more important to our comfort and to our spiritual healthfulness, than that we should consider well the character of Christ, and our own characters in contrast therewith. Few things are more to be dreaded by the believer than a dull or hardened conscience; and the conscience will soon become hardened if it resolves to merge every thought in the one great fact of accomplished salvation and is careless of all that gives to character deformity or beauty in the sight of God. In such a case, natural qualities will be mistaken for grace : honey will not be distinguished from salt: and leaven will be unrecognized as bitter, not because it has lost its bitterness, but because the taste has become vitiated, and is unable to discern. The heart, whilst in this condition, apprehends neither the excellency of the qualities it lacks, nor the malignity of those it cherishes. It cannot estimate the character of Christ, nor appreciate what his grace may have wrought in others. "Inexperienced in the word of righteousness," and failing in all priestly discrimination—for the heart of the priest should keep knowledge—it will censure where it ought to praise, and praise where it ought to condemn. Its powers of service will decay—it will either become listless and cold, or else active with misdirected energy; feeding on things other than the food which God's altar supplies, and finding its occupations in the house of the stranger rather than in the Tabernacle of God.

We must seek, therefore, to consider well the

character of the Lord Jesus as the Meat-offering. It is true, indeed, that we must be perfect ourselves before we can rightly estimate perfectness. Our senses *here* are, and ever will be, too dull to recognize fully either the bitterness of the leaven, the fragrance of the frankincense, or the savor of the salt. We fail, therefore, even in *appreciating* the excellency of a condition in which all evil is absent, and all good present. Nevertheless, as we grow in grace, our ability to estimate these things increases. We find it humbling, yet happy, to think of our own leavened characters by the side of that altar where the unleavened One has been offered for us. We meekly thank God that he feeds us with this food, and makes us partakers of his own joy.

Thus, too, we are encouraged to copy the example of him who is our Meat-offering. We must remember, indeed, that if all the grace of which we could conceive as capable of being communicated to a creature, were ours, our characters could never be as *this* Meat-offering: first, because it was positively and negatively perfect; secondly, because it was presented and burned on the altar *for others.* Moreover, the character of Christ was the development of an excellency that *essentially* pertained to him as the Holy One; whereas our characters, in their best developments have not only flaws unnumbered, but are always the result of a power implanted in us by him—a power which is so far from being naturally ours, that the moment it is implanted it finds itself resisted and opposed by every energy that nature gives. For these and various other reasons, we can never speak of our characters—not even after "the new man" has been created in us—being as the Meat-offering. Nevertheless, if we habitually test our ways by the character of Christ, and acquire an aptitude for distinguishing leaven and honey, and salt and frankincense—if we accustom ourselves to say, "How would Christ, in these circumstances have thought or acted, or spoken or felt?"—actions based on such remembrance of Christ will not indeed be Meat-offerings, but they will be accepted through him who was the Meat-offering, and so will have an excellency attributed to them which is not intrinsically their own.

Reflection, too, on the hinderances which at present obstruct, both in ourselves and others, those developments of character which our consciences approve and our spirits perhaps desire, will quicken our apprehensions of the blessedness of that hour when, being changed into the likeness of him who is risen for us, we shall find even our characters perfect because like unto his. "I shall be satisfied when I awake in thy likeness." This thought, though not properly the subject of this chapter, is nevertheless introduced into it by a verse, evidently parenthetic but intended to remind us that earth is not the only scene in which living character is displayed. It teaches us that there is another sphere, eternal in the heavens, into which Christ, as our first-fruits and forerunner, hath already entered, and there liveth unto God. The parenthetic verse is this: "As for the oblation of the first-fruits, ye shall offer them unto Jehovah, but they shall not be burned upon the altar for a sweet savor." The oblation of first-fruits here referred to is described in Lev. xxiii. 10, 11, and is said by Paul to typify Christ raised from the dead and made the first-fruits, of them that sleep. 1 Cor. xv. 20. First-fruits, as thus applied to Christ, is a word of exceeding blessing, for it implies the sequence of ourselves into a condition similar to that into which he—our first-fruits—has been already brought. When Christ was here, his service was to satisfy for us at the altar. Then he became as the Meat-offering burned for a sweet savor. But he will never more be this. "Christ being now raised from the dead dieth no more, death has no more dominion over him." Accordingly the "first-fruits" which represent him in resurrection were not burned on the altar; they were only presented to the Lord and waved before him—the typical pledge of that blessing which he afterwards expressed in words such as these, "Because I live ye shall live, also;" or again, "The glory which thou hast given me, I have given them, that they may be one as we are." This, as I have already said, is not the subject of the Meat-offering chapter; but it is one so clearly connected therewith, there is so manifest a connection in thought between Christ accepted for us here at the altar, and Christ accepted above, as "the first-fruits," that we might expect that our minds should be led on from the scene, where we have yet to consider ourselves and our characters in painful contrast with the Holy One offered for us, to that coming hour when this sorrowful contrast shall cease to be—when sin and mortality shall be alike swallowed up of life, and no leaven nor any honey, nor any thing short of the perfectness of Christ shall any longer be found in the characters of the risen saints of God. We shall no longer then use, as now, this chapter; but it will not be forgotten. All that we then shall know and feel and exhibit—all the living powers of our new and excellent being, will be recognized as part of the results of HIS having been accepted for us who is our MEAT-OFFERING.

CHAPTER IV.

THE PEACE-SACRIFICE.

LEVITICUS III.

No awakened heart can solemnly consider the claim that God has on the service of his creatures, without being sensible that its failure in devotedness must have sunk it into destruction forever, if God had not, in the exceeding riches of his goodness, provided for it the grace of the BURNT-OFFERING. Nor will a faithful examination of our characters in their more minute features, lessen the sense of our deficiencies. It will only deepen the apprehension of our guilt and would leave us in hopeless despair forever, if the perfectness of Another's character had not been provided on our behalf, to be accepted for us as the MEAT-OFFERING. It is not, however, in the lack of devotedness, nor in the multiplied imperfections of our characters, that we find the root of our misery. The great secret of our moral disease lies, not in the developments of our nature, but in the fact of what our nature in itself is, as fallen and depraved—that nature from which all development springs. In God and in his nature, we find light, purity, holiness. "Holy, holy, holy, is the Lord God of hosts." "He is Light, and in him is no darkness at all." The emblems which he has chosen to denote the excellency of his own heavenly dwelling-place—such emblems as "crystal mingled with fire," or "pure gold like to transparent glass," or "a firmament of terrible crystal"—are but the expressions of what his *nature* essentially is. But when we turn to the condition of *our* nature—that nature which we bring into the world with us—what do we there find? Before any apprehension of good or evil has dawned upon our hearts, before any notion respecting God has been formed in our souls, before we have uttered a word or conceived a thought, sin—essential SIN is found to dwell within us. He who "searcheth the reins and the heart" finds it there. From the first moment of our existence it is the tenant of our frame. Bound up with our being, it enters into every sensation, lives in every thought, sways every faculty. If the senses, by means of which we communicate with the external world, had never acted—if our eye had never seen, and our ear had never heard—if our throat had never *proved* itself to be an open sepulchre breathing forth corruption—if our tongue had never *shown* itself to be "set on fire of hell," still Sin would have been the mistress of that secret world of thought and feeling that is found within us; and every hidden impulse there would still have been enmity against God. God alone understands what SIN is; he alone has the title to speak authoritatively respecting it; and such he declares to be its relation to the nature of fallen man. "Flesh" is the moral name given by the Scripture to all that we naturally are, in body, in soul, and in spirit; and it is "flesh" of which the Apostle saith that in it no good thing dwelleth: and again, "the mind of the flesh* is enmity

* As our translators have very properly translated *To phronema tou pneumatos*, in Rom. viii. 27, "*the mind of the Spirit*," it seems strange that they should not have rendered *To phronema tes sarkos*, "*the mind of the flesh*," in the sixth and seventh verses. Thus the ambiguity of the expression "carnal mind"

against God; it is not subject to the law of God, neither indeed can be." "The flesh lusteth against the Spirit." "Flesh," when thus used morally, is the distinctive name of fallen humanity.

"So soon as Adam"—I quote the words of one of our English Reformers—"was defiled with that spot of sin, out of the root and stock corrupted there sprung forth corrupted branches, that conveyed also their corruption into the other twigs springing out of them. Thence came the horrible blindness of our minds and perverseness of our hearts. Thence came that crookedness and corruptness of all our affections and desires. Thence came that seed-plot, as it were, a sink of all sins, with the fault whereof mankind is affected and tormented." *

would have been avoided—an expression which has caused some to suppose that the mind spoken of may be sometimes not carnal; and that it is only *when carnal* that it is declared to be enmity against God; whereas the object of the passage is to show that the mind of the flesh (and we have nothing else naturally) is essentially and always "enmity against God."

* Nowell's Catechism

The relation of man's ruined nature, first to the law of God, and afterwards to the Spirit of God, is largely dwelt on in the Scripture. If God meets it with his law, which is "holy, just, and good," instead of that law being welcomed and obeyed, as soon as any of its commandments are apprehended, they instantly awaken within us a desire after the very things which God commands us *not* to desire. In vain the law reiterates, "Thou shalt *not* desire;" SIN within us *does* desire. "Sin taking occasion by the commandment," excites to disobedience, and "works all manner of concupiscence." Rom. vii. 8. Dwelling in us like an unclean demon habitually and essentially opposed to God, it hates every thing that God loves, and loves every thing that God hates. Even after "the new man" has been created in us, and after the Spirit of God dwells within us, the enmity of Sin in our flesh remains unchanged—it still struggles against the Spirit. "The flesh lusteth against the Spirit and the Spirit against the flesh, and these are contrary the one to the other." Gal. v. 17. Such is naturally the condition of those whom nevertheless

God has loved, pitied, and met with the grace of the PEACE-SACRIFICE.

The parts of the Peace-sacrifice that were burned on the altar sufficiently indicate the specific object for which they were presented. "The fat that covereth the inwards, and all the fat that is upon the inwards, and the two kidneys, and the fat that is on them, which is by the flanks, and the caul over the liver, with the kidneys, it shall he take off, and Aaron's sons shall burn it," etc. No types could be chosen more strongly expressive of *inward* being. Those parts were selected, that form the seat of the innermost and most deeply seated of the animal feelings and affections often mentioned in Scripture under the general expression "reins and heart"—known only to him, who, because he searcheth all things, searcheth them also, and finds in their condition the evidence of what the *nature* of those to whom they pertain, morally is. In the Burnt-offering, where devotedness proved by outwardly-developed action was in question, we find none of the parts *specified*, to which exclusive prominence is here given. Even where "the fat" is mentioned, which denotes the vigor and healthfulness of the parts with which it is connected, there is a contrast. In the Burnt-offering it is the fat which is connected with the limbs and external parts; whereas, here it is* the *inward* fat or *suet* which covers the vitals. The parts selected to be burned in the Peace-sacrifice were those which determine the condition of the *inward* being. Their presentation on the altar marked the condition of that being, as pure, undefiled, and acceptable before God.

The inward parts of a "clean" animal could not be taken to represent the condition of *our* nature. If *our* type be sought among the living things of creation, it must be sought among things defiled and evil, such as dogs, or swine, or vultures; or creeping things tortuous and slimy, like the viper, or the unclean creatures that move at the bottom of the great deep. The vital parts of such might well be used to represent *our* nature; but they never could be brought to

* The words employed in the original point out this distinction.

the altar of God. They never could be burned there for a sweet-savor.

But it was otherwise with our Substitute. His nature as a man was not less perfect than his nature as God. In both he was equally pure, equally holy. His devotedness, the perfectness of his character, all that he manifested in word and deed, was but the result of his being what he essentially was—the Holy One—One *inwardly* as well as outwardly perfect—One who could say from his youth up, "I delight to do thy will, O my God; yea, thy law is *within my heart*." And when he in whom this inward perfectness was, submitted to die; when that perfectness was presented for us on the cross; when reconciliation and peace became the declared result of that offering—such reconciliation that God bids us rejoice in Christ, and grants us communion with his own joy in him—we find in these things the antitype of the Peace-sacrifice.

Few things are more important to the soul that desires to be established in grace, than acquaintance with the truths taught by the Peace-sacrifice. If our inward condition were marked merely by a distaste for holiness, and a desire to avoid the presence of a purity for which we know ourselves to be unsuited, even that would be a state of sufficient misery. But when, in addition to this, we detect within ourselves an habitual hatred of Him from whose purity we shrink; when we discover that the whole framework of our inward being is marked by living enmity against him, and yet find ourselves brought nigh to God by an act of his sovereign grace with our nature in all the depths of its depravity judicially set aside, and instead thereof the inward purity of Christ presented and accepted for us, we may well marvel and say that "God's ways are not as our ways, nor his thoughts as our thoughts." Such is the lesson taught by the inward parts of an unblemished victim being burned on the altar. The essential sin that dwells within us is not remembered, save as being covered by the mightier efficacy of a holiness that has given itself for us—so covered that God is able to meet us in the fullness of peace and to grant us for our food a part of that offering that has fed the holy fire of his own altar.*

The provision of a table for the offerer—a table furnished by part of the same sacrifice that had been presented on the altar, is one of the distin-

---

* I scarcely need refer to the many declarations which the Scriptures contain respecting the depravity of all that naturally characterizes our inward being: "The heart is deceitful above all things, and desperately wicked; who can know it?" Jer. xvii. 9. "Every imagination of the thoughts of man's heart is only evil continually." Gen. vi. 5. "In me, that is, in my flesh, dwelleth no good thing." Rom. vii. 18. The more there is of inward vigor in us naturally, the more there is found of strength of enmity against God.

In Christ, on the contrary, even after he became flesh, all was perfect, pure, and holy. He was not more truly Light when he was with the Father before all worlds, than he was after he became man and tabernacled amongst us here. The perfectness of his devotedness, and of all his developed character, was but the result of a perfectness that was found within. The purity that pertained to him as man was as the purity that pertained to him as God. Hence, we can easily understand the joy of that soul that discerns how this purity has been substituted for its own depravity, and presented for it on the altar for a sweet-smelling savor.

guishing characteristics of the Peace-sacrifice. After the inward parts of the victim had been burned on the altar for a sweet savor, the offerer was allowed to spread a table, to be supplied from the sacrifice which had been presented at the altar, but had not been burned thereon. On this the offerer and others associated with him were allowed to feed in fellowship together. Yet this, their fellowship with each other, was not the chief thought connected with their feeding on the Peace-sacrifice. To feed at the table of the Peace-sacrifice was the token of fellowship *with God;* for they fed on that on which his altar had fed; and to feed on the same thing is the token of fellowship and peace. Thus, whilst the Peace-sacrifice in being slain and having its inward parts burned for a sweet-savor affords the type of that which has supplied its own excellency in the room of the depravity and defilement that inwardly characterizes our nature, the type terminates not with this. It typifies further a ministration *from* God towards those thus atoned for and accepted; and represents him as ministering *to* them from his own altar, and from his own joys. The other offerings, especially the Burnt-offering, direct our minds to that which has satisfied God; but in the Peace-sacrifice we think also of that which God, *after* having been satisfied, ministers to us. It may be necessary for God, when all the principles of his government have been outraged, to vindicate his holiness before angels and men and Satan, by requiring satisfaction. This may be and is necessary; but it is a necessity arising from sin; whereas impartation and bestowment of blessing pertains to him, as his own proper characteristic in his own sphere of heavenly blessedness—even as he who was manifest in the flesh once said, "It is more blessed to give than to receive."

In considering the relations into which redemption brings, our attention may be so fixed on that *from* which we have been delivered, as greatly to hinder our acquaintance with the new blessings *whereunto* we have been brought. On our first conversion our thoughts are often unduly retrospective. Israel, when brought out of Egypt, felt themselves far better able to appreciate the condition *from* which they had been rescued, than to understand the new circumstances into which they had come. And after we have advanced in our Christian course, if, as believers, we have tampered with evil, and then been, through God's grace, recovered, however thankful we may be for the deliverance—however truly we may recognize many of those relations of blessings which the ceremonies of the Peace-sacrifice typify, yet we shall commonly find, in such cases, that our apprehension of the blessings *into* which we have been brought is far less lively than our appreciation of the mercy that has delivered us from danger. The perils he had known in Sodom would be likely to occupy the soul of Lot, whilst Abraham would be employed with the blessings he had found with God. They who have walked most closely with God will find themselves best able to appreciate the blessings to which grace has gathered them. In such a condition of heart we shall find ourselves able to enter most into the grace of the Peace-sacrifice; for the peculiarity of its joy is grounded not so much on the attainment of pardon, or of acceptance, as on the results of that acceptance received in communion with God, and ministration of blessing from his hand.

Nothing can be more important for the right comfort of our hearts, than to meditate well on this relation of God thus ministering to us. "Having been justified by faith," says the Apostle, "let us have peace with God" *—in other words, being at peace with God, let us enjoy the peace which God has provided—let us feed on the Peace-sacrifice. The table spread therewith is an evidence that every claim of God and of his holy altar has been fully satisfied, and that the results are now before us—results of peaceful fellowship with God forever. The offerer seated at the table thus spread by the gift of God is a type of the condition which attaches to every believer in Jesus, however feeble he may be—however slow in apprehending the blessings that are his. He is reconciled to God, and the subject of his everlasting ministration in grace and love; and whenever the great day of eternity breaks, he will be recognized as one who

* Such, according to some manuscripts, is the right reading in this passage.

is in fellowship with God at the table of Peace-sacrifice.

We cannot wonder, therefore, that a specially eucharistic character should attach to this sacrifice. It was offered "for vows or thanksgiving or voluntary offering," Lev. vii., and consequently was always connected with seasons of triumph or festive joy in Israel. To such occasions the Peace-sacrifice peculiarly belongs. Thus, when the temple was dedicated with joy and gladness, "the king and all Israel with him *sacrificed sacrifice* before the Lord. And Solomon *sacrificed* peace-sacrifices, which he sacrificed unto the Lord, two and twenty thousand oxen and one hundred and twenty thousand sheep. . . . On the eighth day he sent the people away; and they blessed the king, and went unto their tents joyful and glad of heart for all the goodness that the Lord hath done for David his servant and for Israel his people." Nevertheless, although so peculiarly a sacrifice of joy, and although the feeding thereon was so distinctly the sign of peace ratified by God; yet it was a peace made with those who had been enemies—persons in whose flesh sin still dwelt—a peace reached only through the shedding of blood. The *feeding* on the sacrifice was a scene of peace and joy only; but with the presentation at the altar was connected confession, self-judgment, and recognition of the claim of the divine holiness—a claim that could be satisfied only by vicarious death. Lest, therefore, any should virtually dissever the table from the altar, and should seek to enjoy the peace without remembering how that peace was purchased, and how undeservedly it came, it was strictly commanded that the Peace-sacrifice should only be eaten two days at the longest after its presentation at the altar. If any should desire to have the joy of the table continued, they must recur to the altar again. Nor is the application of this to ourselves difficult. Some who recognize the cross as the basis of their hopes, have attempted so to occupy themselves with the ulterior results of redemption as to leave, as they have said, the cross behind them—wishing to enjoy the blessings without the continued humbling remembrance of the condition of those to whom they are given. In heaven, indeed, it will not be necessary, as now, to place ourselves as sinners before the cross, and painfully to contrast our nature with the nature of him who dwelleth in the light, and so to judge ourselves; but whilst we remain in the flesh such self-judgment is necessary for the right healthfulness of our souls. If we attempt to have communion only with the joy and peace of redemption, without the recognition of those truths which pertain to our practical condition whilst yet in the flesh, with sin in us and sin around us, the result will be an arrogant and presumptuous use of the mercies of God, that will turn our blessings into a snare. We can easily understand, therefore, why it should be said, that if the flesh of the Peace-sacrifices were eaten at too great a distance from the time of presentation on the altar, "it shall not be accepted, neither shall it be imputed to him that offereth it; it shall be an abomination, and the soul that eateth it shall bear his iniquity." Lev. vii. 18.

If we examine the nature of the ceremonies appointed when the Peace-sacrifice was presented, we shall see additional reason for guarding against a neglect of the altar. Not only was there the confession of the offerer's own depravity implied by the presentation of a substituted victim—not only was the cleanness of *its* nature brought into contrast with the impurity of *his own*, but a Meat-offering also was presented—a memorial of the character of Christ—" He shall offer with the sacrifice of thanksgiving unleavened cakes mingled with oil, and unleavened wafers anointed with oil, and cakes mingled with oil, of fine flour, fried." Lev. vii. Here was a very full memorial of the character of Christ; but, besides this Meat-offering, *leavened bread* also was commanded to be brought. It was brought as the memorial of *our* characters—brought as the contrast between our characters and the character of Christ, that we might consider them together, and compare them as in the presence of the holiness of God. The "*leavened bread*" was neither burned on the altar, nor fed on by the priest—it was merely offered with the Peace-offering and with the Meat-offering, as something protected by their excellency. Such is the type of our condition. It teaches us a lesson full of grace, yet humbling. To be required to judge ourselves—to own the leaven that lurks in our character and ways—to contrast this leaven with the perfectness of Christ and the requirements of God—to be called on to watch against, and to restrain the developments of that which is thus detected—all this cannot be otherwise than painful; it is an employment of earth, not of heaven; yet it is necessary. Will there be poverty of spirit otherwise? and is there any thing to be dreaded more than that we should feed on the Peace-sacrifice, and seek to rest in its grace, with self-complacent and unhumbled hearts?*

---

* The second day from the time of presentation at the altar was the longest period allowed for retaining the flesh of the Peace-sacrifice. On the *third* day it was not to be eaten at all. *Three* is frequently used in Scripture to indicate *continuous* repetition; just as *two* signifies simple repetition. It was only, however, in the case of "vows, or voluntary offerings," that eating on the second day was allowed. If offered for thanksgiving, it could only be eaten on the same day on which it was offered: "The flesh of the sacrifice of his Peace-offering for thanksgiving shall be eaten the same day that it is offered; he shall not leave any of it until the morning. But if the sacrifice of his offering be a vow or a voluntary offering, it shall be eaten the same day that he offereth his sacrifice, and

None but "clean" persons were allowed to eat of the flesh of the Peace-sacrifice. If any one, "having his uncleanness upon him," or if any one, being clean, had defiled himself by touching any unclean thing, if any such ate "of the flesh of the sacrifice of Peace-offerings, which pertain unto the Lord, even that soul shall be cut off from his people." Professing Christendom teems with examples of persons unsanctified by faith in Jesus, and therefore "having their uncleanness upon them," attempting to feed at the table of Peace-sacrifice. To such these solemn

---

on the morrow also the remainder of it shall be eaten." Lev. vii. Faith is always regarded as being most vigorous in the case of *voluntary* service or worship, and then the soul can be longer confided in for not misusing its mercies. "Thanksgiving," it will be observed, is not here regarded as a voluntary service. Whenever the call of duty is so imperative that the refusal to recognize the claim would be a sin, then, of course, there is not the same opportunity for voluntariness, as in cases where there is no such claim. For this reason thanksgiving, which becomes a positive *duty* when special mercies are received, is not classed with voluntary services, and the soul that renders *it* merely, is not regarded as being beyond the ordinary condition of faith.

words in their full force apply—"That soul shall be cut off from his people." And if any who have believed, and are therefore "clean," John xv. 3, tamper with evil, and yet seek to comfort their hearts, *whilst unrepentant*, by the peace of this sacrifice, against them, too, judgment is written. Of such the apostle spoke, when he said to the Corinthians, "for this cause many are weak and sickly among you, and many sleep; for if we would judge ourselves we should not be judged." 1 Cor. xi. 30. It is true, indeed, that such, seeing that they are under grace, and not under law, shall never come under that judgment of condemnation which shall fall upon the world of the ungodly and end in the second death. The judgment of chastisement here, however severe, is not to be confounded with judgment unto damnation. The one is from a Father towards his children, and is in love; the other is from an unreconciled God towards rebels, and is in the power of everlasting wrath. Nevertheless, the apostle spoke of chastisement from the Lord being a solemn thing, even though grace enabled him to add, "but when we are judged we are chastened of the Lord, that we should not be condemned with the world." The knowledge of this mercy must not prevent our saying, "Judge therefore yourselves, brethren, that ye be not judged of the Lord."

It will be seen from what has been already said, how needful it is to distinguish between the altar on which the sacrifice was *offered to God*, and the table on which the remaining part of the sacrifice was fed on by the offerer. Nothing could be more contrasted than the altar and the table. The altar was the place at which the blood *was shed for expiation*, and where *satisfaction* was made unto God. All the ministration there was toward God. It was the recognition of the claim of *his* holiness, and unless that were satisfied, rejection and wrath, not acceptance and peace, must have been the portion of all who drew nigh. But when the services at the altar were finished, then God could act toward the worshiper as reconciled; and the table became the place, not of the offerer's ministration to God, but of God's ministration to him. There was no atonement at the table—no propitiatory sacrifice was offered there ; all this had been completed before ; and the flesh of the Peace-sacrifice, fed on at the table, was only a memorial of the sacrifice already finished at the altar.

I scarcely need observe that there is a marked resemblance between the relation of the table of Peace-sacrifice to the altar, and that of the Lord's table to the cross. This analogy is distinctly referred to in the New Testament; and if remembered, would sufficiently preserve us from the destructive error of confounding between an altar where expiatory sacrifice is offered, and a table which only exists on the ground of expiation having been complete. The table is indeed connected with an altar, but that very connection shows *that it is not itself an altar.* Nor could this obvious truth have been forgotten, if professing Christianity had not lost the apprehension of what the cross is, as the place where the true Peace-sacrifice has been once and forever offered. Otherwise, the table of the Lord could never have been spread; the very fact of its continuous existence implies that the sacrifice on which it has been founded is finished and accepted forever. This however, was soon forgotten in the professing church. The doctrine of completed atonement was lost almost as soon as the apostles died. The thought expressed in "SATISFACTION"—that word which embodies the keystone truth of the gospel—was banished from the writings of the early centuries, until at last the table of the Lord was avowedly changed into an altar, and blasphemously surrounded by sacrificing priests, in daring defiance of every truth that the ninth and tenth chapters of the Hebrews contain. No peace can dwell in a heart that, even indirectly, gives itself over to such things.

We are able, through God's abounding grace, to say that our Peace-sacrifice has been slain, offered, accepted forever; and that the feeblest believer is regarded by God as being under its power and having fed thereon. He is regarded as a guest at the table of God (for the Peace-sacrifices were the Lord's. Lev. vii. 20), and the fact of his being a guest there is a proof that, *as to acceptance,* he is perfected forever—so perfected that there remaineth no more offering for sin. He never, therefore, seeks to offer for sin again. He may recur to the remembrance of the sacrifice once offered, and to every thought connected with the altar; yet he never seeks to make atonement at that altar again. The cross of the Holy One cannot be erected afresh. To speak in any sense of the repetition of atonement is to dishonor the work which Christ has wrought —it nullifies that by which God has declared that he perfects forever all who believe, and is a rejection of the one only propitiation.

It is, then, the sin of our nature—that which of all things is most depressing—most terrifying to an awakened heart—it is this that is met by the grace of the Peace-sacrifice. Wherever we go, whatever we do, by night or by day, in public or in private, in the church or in the world, we carry *sin* within us. It besets us always, and is often chiefly felt when we seek to worship or to serve God. Watchfulness and experience may enable us to restrain its violence, and to gain victories over its outbreaks, and he who is best able to bridle his evil is pronounced by the Scripture to be most practically perfect; but such perfectness is not the perfectness of heaven, neither is it a perfectness on which we can rest as the ground of acceptance before God. The knowledge of our inward defilement must have made us shrink from God forever, and would have hopelessly shut us out from his presence, unless he had provided for us this offering. But there we see the inward perfectness of the Holy One presented on our behalf; and ourselves not only accepted but *ministered to* by God. Thus sorrow is turned into joy, and the cry of hopeless despair exchanged for the voice of thanksgiving. We are enabled to say, "The Lord hath done great things for us, whereof we are glad"—that "He hath given us the garment of praise instead of the spirit of heaviness." The more we examine ourselves, and probe the source of our woe, the more do we find reason to bless him for that grace which has found in the exceeding depth of our sin the occasion for the display of its own more abounding fullness. The soul willingly consents to be honest in self-examination then. It need not hide from itself the condition of its nature, when it finds in that condition the very thing that has drawn forth the grace of the Peace-sacrifice—grace that causes us to recognize the essential evil that dwells within us, only when it makes known to us essential good as our everlasting portion.

CHAPTER V.

THE SIN-OFFERING.

LEVITICUS IV.

THE former chapter has directed our thoughts to the manner in which grace has met the deep intrinsic evil of our nature—that nature which, even if its energies had never been aroused into development, would still have remained "enmity against God," and therefore have justly merited everlasting wrath. What can merit wrath more than that which is inherently opposed to essential perfectness? What can be more surely the heir of woe than that which is so evil as necessarily to be miserable in the presence of good? Such a condition is in itself misery, apart from the superadded inflictions which fall on it from the righteous judgment of Good: and such is the condition of our nature—truly, in every sense, the rightful heir of anguish and of indignation. Yet, in order that we might not inherit these things—in order that we might know blessing instead of curse, joy instead of anguish, peaceful communion instead of the alienation of eternal enmity—the Peace-sacrifice is given. So, standing as in the presence of God's own holiness, we are able to consider our nature in all the depth of its corruption, and yet to say that instead of having it and its judgment as our portion, we have reckoned to us, the perfectness of One, whose excellencies are the exact converse of our abominations. Such is the result of Jesus being the Peace-sacrifice. In virtue thereof, peaceful communion, as if at the same table and over the same sacrifice, becomes the abiding relation into which the whole family of faith are brought with God.

But our knowledge of evil is not limited to that which lies hidden within us. Our nature does not slumber; it acts. "Dead," as regards all power of living to God, it is full of untired energy in living according to the prince of this world—"the spirit who worketh in all the children of disobedience." Cain and his children were "dead" towards God—no principle of purity or holiness, or light or love, acted in them towards him; but out of his presence they were full of enterprise and activity—they builded cities and invented arts, living to Satan and to themselves. What they *were*, that naturally we *are*. We are *committers* of sin—*doers* of iniquity. No remedy, therefore, commensurate with our need, could be found in any thing that failed to meet the consequences of *committed* sin. Accordingly, for this the Sin-offering and the Trespass-offering were appointed.

Committed sin may be distributed into two principal divisions: first, sins committed in ignorance; secondly, sins committed consciously. It is of the first of these classes that the fourth chapter of Leviticus treats.

There is a prevailing disposition in the hearts of many to think of the sins of ignorance as if they were no sins; or if they are to be called sins—if it be allowed that they need mercy, such mercy is regarded rather as a right than as the free and unmerited gift of grace. Ignorance in the minds of such persons becomes synonymous with guiltlessness; to act conscientiously, however dark or dead the conscience, is to act blamelessly. The thought of the responsibilities that attach to knowledge, becomes secretly a reason why knowledge is eschewed. In a word, darkness is loved rather than light, because darkness brings quiet; but light has awakening and convicting power.

I scarcely need remark how all that we have been considering in relation to the Sin-offering, and sins committed in ignorance, destroys that evil and infidel thought, of every man being to himself a sufficient rule for his own actions. If culpability only attaches where conscientious conviction is transgressed, he who has the most darkened or hardened conscience would have least of guilt, for he would sin conscientiously. We are sufficiently disposed to avoid light without this additional incentive to love darkness. What is conscience in a fallen being, without rectification according to the word, and by the Spirit of God ?*

---

* "Neither our conscience, nor our measure of light, nor our ability, but the truth of God is the standard by which both sin and trespasses are to be measured. '*Though he wist it not, yet is he guilty,*' Leviticus v. 17.

A sufficient answer to all such thoughts is this —that the especial reason for the appointment of the Sin-offering was, that it might meet sins committed in ignorance. No one who reverences the word of God, will speak lightly of sins of ignorance, after he has once read such words as these: "If a soul shall sin through ignorance

---

If man's conscience or man's light were the standard, each man might have a different rule. And, at this rate, right or wrong, good or evil, would depend, not upon God's truth, but on the creature's apprehension of it. At this rate the filthiest of unclean beasts could not be convicted of uncleanness, while it could plead that it had no apprehension of that which was pure and seemly. But we do not thus judge in the things of this world; neither does God judge so in the things of heaven. Who argues that because swine are filthy, therefore the standard of cleanliness is to be set by their perceptions or ability; or that because they seem unconscious of their state, therefore the distinction between what is clean and unclean must be relinquished? No; we judge not by their perceptions, but our own; with our light and knowledge, not their ignorance, as our standard. God, in like manner, though in grace he finds means for pardoning it, still judges evil as evil whenever he finds it. Our blindness does not alter his judgment; for it is our sin and that alone which has caused the blindness."—*Gukes on the Offerings.*

against any of the commandments of the Lord, concerning things which ought not to be done, and shall do against any of them, . . . then let him bring for the sin that he hath sinned," etc. The heinousness of such sins of ignorance depends, not so much on the character of the deed done, as on that condition of heart, which is capable of committing sin without knowing that it is sin; and commits it, perhaps exultingly, triumphing in it as good. What must angels in heaven think of the state of that soul which is so thoroughly blinded—so utterly astray from God as to violate his commandments, and resist his will in total unconsciousness that it is doing wrong! It was thus that multitudes in Israel hated and persecuted the Lord Jesus—it was thus that Paul shed the blood of Stephen, resisting the full testimony of the Holy Ghost from one, whose face shone as he spake, with heavenly brightness. All this was ignorance. Paul verily thought that he was doing God service; yet that very thought argued such thorough blindness of soul—such entire alienation of heart from God, that it was alone sufficient to make him "the chief of sinners."

Nature, if left to its own native blindness, would always sin, and sin in ignorance—such sin being the embodiment in action of those dark principles of enmity against God which lie embosomed in the human heart. In order, however, that the character of sin might be fully manifested, and that want of light might never be pleaded in palliation of transgression, God has never left himself without witness. Throughout the heathen world, the eternal power and Godhead of God are borne witness to by the works which his hand has made. "The heavens declare the glory of God, and the firmament showeth his handy-work." Ps. xix. "He left not himself without witness, in that he gave them rain from heaven and fruitful seasons, filling their hearts with food and gladness." "The invisible things of him from the creation of the world are clearly seen, being understood by the things that are made, even his eternal power and Godhead, so that they are without excuse." Rom. i. 20. The Jews, in addition to this testimony of creation, had also the written word. "To them were committed the oracles of God." They had also many a prophet, many a teacher, line upon line and precept upon precept. The consciences both of Jews and Gentiles were often made to feel the appeals of God. As Paul spake Felix trembled. Nevertheless, they rejected these appeals. Satan and their own evil quenched or obscured the light. As they turned from it, their conscience became more hardened; and as it hardened, sins of ignorance were multiplied, and committed with a higher and more reckless hand. Shall we speak lightly of sins of ignorance like these? One evidence of their character will be found in this, that such sins chiefly abound where the conscience is most hardened, either by long continued evil, or by the judicial infliction of God. What can be more terrible than a conscience so hardened?

Nothing has a greater tendency to bring the conscience into this state, and to lead to the daring commission of sins of ignorance, than religious truth perverted. Revealed truth had been received by Israel, but received to be betrayed. Their influential systems—the systems which they worshiped, were based on perverted truth. From their childhood they drank of a cup of error ministered to them in the name of God. In vain the Scriptures spake of Jesus; in vain John, his forerunner, testified; in vain the Lord himself proved by his words, his character, his miracles, that he was indeed the Son of the living God. The light of holiness and of grace shone fruitlessly upon hearts, whose natural darkness was deepened by the systematic influence of a religious corruption, that had sanctified error by holy titles, and had blessed wickedness in the name of God.

Nor has it been otherwise in Christendom. The past and present history of the church of God supplies countless instances of souls, so nurtured from childhood in the atmosphere of error, as to be deadened in every power of right discernment and apprehension. If a lamp that man or Satan have kindled from beneath be early put into our hands; if we are taught to regard it as a light kindled in the sanctuary of God; if our ear welcomes the deceiving tale, and we refuse to test it by the true light of God's written word, what wonder if we are deceived? What wonder, under such circumstances, seeing that our hearts naturally love darkness, that sins of ignorance should abound? Shall we say that there is no heinousness in sins of ignorance like these?

It would be happy, indeed, if we could assert, even of real Christians, that they are free from these fearful sins of ignorance. But whenever they give themselves up to the guidance of any individual, or of any system whose influence is not strictly according to the revealed truth of God, they will surely act against Christ and his commandments ignorantly. The practices that he favors, they will discountenance; the doctrines he teaches, they will reject; the persons whom he commissions, they will resist; they will substitute error for truth; and ignorantly throw the weight of their character and their gifts into the scale of falsehood. There is nothing, perhaps, at this present moment, that is operating more terribly against the progress of truth, than the misdirected energies of real Christians, ignorantly sustaining error, ignorantly resisting light.*

Paul was keenly alive to the danger of these sins of ignorance. He knew how easily the souls, even of believers, can be bewitched. "O foolish Galatians, who hath bewitched you?" He knew how easily Satan can transform himself into an angel of light; and how hard it is, while in the midst of "man's day," to judge of persons and things in the light of the day of God. Even, therefore, when he was walking most blamelessly, in much maturity of grace and knowledge, he refused to pronounce any certain judgment on his own character; for there might be blemishes in it which he was unable to discern, and decision respecting this pertained to the Lord, not to him.

---

* Of course I do not mean to imply that all the sins either of Christendom or Judaism are sins of ignorance. But in a period of religious declension or apostasy, when the early pattern given by God to the churches has been long departed from, it must be that ignorance will abound. And as the dispensation draws nigh to its close, and the conscience becomes more obdurate, and judicial blindness increases, sins of ignorance will necessarily multiply.

"I am not," said he, "conscious to myself of any thing;"* that is, I am not conscious of any allowed transgression; "nevertheless am I not hereby justified; but he that judgeth me is the Lord." If, then, there may be sins of ignorance, even where there is most diligence and watchfulness, how much more where there is negligence or slumber, or acquiescence in the prevailing evil of the age? There has been only One on earth free from sins of ignorance, even he who said, "I have set the Lord always before me;" and he came to be our Sin-offering—to bear the wrath due to these very sins of ignorance: otherwise, they alone would have sunk us into perdition forever.

The chapter before us, as being addressed to those who were ostensibly the separate people of God, teaches us especially respecting sins of ignorance committed by *believers.* The greater our privileges, the nearer we are brought to God; the more intimately we are connected with his

* "I know not that I am guilty of unfaithfulness." 1 Cor. iv. 4. Coneybeare and Howson's Translation.

service, the more terrible must be the consequences of transgression. The sin of an Israelite had a greater heinousness in it than the sin of an uninstructed Gentile—the name of God was more dishonored thereby. Again, the sin of a priest or of the whole congregation of Israel, seeing that with such should have been found understanding, and the fear of the Lord, was greater than the sin of an individual among the people. To the sin of an anointed priest and to that of the congregation equal heinousness attached. In each of these cases, the full consequences of the sin of ignorance were developed: and therefore, in meeting these consequences, the full efficacy of the Sin-offering was displayed.

The priests were anointed that they might minister in the near presence of God. Their employment was in holy things—their place the sanctuary. As instructed in the ways of the Lord of Hosts, as acquainted with the manner of his house, their lips were to keep knowledge; and others, through them, were to learn the ways of the Lord. Sins of ignorance, therefore, were the very sins that should have been absent from the priest. But if they were found in him—"if the priest that is anointed do sin . . . . through ignorance against any of the commandments of the Lord, concerning things which ought not to be done, and shall do against any of them," then his sin was to be estimated by the holiness of the things and places in which he ministered, and by the disastrous consequences to others, as well as to himself, that flowed from its commission. His sin had penetrated, as it were, the holy place; it had entered before the vail; it had tainted the place of his ministration; it had defiled the altar; it had involved others in its consequences; and the stain must be effaced, either by vengeance consuming him, or it must be expiated by the blood of a substituted victim.

It was for this that God, in the unsearchable riches of his grace, appointed the Sin-offering. The offending priest brought the victim to the door of the Tabernacle before Jehovah, and there "leaned" his hand upon its head, and slew it. The blood was then borne into the holy place, and there sprinkled seven times before the Lord, thus specially recognizing *him* as the person against whom the sin was committed. "Against thee, thee only, have I sinned, and done this evil in thy sight: that thou mightest be justified when thou speakest, and be clear when thou judgest." The ground on which he was accustomed to stand when he ministered was thus sprinkled, and also the golden altar of incense, at which he served. Thus the taint was covered over; himself purchased back from destruction; the places of his honorable service preserved unforfeited. The remainder of the blood was then poured at the bottom of the altar of Burnt-offering, as a memorial that the just requisition of holiness had been met—met by death. The blood was not, as in the Burnt-offering and Peace-sacrifice, scattered *on* the altar, in token of its acceptableness there; for now it was regarded as the result and token of vengeance deservedly falling upon sin. The reality of the death by which the sin was expiated, and the certainty of that expiation being recognized in the very sanctuary whose holiness had been violated, was proved by the blood being poured, and allowed to *remain*, at the bottom of the altar. There it could be seen as the token of accomplished and accepted atoning death. It was blood *shed*.*

But whilst these ceremonies within the holy place and at the brazen altar thus supplied the memorial of reconciliation as the result of wrath appeased, there were other ordinances without the Tabernacle, which teach us respecting that wrath whilst in process of being inflicted. The principal parts of the victim, viz.: "the skin of the bullock and all his flesh, with his head, and with his legs, and his inwards, and his dung,

* There is, probably, nothing that the consciences of believers feel more acutely, than the extent of the dishonor done to God, when they have sinned in positions of high and honored service. They know that the dishonor done to God is commensurate with the dignity and holiness of their position. They know, too, that Satan, and holy angels, and men in their measure, understand this. The sense of such guilt would be overwhelming, if there had not been provided in the Sin-offering, grace adequate to meet the depth even of this need. Happy are they who, in such circumstances, fly to the true refuge, instead of having recourse to idle extenuations, which have in them the guilt of hypocrisy.

even the whole bullock, shall he carry forth without the camp, unto a clean place where the ashes are poured out, and burn him—literally, burn up or consume—on the wood with fire; where the ashes are poured out shall he be burned up."

It should be observed how remarkably this passage respecting this first class of Sin-offering ends with the word "*burn up.*" This is very unusual. We commonly find at the conclusion some words that intimate forgiveness attained, or which speak of the offering as a sweet savor. But here no such results are mentioned; the object being to bring out in strong relief the great truth that sin deserves and receives consuming wrath. This thought may be and should be *conjoined* with other thoughts; but other thoughts should not be *commingled* with it, for so none will have their own proper completeness. This, however, is seldom the case in our experience; we continually neutralize one truth by another. It is right to combine, but combination is not confusion. In the rainbow, colors are combined, but they are not neutralized nor confused.

The mind is evidently intended to rest on the solemn truth taught by the word with which these directions conclude—BURNT UP. He who has considered the heinousness of sin as estimated in the sanctuary in relation to the holy vessels and services there, will best apprehend the reason of the devouring wrath which this word expresses. In the Passover our minds are chiefly directed to the deliverance; in the Peace-sacrifice to the peace into which we are delivered; in the Sin-offering to the satisfaction rendered to WRATH. The manifested infliction of destroying wrath, though deserved by indwelling sin, is delayed in the governmental order of God, uutil sin has been *committed.* This is a sufficient reason for the great type of wrath *inflicted* being found in this chapter.

A very different type this, from that in which the whole offering was lifted up on the altar of God as an offering of sweet savor; or from that in which, as in the Peace-sacrifice, these parts, or the greater number of them, were fed on by the offerer. Here fire kindled, not on the altar, not within the Tabernacle, not even within the camp, but kindled "without the gate"—the place of dishonor and reproach—devoured, like the fire of Gehenna, that which was counted as if it were an accursed thing. In the case of the altar, the fire that was thereon kindled, fed gratefully on that which satisfied it by its excellency; but here, a fire, kindled without the camp, burnt up, as in fury, that which was given it to be consumed. Such was the type of him, whom, though he knew no sin, God made sin for us. 2 Cor. v. 21. In other types, we have seen him, as the One who "gave himself for us, an offering and sacrifice to God for a sweet-smelling savor;" but in this burning without the camp, we see him stricken—"bruised"—made a curse for us—made sin for us.* It was then that he

* It is not easy to recognize vengeance and wrath, either as due to our sins, or as endured by our Substitute for us. Often, after we have apprehended that the Holy One has been stricken for us, and that he has become for us a sacrifice of sweet-smelling savor, we form but a feeble estimate of the wrath he sustained for us, or of the reasons why that wrath was due. It is well for us that our safety depends not on the clearness or comprehensiveness of our faith, but

uttered that bitter cry, "My God, my God, why hast thou forsaken me, why art thou so far from helping me, and from the words of my roaring?" Thus, too, we can understand the words of the apostle, "God sending his own Son in the likeness of sinful flesh, and for sin, judged—damnatorily judged—sin in the flesh." The flesh of the Lord Jesus was holy: in him was no sin; but the sin of our nature, here called "sin in the flesh," was reckoned to him as our Substitute, and when he died upon the cross was there damnatorily judged. There it received its award. This is the lesson that faith learns, as it stands by the fire without the camp, and gazes on it, whilst the devoted parts of the Sin-offering are consumed. There it beholds the memorial of what Christ became on account of his people. There it sees not only their sins but their sin judicially ended. We may stand, as it were, by the side of that burning pile. We may see the flame fiercely raging in the full intensity of its

simply on the fact that our souls have indeed said, "Lord, to whom shall we go? Thou hast the words of eternal life."

devouring power; at length we behold it lessen; at last, flicker and decay, till it smoulders among the embers. We may watch the last expiring spark that glimmers there, and when that ends—when nothing but the cold ashes remain—we see an emblem of the relation which the fire of holy wrath bears to all the believing people of God. Its power is expended; it hath burnt itself out; ashes only remain.

Yet at the same moment when the real power of wrath bore on the Holy One—our Substitute—even whilst he was being stricken *as if* he had been sin, there was, nevertheless, found in him all that perfectness of heavenly excellency, which was inseparable from him, even whilst being made a curse for us. God still beheld in him his only beloved Son in whom he was well pleased; whose obedience and devotedness and perfectness in life and in death, remaining unchanged even whilst wrath thus preyed on him, ascended still as the "odor of a sweet-smelling savor." This truth is carefully preserved, not only in the types of the Burnt-offering, and Meat-offering, and Peace-sacrifice, but also in the ordinances of the

Sin-offering itself. Whilst the body of the Sin-offering was carried without the camp to be consumed, the internal parts, that is to say, the internal fat, kidneys, etc., were placed on the altar, and there burned. These, it will be observed, were the same parts that were burned in the Peace-sacrifice; here, too, intended to typify those excellencies of nature in Christ, which shone in him always, and manifested his nature as man, to be the exact opposite to ours, as inhabited by, and subjected to sin. Sin committed in ignorance is so connected with the condition of our nature, inwardly; it is so impossible to meditate on the one without tracing it to the other, that we can easily understand why this part of the ceremonies of the Sin-offering should direct our thoughts to the condition of our nature, and to the satisfaction made on its account. Conscience, whenever it truthfully meditates on sin committed, goes back to the root from which it springs, and finds that root within us. And when that is once seen, how could there be any rest, unless God had provided for us One, whose excellencies are here also substituted for our vileness? In atonement, divine holiness requires in the Surety, not only that he should bear every penalty, but that he should also present a substitutional perfectness for us.

If we compare the *fourth* and the *sixth* chapters of Leviticus, it is very evident that the first broad distinction between them is, that the former treats of sins committed ignorantly; the latter, of sins committed knowingly. In the one, it is said, "if a soul sin, through ignorance, against any of the commandments of the Lord." Lev. iv. 1. In the other, "if a soul sin, and commit a trespass against the Lord, and lie unto his neighbor in that which was delivered to him to keep, or in fellowship, or in a thing taken away by violence, or hath deceived his neighbor, or have found that which was lost and lieth concerning it, and sweareth falsely," etc. Lev. vi. 2. In such cases it is very evident that the action is willful.

The division, however, into sins ignorantly, and sins knowingly committed, is not alone sufficient. Sins committed ignorantly greatly vary, not only in the degree, but also in the kind of ignorance; and for such ignorance, we may be in different degrees responsible. In order, therefore, to mark that such differences are appreciated by God, and that he desires that we, too, should appreciate them, various classifications of sins of ignorance are given in the fifth chapter; in some of which, there is so much of self-caused ignorance, that they very nearly approach, in the character of their guilt, to sins knowingly committed. Nevertheless, whatsoever the character of sin, we have ever to remember that the one sacrifice once offered "covereth over" forever *all* sin, for all who believe. If believers analyze the character of their sins, it is not that they might be more secure, but more wise, more able humbly to serve and to thank him, who teaches them the character of their sin *after* he has brought them, through the blood of the sacrifice, into everlasting reconciliation.

Sins of ignorance greatly differ in kind as well as in degree. He who transgresses because he is ignorant that any commandment exists forbidding him to do what he does, commits a sin very different in character from that of one who, *knowing* that certain things are forbidden, nevertheless disobeys, either unawares, or because he deceives himself into the belief, that the particular case in question may be made an exception to the general rule, on the ground of necessity, or pardonable expediency; so that with a *good* conscience (as men say), in other words, with a perverted conscience, he ignorantly does evil. Ignorance of this kind, that is, ignorance which respects the particulars of action, is often self-induced, in a sense in which general ignorance, that is ignorance which affects the general *principles* of action, is not self-induced. To be ignorant of some general principle whereby a whole class of things is universally proved to be evil, differs greatly from an ignorance which only affects the question whether such and such a particular case falls, or does not fall, under that class. Thousands, for example, like Luther in his earlier days, render religious allegiance to bodies falsely claiming authority from God, because, from being educationally, or otherwise blinded, they discern not the principle whereby, in the word of God, all such bodies are condemned; whilst others, well knowing that any recognition of such bodies is forbidden, do, nevertheless, give themselves to practices whereby, unconsciously or carelessly, or for expediency's sake, they recognize them. The first are ignorant as to the principle of their action; the latter of its circumstantial particulars. The first kind of ignorance is chiefly marked by the extent and depth of the darkness by which it is accompanied; the second derives its criminality, chiefly, from the carelessness or willingness to be deceived, by which it is almost always characterized. The sins of the *fifth* chapter belong to this latter class. They are, indeed, done in ignorance; but so much of voluntariness mingles with the ignorance, that they verge towards the willful sins of the sixth chapter, and so stand contrasted with sins of ignorance properly so called, of which the *fourth* chapter treats. Such sins, therefore, have a mediate character. They are committed in too much ignorance to be classed with the willful sins of the *sixth* chapter; whilst, on the other hand, there is too much of voluntariness in that ignorance, to admit of their being classed with such sins of ignorance as are treated of in the *fourth* chapter. Accordingly, whilst the sins of the *fourth* chapter, that is, sins done in ignorance, and arising mainly from ignorance, are met by the Sin-offering; and whilst the sins of the *sixth* chapter, that is, willful transgressions, are met by the Trespass-offering; the sins of the *fifth* chapter—from verse 1 to 13 inclusive—are met by *a Trespass-offering of a peculiar character*, viz., a Sin-offering* offered for a Trespass-offering; whereby the mediate character of such sins is plainly signified.

The sins treated of in the fourth chapter—met by the Sin-offering properly so called—derive their predominant feature from the circumstance of ignorance being their root. They so manifestly spring from ignorance—ignorance is so distinctly their parent, that they stand morally contrasted with other sins, which, even if committed ignorantly, cannot, in the same sense, be said to spring from ignorance. The ignorance which once

* And sometimes by a Sin-offering *and* Burnt-offering *offered for a Trespass-offering;* sometimes by a Meat-offering *offered for a Trespass-offering.*

caused St. Paul to venerate Judaism; and caused Luther, for a time, to bow before the false pretensions of Romanism, is very different in character from that ignorance which tampers with something that is unclean or evil, because it is too careless, or too inexertive to rouse itself to inquiry; or because it fears what it may discover, if it should probe too deeply. In the first case, there is no dread of inquiry or deliberation, because the mind is so thoroughly blinded, that it suspects not its condition; but in the second case, carelessness or disinclination to know the truth prevents examination. Ignorance, in fact, is *consciously* cherished; so that every one who honestly examines an action so performed, feels that, however much it may be committed ignorantly, yet that its root is not ignorance, but a certain disposition of heart that entails on itself an ignorance which it knows that it might readily escape.

There are few chapters worthy of more solemn consideration than the fourth of Leviticus. It teaches us the deep responsibility of all positions of ostensible service—especially such as are influential over the minds and habits of others. Any influence we may possess, any ability of instructing, comforting, or in any way helping others, by word or by example, is a talent which we cannot escape the responsibility of using. We dare not hide it in a napkin. The priests of God, and all believers are priests, *must* act, and that, too, openly. But how needful that they should well consider the responsibility of their position; the danger in which they are of acting ignorantly, and the disastrous effects of such ignorance, in dishonoring God, and injuring others, who may be involved in the consequences of their sin! Honest-hearted reception of the word of God can alone preserve us from such ignorance. But is there acquaintance with the Scripture now; or is its light hidden, and other lights substituted instead? Think of the general delusion that has pervaded Christendom, as to this present time being one of holy progress, whereas, the Scripture over and over again declares, that it is one of declension, disobedience, and dark iniquity —iniquity that will bring on a visitation of judgment, the like to which has never yet been.

Think of the manner in which ceremonial rites—many of them mere inventions of man—ministered, too, by unholy hands, have supplanted the true and saving ministration of the gospel of the grace of God. Think of the multitudes, yet in their sins, because unsanctified by faith in Jesus, who are taught, even whilst they are yet strenuously serving the god of this world, falsely to say to the great Shepherd of Israel, "We are thy people, and the sheep of thy pasture." Think how many, uncommissioned of God, unacquainted with his truth, and untaught by his Spirit, have usurped the place of ministers of Christ, and are so owned and honored. Think of the manner in which Judaical position and Judaical principles have been assumed by those who have forgotten that Christ, and not Moses, is their master; so that they whose feet should have been shod only with the preparation of the gospel of peace, have rushed into the battle-field, crying, "The sword of the Lord and of Gideon;" whilst others, who should have remembered that the place of discipleship now is to follow Jesus of *Nazareth*, and to become, it may be, as the off-scouring of all things for his sake, have eschewed this place of lowliness, and have sought to reign as kings, building for their worship gorgeous temples, and for themselves pleasant palaces; as if Solomon on the throne of his glory, instead of Jesus in rejection and reproach, were the pattern of Christian condition now. Think, too, of the blindness that prevails, as to the prospects of Israel, of the nations, and of the church, as to the nature of the last great Apostasy, and the coming and reign of the Lord Jesus; and then say, whether there was ever an hour when sins of ignorance more abounded—an ignorance, the depth of which, and the sinfulness of which, One only can appreciate.

There is a natural tendency in the heart of man—and it operates abundantly even in real Christians—to bow to the influence of perverted and falsely assumed authority. "The prophets prophesy falsely, and the priests bear rule by their means, and my people love to have it so." That honored place of authority and influence, once held by the unfallen church, whilst it yet stood as "the pillar and ground of the truth," has been seldom claimed by any, without the claim—however false and presumptuous—being willingly owned, and sometimes welcomed, even by many who are really Christ's. But all such authority, seeing that it is neither based on nor guided by truth, can only lead into the darkness to which itself belongs. What wonder, therefore, that ignorance should settle in upon that soul that has made itself the slave of such authority; what wonder if, unconsciously, it should welcome falsehood, and fight against Truth; and congratulate itself most when furthest distant from the principles of Christ. Individuals, too, as well as collective bodies, may claim an authority which God has never given; and not unfrequently fear, or affection, or self-interest, or a disposition to lean upon others, causes it to be gladly recognized. But such authority, seeing that it is not in the power of Truth, that it directs not to the Scriptures alone, that it will not bear the test of the "law and of the testimony," can only, as in the former case, lead towards, if not into, darkness. Nothing but close adherence to the Scripture can preserve us from such results in a day like the present. Is that which we hear false or true? Is it or is it not the word of God? Such are the great questions we have to ask ourselves now. The faithful use of the Scriptures will no doubt expose many an error, detect many a sin of ignorance, and show us much that we have no sufficient grace to attain. Thus, after years of dark declension in Israel, when at last the faithful energy of a few led them back again to the neglected Scripture, the first result of their return to it was this—that all the people "wept;" for they discovered how they had offended, and in what they had long and ignorantly sinned. Yet their tears were not allowed long to flow. The voice of compassion said to them, "Weep not; let joy in Jehovah be your strength." God can ever comfort truthfulness and confession.

The amount of responsibility that may attach to individuals on account of these sins of ignorance, there is One, and One only, that can determine. An all-seeing eye that traceth the end from the beginning, is alone able to detect how, and when, and where the various streams of error first emanated; and who they are who have since most labored to swell them, or to prepare channels for their diffusion. Some diffuse error because they love it; others, because they are deceived into believing it a duty. Some, through indifference, or timidity, or dislike of truth, refuse to avail themselves of instruction, even when it is brought to their very doors; others, again, seem deprived almost of the opportunity to learn, entombed in a darkness which light seeks in vain to penetrate. The determination of the various proportions of guilt must be left to the great final day. All that we can at present say is, that the value of the Sin-offering can never fail; and that all who are under it, that is, the whole family of faith—all who have not rejected the record which God hath given of his Son—are surely protected from condemnation by its everlasting efficacy. But although the believer in Jesus shall never be plucked from the hand of the Almighty Shepherd, yet the effect which sins committed by us in ignorance may produce upon others, who, through our example, may continue in darkness, and perhaps perish with a lie in their right hand; the effect which such sins must produce in darkening our powers of spiritual apprehension, and destroying the proper comfort of our hearts; the effect, too, upon our service in hindering fruitfulness, and causing "wood, hay, and stubble" to be the result of our labors;—these, and other such consequences, who can appreciate? They will be understood only in the day which revealeth all things; when "we, too, shall know even as also we are known."

Instruction, exhortation, discipline, chastisement, are employed by the grace of the great Head of the church towards his people, to free them from sins of ignorance, and their disastrous consequences. But Satan and the sin that dwells within us put forth their energies to resist. They struggle to increase darkness and to confirm error; and we cannot be surprised that their plans should prosper during a period marked by our Lord himself as one in which "iniquity shall abound."

Yet, the greater the darkness, the more precious is any light that is available in its midst.

Amid all the dark and shifting scenes through which the fierce passions of men under Satan are hurrying, alike, the church and the world, the word of God remains unchanged and unchangeable, as the one steady light appointed to shine on in the darkness, until the day dawn. Happy are they who stand most apart from the tumultuous scene, and cleave most closely to the Scripture, and most meditate therein. If, as the history of Christianity peculiarly shows, the perpetual effort of Satan be to hide, or to veil, or to distort the light of Scripture, let our effort be to unveil it, and to give steady direction to its beams. Even if weak ourselves, we may be able very effectually to aid others. He will not have lived in vain, who shall have caused one ray of light from the word of God to rest steadily on a heart that was dark to it before.

But how could we have any courage to use, or to approach a light that will surely manifest ignorance and sins of ignorance, both in ourselves and others, if there were no SIN-OFFERING? What hope could we have unless we were able to say that the whole family of faith are protected forever under its efficacy? We have not again to offer it: it HAS BEEN offered, once and forever offered—every ceremony fulfilled—every ordinance obeyed. We find in it a work that has been finished—a grace that has been perfected. May we use it, not to nurture ignorance, and listlessness, and slumber, but to encourage ourselves to cleave to, and maintain that light of revealed truth, which, however beset by evil, however much it may be for a time shrouded, shall never have its essential brightness marred by the admixture of one element of darkness, on to the hour when it mingles with the light of the eternal day.

There, none will pretend that there are many standards of right and wrong; or that a fallen creature may find a safe and sufficient guide in the convictions of his own dark bosom. As soon as the redeemed are personally sinless, they will fully recognize the blessedness of owning and bowing to one sovereign will. Sins of ignorance will be fitly appreciated then; and habits of extenuating and excusing evil will no longer hinder the apprehension of the fullness of the grace, which, refusing to palliate iniquity, or to call darkness light, has itself bowed beneath the curse due to evil, and there proved itself to be almighty—almighty in vindicating holiness—almighty, also, in delivering the sinner who despises not the Sin-offering.

CHAPTER VI.

THE TRESPASS-OFFERING.

LEVITICUS VI.

If we read the commencing verses of the sixth chapter of Leviticus, it is evident that the sins they describe are sins that must have been committed knowingly. "If a soul sin, and commit a trespass against the Lord, and lie unto his neighbor in that which was delivered him to keep, or in fellowship, or in a thing taken away by violence, or hath deceived his neighbor; or have found that which was lost, and lieth concerning it, and sweareth falsely," etc. In the cases here supposed, there is evidently no ignorance—the deed is knowingly and deliberately done.

Our first impulse, in thinking of sins thus committed, is, to attach to them a far higher degree of heinousness than to sins committed in ignorance; and in many cases this impression is just. I say, in many cases, because sins ignorantly committed *may* imply a condition of more obdurate evil than is indicated by some sins that are knowingly committed. Violence of temptation, terror, or the desire of escaping some threatened danger, may sometimes overpower a heart whose disposition, radically, still remains true to God. It is thus that martyrs have sometimes foregone their previous confessions, and disavowed, momentarily, the truth which their souls still loved. It was thus surprise and terror caused Peter to deny his Lord; whilst nevertheless his faith in him and his mission failed not. Satan never so far prevailed as to banish from the heart of Peter the conviction that Jesus was indeed the Christ, the Son of the living God—worthy of all reverence, all reliance, all love. That conviction was never driven from Peter's soul. If it had been, he must have been separated from his Lord forever. Ignorance, like the ignorance which was resting on the people of God's wrath around him, would, in that case, have rested on him also. But it was impossible. Though he was sifted as wheat, yet Jesus prayed for him, that his faith should not fail; and it failed not. His heart was never driven back into utter darkness: he still confided in and loved him whom he was denying—otherwise, when Jesus looked on him, would that look have pierced? Would he have gone out and wept bitterly?

How different the state of Peter, even whilst knowingly committing that sin, and the condition of another, who, even at that very moment, was preparing—ignorantly, indeed, but deliberately—to enter on his course of resolute and blasphemous defiance of Christ. Paul was in Jerusalem, learning at the feet of Gamaliel, during the time that the Lord himself was ministering in the midst of Israel. He had the opportunity therefore of hearing and owning that Holy One—him of whom God had said, "Behold my servant, whom I uphold; mine elect, in whom my soul delighteth." It was open to Paul to have owned him and comforted him; for though he was the One "who clotheth the heavens with blackness, and maketh sackcloth their covering," yet he had humbled himself, so as to need sympathy and find refreshment in the love, even of the creatures whom his own hand had made. But Paul rendered to him no sympathy, nor any love: on the contrary, he despised him, hated him, and virtually, if not actually, joined in the cry of those who said, "Crucify him! crucify him!" And afterward, when the Holy Ghost was sent down from heaven, and many, even of the murderers of Jesus, quailed before its testimony and resisted no longer, the heart of Paul still refused to bow. He heard the words of Stephen, full of the Holy Ghost and of power—saw his face shine as the face of an angel, and yet joined in slaying him. All this, indeed, was done in ignorance; but it made Paul the greatest of pardoned sinners. The greatest, therefore, of pardoned sins recorded in Scripture, was a sin committed in ignorance.

If Paul had not done these things in ignorance—if he had blasphemed, as he did, the testimony of Stephen, whilst secretly in his conscience recognizing it as being from God—he would, in that case, have passed the limits of forgiveness, and would have committed the sin that never can be forgiven, either "in this world or in the world to come." It may seem difficult, perhaps, to conceive of wickedness so intense as for the soul deliberately to blaspheme as evil that which it *knows* to come from the almighty Source of all good; yet so it may be. Light may dispel darkness, but light has in itself no power to change the nature of man's perverted will. It is a fearful thought, that when the soul has long loved darkness and avoided light, and cherished its delusions, and hardened itself in willfulness, even if God should be pleased, by a sudden exercise of almighty power, to sweep in a moment every cloud from the soul, and to scatter every web that dissimulation or hypocrisy have woven, the unregenerate heart would nevertheless still remain as full of willfulness as ever, and would only use the light given to assist it in committing the unpardonable sin. It would still blaspheme, and blaspheme knowingly. Such will be the character of that closing hour, when men, well conscious of what they are doing, will say both of Jehovah and his Christ, "Let us break their bonds asunder, and cast away their cords from us"—when "they shall make war against him that sitteth upon the horse, and against his army." Rev. xix. Thus, whilst the greatest sin recorded as pardoned is committed ignorantly, the greatest of sins is committed knowingly.

It is not, therefore, from the mere fact of a sin having been knowingly committed, that we can infer the greatest insubjection of the will. Abraham sinned knowingly when he wandered from Canaan into Egypt, and endeavored to protect himself by falsehood and the abandonment of his wife. Gen. xii. Moses sinned knowingly when he smote the rock in anger, and forgot to honor God in the sight of Israel. Peter and Barnabas transgressed knowingly when they dissembled at Antioch and compromised the truth of the gospel. Paul disobeyed knowingly when, being warned through the Spirit not to go up to Jerusalem, he went. Acts xxi. 4. Martyrs have sinned knowingly when, overpowered by terror or seduced by flattery, they have sometimes fallen for a season, and abjured the truth for which they have been suffering. Yet how many a sin committed in ignorance indicates to the eye of God a degree of willfulness not found in these his servants, even though they knowingly turned from the straightforward path! When we willfully cause, or willfully deepen our own ignorance, or avoid the light whereby it would be dispelled, or cleave to our ignorance because we love both it and its results, we are in a worse condition of heart than many, who, under the force of circumstances, may commit conscious and deliberate transgressions. Accordingly, though the transgressions mentioned in the sixth chapter of Leviticus are distinctly such as must have been knowingly committed, yet not a word is said that implies that they are more heinous than the sins of ignorance mentioned in the preceding chapter. They may be, or they may not be. The degree of heinousness that attaches to any transgression depends really on the inward condition of the will; and that, who, excepting God, can judge?* Yet, though sins may thus differ in their character and in the degree of their heinousness, we must remember

* The transgressions which *we* are accustomed to judge most severely are such as are deliberate and

that every sin is a breach of God's holy law—a law whose holiness adjudges wrath to *all* transgression. Every sin, therefore, of whatsoever kind it be, needs to be met by the same grace, exercised through the same everlasting sacrifice.

The cases of trespass mentioned in this chapter

---

willful; yet it may happen that one, who sins in ignorance, may have a will more stubborn, rebellious, and wicked, than one who may commit knowingly a very great trangression. A willful transgression does not always prove the greatest willfulness of soul; nor does the committal of the very same sin prove, necessarily, the same alienation of heart from God. Adam, though he committed the same sin as Eve, was not in the same depth of transgression; for he was not deceived as she. He did not believe the lie of Satan, that Satan could make him happier than God had made him. The apprehension of God and of his goodness were not blotted out of his remembrance in the same manner as in Eve. "Adam was not deceived, but the woman being deceived was in the trangression." 1 Tim. ii. 13. We must not, therefore, judge by the outward appearance merely—there may be distinctions that we cannot discern. The direst form of sin is when willful transgressions are the direct result of habitual willfulness of soul; and this is often the result of long perseverance in sins of ignorance.

are all of them trespasses against a neighbor. Nevertheless such trespasses are also trespasses against the Lord. "If a soul sin, and commit a trespass against the Lord, and lie unto his neighbor," etc. Wherever government is perfect, wrong done to a subject is regarded as wrong done to the sovereign; and so it is here. If a man injure his neighbor, wrong is considered to be done to God as the Legislator and Governor of his people; and wrong is of course done to the neighbor—wrong, too, of double character: first, in that he is deprived of that which is his own; secondly, in that he is deprived of it by fraud or deceit or violence, so as thereby also to be injured and dishonored. Accordingly, *compensation* becomes a predominant and distinctive feature in the Trespass-offering. The stern eye of Moses, who, as the minister of law, could abate nothing from the full claim of perfectness, examined the victim and estimated it by shekels of silver; and if it fell short of the appointed value, it was rejected. "And he shall bring his trespass-offering unto the Lord, a ram without blemish out of the flock, with thy (that is Moses') estimation;"

the victim must be of a value that would adequately compensate for the wrong done to the government of God. Moreover, all that was taken from the neighbor was to be restored. There was to be the compensation of restitution —"He shall restore that which he took violently away," etc. And lastly, in order that the injured person might be compensated for the manner in which he had been defrauded, a fifth part of the value was to be added to that which was restored. "He shall even restore the principal, and shall add the fifth part more thereunto, and give it to him to whom it appertaineth, in the day of his trespass-offering." Unless all this were done, and the victim duly offered, the sin was not atoned for, and wrath remained as the portion of the guilty.

Such were the severe but just ordinances of the law respecting trespass. And here again we have to observe the contrast between the requirements of Sinai and the grace of the New Covenant—the Covenant of Zion. What if such compensation were exacted from *us?* Could we provide any offering that would meet the estimation of the sanctuary of God? Could we make restitution, and not restitution merely, but full compensation to all whom we may have injured by thought or word or deed, and then rest our claim for immunity from wrath on the completeness of the satisfaction thus rendered to God and to man? If such things were required of us, wrath must have remained as our irreversible portion forever. We should not have been able suitably to compensate man, much less to satisfy God. But we have not thus to provide. God has not forgotten that he is Jehovah-jireh True to that covenant name, he has himself provided for us a sacrifice, by whose perfectness every claim is satisfied: so that nothing as regards the putting away of guilt remains to be effected either towards God or towards man. "By one offering" Christ "hath perfected forever" all who come unto God by him. The remission is so complete, says the Apostle, that "there remains no more offering for sin." This is salvation.

If compensation to those whom we have injured were, under the gospel, made *necessary to the attainment of forgiveness*, then we should, in part, become the authors of our own salvation.* Not but that it is just and meet, whenever it be possible, to make restitution to any whom we have wronged. The fitness of such restitution, nature itself teaches. The first thought of Zaccheus, after the Lord had entered his house bringing salvation, was, "Behold, Lord, the half of my goods I give to the poor, and if I have defrauded any man by false accusation, I restore him four-fold." A right and fitting thought, if such devotedness be made a thank-offering for salvation; but pregnant with destruction if made the prerequisite or procuring cause.† Yet how often on this and kindred subjects does error

* The author means here to draw a distinction between the offering of compensation, as a work in order to obtain the forgiveness of God, and the making of restitution as a result of the forgiveness and cleansing freely granted through the sacrifice of Christ. The latter is the exercise of one saved by grace and taught by the Spirit to exercise himself, "to have always a conscience void of offence toward God and toward men."—Am. Ed.

† It should be observed that, in our Lord's reply, he makes no reference to the intentions that Zaccheus had expressed. He simply said, "this day hath SALVATION come to this house." The emphasis is on

feign the accents of truth! Naked falsehood is not the only instrument whereby Satan deceives. He deceives chiefly by perverting truth or deranging its proper order; and therefore one of the employments of the Great Head of the church —the Bishop of the souls of his people—is to give them, through the Spirit, *rightly ordered* apprehensions of his truth. None who have the Spirit of Christ can fail to recognize that restitution and compensation are principles holy, just, and true—they are principles which all who honor Christ will seek practically to embody in their ways whenever occasion may require: but how different this from making them the prerequisites of salvation! To that we say, God forbid. If salvation be of grace, then it is no more of works. We desire not to be "teachers of law,

---

salvation. That was the word intended to arrest the attention of Zaccheus and all who were observing these things. The fact that full and free salvation had suddenly come to a most undeserving dwelling was not to be obscured by Zaccheus' proposals for the future—however sincere such proposals—however right as a *result* of salvation.

understanding neither of what we speak nor whereof we affirm."

But it may be asked, are we, by this type, authorized to expect compensation from those by whom we may have been injured? If we were under law and were claiming "an eye for an eye, tooth for tooth," we should, of course, whenever injured, expect reparation. But we are not under law: we are sinners saved by grace, and as such, deserve nothing, and claim no compensation.* Compensation, in this sense, is a word banished from the lips and from the heart of every one who knows what grace is. Could the redeemed, in the day when grace shall be fully apprehended and its results known, desire—even

* If the Old and New Testaments mean any thing by what they teach on this point, *the trespasser is the wrong man to contend for rights.* Because we are converted trespassers, and trespassers who make our boast in grace, we are called, as the very witnesses of that grace and of our need of it, to deal in what we call grace to others. * * But how far is this acted on by many who profess to be one with Christ? Provided we have been *just,* who asks have I been *gracious,* in my dealings to my fellow-men.—*Gukes.*

if it were possible—to exact any thing from their then perfected brethren? Did Joseph wish it, when his brethren stood around him and he comforted them? Even here, grace "frankly forgives" whenever any are brought to the recognition and confession of the wrong. Not indeed that the saints will lack recompense; but the recompense of grace through Christ is not to be confounded with the exacted compensation of law. The redeemed in that day will be recompensed, and more than recompensed, for every past suffering and for every woe. However they may have been persecuted, or maligned, or injured—however they may have been hated or outcast even by their brethren—however they may have found treachery where they expected faithfulness—all will judge themselves to be more than recompensed, when they find themselves surrounded in glory by all the results of the righteousness and excellency of the Son of the Father. It is true, indeed, that he who putteth every tear into his bottle, and noteth all their sorrows in his book, may in the abounding riches of his grace meet every past grief by some corresponding joy, and make every injurious word or violent deed that they have meekly met for his name's sake, an added jewel in the crown of their glory. "Blessed are ye when men shall revile you, and persecute you, and shall say all manner of evil against you falsely, for my sake. Rejoice and be exceeding glad, for great is your reward in heaven." I do not limit the superabounding bountifulness of grace towards those whom God has been pleased to love in Christ Jesus. But I say, that no superadded recognition or reward of this kind will be needed, in order to make every heart feel that its recompense is not merely complete, but infinite, the moment it stands in glory numbered among the saved. Every heart will spontaneously and joyfully acknowledge then, that whatever claim brother may have had against brother, all has been answered to infinitude by Him who, as the kinsman and representative of all his brethren, will have given to each, more than could ever have been taken away from any one among them, even if all the combined energies of evil, that have ever worked in the church and in the world, had been concentrated on one individual head. Thus grace, without acting on the Sinai-principles of retribution, is able to appropriate every principle that is holy, just, and true, and to apply it in its own new manner, in the power of blessing.

In the preceding observations, I have chiefly dwelt on the trespasses described in the sixth chapter, because they, being knowingly committed, seem to stand in most palpable contrast with the sins of ignorance described in the fourth chapter. I have, however, already remarked that a Trespass-offering was not only required in cases in which the deed was knowingly done, but on every occasion in which the attention is primarily directed to the nature of the act, rather than to the moral condition of the agent.

Indeed it is on this, and not on the circumstance of the sin being ignorantly or knowingly committed, that the true distinction between the Sin-offering and the Trespass-offering must be made to rest. We well know that there are occasions on which the general moral condition of the person who has sinned is regarded far more than the particular act of transgression he may have committed. On the other hand, there are cases in which the deed done and its consequences are made the primary object of regard. In the first case the Sin-offering, in the latter the Trespass-offering, would be required.

Nothing can more clearly show that the distinction between the Sin-offering and Trespass-offering is not founded on the sin being knowingly or otherwise committed, than the fact that the first instance in which the Trespass-offering proper is commanded to be brought, is one in which the wrong is done *ignorantly.* See the fourteenth verse of the fifth chapter, where the words, "And the Lord spake unto Moses," marking a fresh division, are again found. "And the Lord spake unto Moses, saying, If a soul commit a trespass, and sin through ignorance in the holy things of the Lord," etc. The trespass referred to in this passage is done in ignorance and is committed against the Lord only. In this case, as in the case of a trespass against a neighbor (see chap. vi.), the victim brought for a Trespass-offering was to be of a fixed, estimated value; and secondly, in addition to the victim, compensation was to be made, not merely by returning an equivalent, but by adding a fifth part or double tithe thereunto. Whenever, therefore, in the relation we hold to God, as his people and servants, we defraud him even ignorantly of that which is his rightful due, a trespass is committed, by which we should have been forever ruined, if there had not been found in Christ a value fully compensatory in all the three aspects here referred to.

It is worthy of remark that, although the ignorance in cases of trespass against the Lord in holy things must be considered as especially *voluntary*—inasmuch as we cannot suppose that the declarations of God respecting his rights are unintelligible or obscure—yet that the only trespasses here mentioned as *ignorantly* committed, are trespasses against the Lord in holy things; whereas the instances of trespass *knowingly* committed are confined to those committed against men. We can easily understand this. We often defraud God of that which is his due, carelessly and without giving it a thought; whereas in trespasses against a neighbor, we are for the most part far too cautious to trespass unwittingly; the fear of man being often more operative than the fear of God. Israel went on for ages defrauding God of that which was his due; for they were commanded several times in the year to appear before him and celebrate his feasts; yet ages passed and they never celebrated them at all. And when at last, as in the times of Ezra and Nehemiah, they gathered together and opened up his word and read therein, they found their omissions so many and so grievous that they all lifted up their voice and wept. In Malachi, too, we find them again described as habitually defrauding the Lord of his due; and yet saying, "In what have we sinned so much against thee?" And if we consider the present condition of the church of God—are they rendering to God that which he claims of them in his word? Is their doctrine, their order, their worship, such as his word demands? Or is there daily a continuance in practices which take from him that which his word declares to be his due? Are there not many real Christians, exact, even to the most minute tittle, in rendering to men their due, who nevertheless—for reasons that will not bear examination—selfish reasons—refuse to search fully into truth; so that they continue voluntarily ignorant of its claims, and never give to it its right pre-eminence nor the proper allegiance of their souls; and so render the practical unity of the children of God impossible? Yet this is often done and persevered in unconsciously.

The seventeenth and following verses of the fifth chapter are worthy of especial attention; because they pronounce all ignorance that has caused aberration from the commandments of the Lord to be in itself *trespass.* "If a soul sin, and commit any of those things which are forbidden to be done by the commandments of the Lord; though he wist it not, yet is he guilty, and shall bear his iniquity. And he shall bring a ram without blemish out of the flock, with thy estimation, for a Trespass-offering, unto the priest; and the priest shall make an atonement for him *concerning his ignorance wherein he erred and wist it not;* and it shall be forgiven him. It is a Trespass-offering." Lev. v. 17, etc. We have before seen ignorance marked as sin—we here see it marked as *transgression.* How different man's estimate, and even the church's estimate of ignorance, and sins of ignorance, from that which is presented to us in these chapters! However trivial the offence committed, the ignorance in which it is committed is marked as being itself *trespass.*

It is interesting to observe how the fifty-third chapter of Isaiah—that blessed chapter of salvation—describes the punishment due both to the sin and to the trespasses of God's people as having alike rested on the head of the great Substitute. "It pleased Jehovah to bruise him; he hath put him to grief; when thou shalt have made his soul an offering for sin (*trespass*), he shall see his seed, he shall prolong his days, and the pleasure of Jehovah shall prosper in his hand." Again in the 12th verse, he is described as the Sin-offering: "He was numbered with the transgressors, and he bare the SIN of many." Thus Jesus is alike the Trespass-offering and the Sin-offering for his people—even all who believe.

CHAPTER VII.

THE OFFERINGS AS A WHOLE.

SUCH, then, is the outline—an imperfect outline, of the five different aspects under which it has pleased God to teach us respecting the one great sacrifice. In separating us from Egypt and leading us into a wilderness—for in following him we find ourselves separated from many an association, and interest, and occupation, which naturally we loved—when thus led into the wilderness, we find not a wilderness merely, but a Tabernacle, within whose holy enclosure we are taught lessons of grace. When, not as in the presence of the fires of Sinai, but with the light which the gospel has supplied, we enter that typical dwelling-place of God, we find every thing there testifying of grace, because every thing speaks of Christ. As we stand by the side of the altar, and think of the guilt of our trespasses, or of our sins of ignorance, or of the sin of our nature, or of our blemished characters, or of our failure in devotedness to God, we find an offering which has not only canceled this guilt, but left the perfectness of its own excellency in its room. It is not only blackness covered over: it is blackness of darkness swallowed up of light —light pure, holy, and perfect as that which is known in the presence of God in heaven. God had so appointed it—it is his gift—we have only to bow the head and worship, and give thanks to him forever.

But while this superabounding of grace is the great lesson of the Tabernacle, the side of the Burnt-offering altar is also a place where instruction of deepest practical moment is received. The apostle speaks of it as an altar, at which we may not only feed—feed on the provisions of its grace—but at which we may also *serve.* "To do good and communicate forget not, for with such SACRIFICES God is well pleased." There is a sense, therefore, in which, through Jesus, even we may bring our gifts and sacrifices to the altar. It is the knowledge of this that sheds a radiance upon the otherwise dark circumstances of life, and gilds many a gloomy scene in the wilderness with the light of heavenly blessing. When the soul discerns how sin and death have entered into all things here, and sees that all is tainted—when it apprehends the truth of that sorrowful cry, "Vanity of vanities, all is vanity"—how it rejoices to find a new sphere in which things that would otherwise "perish with the using" may be employed for God. Even the mammon of unrighteousness may be used for him. "Make to yourselves friends," said the Lord Jesus, "of the mammon of unrighteousness;" that is, so use it that its use may bear witness *for* you and not *against* you in the final day. We may, if we please, spend our time, our energies, our talents on ourselves, and sow to the flesh, and of the flesh reap corruption; or we may bring these things to God, and to his altar, and so sow to the Spirit, and of the Spirit reap life everlasting. Nature uses for itself; Faith for God. Faith has a transforming touch, whereby things which otherwise are worthless as dross, become transmuted into the preciousness of gold. He who most fully knows the ruin that sin has wrought in every thing beneath the skies, and who best appreciates the character of him who is "a rewarder of them that diligently seek him," will bring, like Abel, "the more abundant sacrifice," and find in the service of the Burnt-offering altar one of the chief consolations of the hours of his pilgrimage. And if a regard to the various aspects supplied by these several offerings be needful in forming a right estimate of the One Sacrifice, it is scarcely less needful in preserving us from a certain narrow exclusiveness of feeling, into which we not unfrequently fall in our attempts practically to follow Christ. Ardent and imaginative hearts, young in the faith and ignorant of themselves, struck with the blessedness of being wholly devoted to God, are often wont to make *that* the one absorbing thought, whereby every desire respecting themselves and every judgment respecting others is moulded. It would be difficult, indeed, to over-estimate the value of true devotedness; for it imparts an energy and vigor to Christian life such as nothing else can give; but unless the desire for its attainment be tempered by the knowledge which other relations of Christ supply, nature governs it, and evil fruits—fruits of bitterness, selfishness, and pride, are found in result. Many who have made devotedness the exclusive object of their thoughts, have shown little ability, or else little disposition, to regard either excellencies or blemishes in character. They misjudge both others and themselves. "What," say they, "are a few blemishes in one who has made personal sacrifices and dared hardships and dangers from which others have shrunk back dismayed—what the value of a few quiet, minute, and almost hidden graces, compared with deeds of self-denial that might adorn even an apostle?" Self-denial and suffering become, in the eyes of such, the only bright jewels in the crown of service. Suffering is extolled; but whether truth be the object suffered for is a question unasked and unheeded. It is thus that the toils and sufferings of Xavier have, to many minds, thrown a halo around the wickedness of Jesuitism itself. It is thus that the workings of falsehood and evil, even in real Christians, have been overlooked, and virtually sanctified. It is true, indeed, that that which blinds the world may only dazzle the eye of a Christian; but a dazzled eye is unfit for right practical discrimination. It can neither extend its view to that which is afar off, nor examine that which is nigh. It is not to be wondered at, that such, though they may speak great things respecting the Burnt-offering, should virtually pass over the Meat-offering unheeded, and fail to distinguish salt from honey ; frankincense from leaven.

And again, if any, more experienced than themselves in the evil of the human heart, has found a rest greater than they have ever realized, in the knowledge of the Peace-sacrifice, the desire to speak of that peace and to dwell in that peace, even when combined with true devotedness of heart, is often despised by those whose thoughts respecting devotedness are more like highly-wrought pictures than realities learned in the school of well-disciplined experience. Ripened knowledge and maturity of grace are, by such persons, little appreciated. The undisciplined fervor of youthful energy is valued far more than the wisdom of the hoary head, even when that head has grown hoary in the path of faithfulness and truth. And if such succeed in influencing or guiding the sheep of Christ, they are far more ready to be ever hurrying them, and that by harassing paths over stony places, than to give them, from time to time, their proper rest by still waters and green pastures. They forget that the Good Shepherd "maketh his flock to rest at noon," and "carrieth the lambs in his bosom," and "feedeth that which standeth still."

Yet there may be error on the other side also. Some, attaching exclusive importance to certain displays of character, have undervalued devotedness. If certain features of character are possessed—especially such as belong chiefly to the circle of natural duties—the desirable point of Christian progress is supposed to be attained; although the interests of truth, and the sorrows of those who suffer with it, and the path which is marked with the characteristics of Nazareth, are unthought of, or else eschewed. Or again, the enjoyment of the peace of redemption is sometimes made the one exclusive object of desire. If that be maintained—if the soul, as gathered under the shelter of the Peace-sacrifice, be able to say, "My beloved is mine, and I am his," it is satisfied; whilst all energy of service, and every stimulating principle that is supposed to disturb or to interfere with this rest, is suspected. The true rest of faith is never interfered with by energy, nor by earnest inquiry after truth, nor by going without the gate bearing the reproach of Christ. We read in the Canticles of one who had been brought into the city and was slumbering in its palaces, "her hands dropping with myrrh, and her fingers with sweet-smelling myrrh," whilst her Lord was without, "his head filled with dew, and his locks with the drops of the night." What a contrast of condition! How diverse the circumstances of the bride of Christ, and those of her Lord! Her conscience recognized the dissimilarity; she tried to comfort herself in the thought that her *heart* was awake, even though *she* had laid down to sleep. Vain comfort! for why should there be this opposedness between the practical position and the inward condition of the heart? Yet how often is this diversity found! How prone our hearts to lay aside their soldiership and to sink into listlessness or slumber, forgetting that the true rest of faith is most found when the realities of the conflict of this "evil day" are most realized. "We wrestle not against flesh and blood, but against principalities, against powers, against the rulers of the darkness of this world, against spiritual wickedness in heavenly places." We stand as in the midst of a land which teems with the strongholds of an active and skillful foe. What secular system, what ecclesiastical system is there, influential over the hearts of unregenerate men, in which faith does not recognize the presence and power not of human evil merely, but of Satan? What need, then, of the armor of God! What need of activity and vigor! It is true, indeed, that the great Captain of our salvation is able to grant, and does grant to his people, rest. Israel, from time to time, rested in the wilderness; but they rested in places which God chose; and when he chooses them, the places of rest are always found in the onward path of victory and triumph, where the foe may be successfully resisted, if not overcome. Whilst waiting on the guidance of his hand, we shall not misuse our seasons of repose; we shall not so rest at the Peace-sacrifice table, as to forget the service of the Burnt-offering altar.

Thoughts like these—for these observations are merely intended as suggestive—may be much enlarged by those who desire to pursue such meditations. Yet however important the practical instructions that are connected with every lesson of the Tabernacle, we must never forget that the great primary subject of instruction there, is *grace*—that "grace in which we stand." Well may it be said that they "stand in grace," who are brought within the holy enclosure of the Tabernacle, there to abide under the protection and under the value of all that the One Great Offerer has supplied to the now satisfied altar.

And if it be asked what the instrument is employed by God to bring us into connection with all these wondrous and enduring blessings, the answer is, *Testimony*—the testimony that he himself gives in his word and by his ministers respecting Jesus. How wonderful the condescension and goodness of God, in that he himself consents to become the declarer of that mercy which his grace has provided on the Cross! The gospel is called "the gospel of God," not only because God provided the sacrifice, but because he "preaches" or announces it. God "preaches peace by Jesus Christ." Acts x. 36. Hence God thus testifying concerning Jesus presents himself as the object of saving faith; and therefore believers are described as those, "who, through him—*i. e.* Jesus—*do believe on God,* who raised him up from the dead, and gave him glory; *that your faith and hope might be in God.*" 1 Peter i. 21. And again, "It was not written for his (Abraham's) sake alone that it (righteousness) was imputed to him, but for our sakes also to whom it shall be imputed, that is to say to us *who believe on him that raised up* Jesus our Lord from the dead," etc. Rom. iv. The testimony thus spoken of may be *written* in the Scripture, or it may be *orally* given by the lips of God's servants: in either case it is alike to be regarded as testimony given by God. Of the *written* testimony it is said, "These things are WRITTEN that ye might believe that Jesus is the

Christ, the Son of God, and that believing ye might have life through his name." Of the *preached* testimony it is said, "The word is nigh thee, even in thy mouth and in thy heart; that is, the word of faith that we PREACH; that if thou shalt confess with thy mouth the Lord Jesus, and shalt believe in thy heart that God hath raised him from the dead, thou shalt be saved." Rom. x. 8. And again: "After that in the wisdom of God the world by wisdom knew not God, it pleased God by the foolishness of preaching to save them that believe." 1 Cor. i. Accordingly we read of the Apostle standing before a mingled multitude and saying: "Men and brethren, through this man (*i. e.* Jesus) is preached unto you the forgiveness of sins, and through him all who believe are justified from all things." Acts xiii. What words can be more simple? What more explicit? It is a testimony sent from God. It directs not to ritual observances; nor to observances of any kind; but simply presents God as ready to become the justifier of any who cast themselves on him, through the finished work of Jesus thus declared.

Some receive the message; and them God receives through the name of Jesus, and imputes to them righteousness without works, and makes Christ to them "righteousness, and sanctification, and redemption." Others, either careless as to having any rest for their souls, or else resting in some other hope, refuse the rest prepared of God in Jesus, and they continue aliens—unsprinkled by the blood of the Lamb. It is possible, indeed, that such may have "a zeal of God" that men may magnify and admire. So had Israel. "I bear them record," says the Apostle, "that they have a zeal of God, but not according to knowledge." It was not guided by truth—revealed truth. "Going about to establish their own righteousness, they refused to submit themselves to the righteousness of God"—the righteousness, that is, which he had provided in another; and therefore wrath abided on them, and they died in their sins.

Nor is the forgiveness of the gospel the forgiveness of past sin only. Such is the character of forgiveness among men—it respects the past only: but he who through faith is brought under the grace of the gospel is not forgiven *merely*. His forgiveness is accompanied by acceptance and endowment with grace *in another*. He is "accepted in the Beloved." God is pleased to enter into covenant with every believer, and to engage never more, as regards acceptance, to behold him in his own separate individuality; but always to view him under the value of the service and sacrifice and name of Christ. In other words, the believer obtains a new relation to God in a Representative; and that relation must be measured both as to its value and as to its perpetuity, by the value and continuance of that Holy One by whom he is represented. Hence, though God retains his title to chasten and to correct, yet the believer, from the moment he believes, is judicially pronounced in the courts of God free from the wrath due to his sins, whether past, present, or to come. His standing as recognized in the courts of heaven is in Another. Another is his "Forerunner," Heb. vi.; his "First-fruits," 1 Cor. xv.; his "Priest," Heb. viii.; his "Advocate," 1 John ii.; his "Life," Col. iii. In his Representative, he is already "seated in heavenly places," and brought into the new creation of God: in which sense, also, it is already said of believers, "old things are passed away; behold, all things are become new."

Let none, therefore, who have received the message of reconciliation in the blood of Jesus, and cast themselves on God thereby, fear to appropriate to themselves these mercies, and to take their stand boldly, as those who belong to the Tabernacle of God. The deepening darkness of these latter days requires steadfastness—it demands that we should gird on our armor, and witness a good confession, and contend earnestly for the faith once delivered to the saints. We may be weak; but the faithfulness of God will not fail his people. He has loved them with a love stronger than death, that many waters shall not quench. He has brought them from Egypt, and divided for them the waters of destruction, and guided them by his strength unto his holy habitation, in a sense that Israel's deliverance merely typified. Theirs was a typical separation in the power of fleshly ordinances; ours a real and effectual separation in the power of "an endless life" as seen above the heavens in Christ risen. The one was made dependent on the creature, and it failed: the other rests on him who is "God over all, blessed forever"—the Redeemer as well as the Creator of his heritage, and therefore it is effectual, and abides for evermore.

THE END.

www.ingramcontent.com/pod-product-compliance
Lightning Source LLC
LaVergne TN
LVHW010743120826
845150LV00009B/1647

9781425514334